4 95. 918340

# TEACH YOURSELF BOOKS

# THAI

KU-375-750

# THAI

## A COMPLETE COURSE FOR BEGINNERS

# David Smyth

| WATERFORD CITY LIBRARY | |
|---|---|
| 2453028 | |
| L B C | 930118 |
| | E17.94 |
| | |

**TEACH YOURSELF BOOKS**

For UK orders: please contact Bookpoint Ltd, 130 Milton Park, Abingdon, Oxon OX14 4SB. Telephone: (44) 01235 400414, Fax: (44) 01235 400454. Lines are open from 9.00 – 6.00, Monday to Saturday, with a 24 hour message answering service. Email address: orders@bookpoint.co.uk

For U.S.A. & Canada orders: please contact NTC/Contemporary Publishing, 4255 West Touhy Avenue, Lincolnwood, Illinois 60646 – 1975 U.S.A. Telephone: (847) 679 5500, Fax: (847) 679 2494.

Long renowned as the authoritative source for self-guided learning – with more than 30 million copies sold worldwide – the *Teach Yourself* series includes over 200 titles in the fields of languages, crafts, hobbies, sports, and other leisure activities.

*British Library Cataloguing in Publication Data*
A catalogue record for this title is available from The British Library

*Library of Congress Catalog Card Number:* 94-65936

First published in UK 1995 by Hodder Headline Plc, 338 Euston Road, London NW1 3BH

First published in US 1996 by NTC/Contemporary Publishing, 4255 West Touhy Avenue, Lincolnwood (Chicago), Illinois 60646 – 1975 U.S.A.

The 'Teach Yourself' name and logo are registered trade marks of Hodder & Stoughton Ltd.

Copyright © 1995 David Smyth

*In UK:* All rights reserved. No part of this publication may be reproduced or transmitted in any form or by any means, electronic or mechanical, including photocopy, recording, or any information storage and retrieval system, without permission in writing from the publisher or under licence from the Copyright Licensing Agency Limited. Further details of such licences (for reprographic reproduction) may be obtained from the Copyright Licensing Agency Limited, of 90 Tottenham Court Road, London W1P 9HE.

*In US:* All rights reserved. No part of this book may be reproduced, stored in a retrieval system, or transmitted in any form, or by any means, electronic, mechanical, photocopying, or otherwise, without prior permission of NTC/Contemporary Publishing Company.

Typeset by J.Film Process, Bangkok.
Printed in Great Britain for Hodder & Stoughton Educational, a division of Hodder Headline Plc, 338 Euston Road, London NW1 3BH by Cox & Wyman Ltd, Reading, Berkshire.

| Impression number | 13 | 12 | 11 | 10 | 9 | 8 |
|---|---|---|---|---|---|---|
| Year | 2004 | 2003 | 2002 | 2001 | | |

# CONTENTS

**Introduction**

**Pronunciation**

# ── INTRODUCTION ──

## *About Thai*

Thai is the national language of Thailand and is spoken by approximately fifty million people in that country. Lao, spoken in next-door Laos, is very closely related to Thai (although most Thais from Bangkok would have considerable difficulty understanding it), but the other neighbouring languages, Burmese, Cambodian and Malay, are completely different. Distinct dialects of Thai are spoken in the north, northeast and south of the country, but it is the language of the Central Region and Bangkok which is used throughout the country as the medium for education and mass media and which is taught in this course.

Thai is a *tonal* language. In tonal languages the meaning of a syllable is determined by the pitch at which it is pronounced. **kao**, for example, means *news* when pronounced with a *low* tone, *white* with a *rising* tone and *rice* with a *falling* tone. If tones make pronunciation in Thai seem more complex than in more familiar European languages, the learner will probably find Thai grammar considerably easier to absorb, for there are none of the complex verb tenses and noun endings which seem to dominate many people's experience of language-learning.

Thai is written in its own alphabetic script which has developed from a script originally found in India. It is written across the page from left to right, with certain vowels appearing above the line of writing and others appearing below.

There are no spaces between words and spaces only occur as a form of punctuation, similar to commas and full stops.

## About the book

This book is intended for the complete beginner. It aims to equip the learner with the necessary vocabulary and grammar to cope with the day-to-day situations a foreigner is likely to encounter in Thailand. A further important aim of the course is to provide a solid introduction to the Thai writing system so that the learner will have the means to extend his or her knowledge of the language beyond this course.

Each unit is built around a dialogue (**bòt sŏn-ta-nah**), marked. 🔲 This is followed by a brief cultural background note entitled **pah-sǎh láir sǔng-kom** which draws out aspects of the linguistic or social context of the dialogue. Key phrases and expressions (**sǔm-noo-un**) are highlighted, while the full vocabulary lists, marked 🔑 , and explanatory language notes (**kum, ùt-tí-bai**), marked 🔲 ,will enable you to understand the conversations without too much difficulty. A variety of practice exercises (**bàirp fèuk hùt**), marked 🔲 , reinforce the material covered in the dialogue, and the Key at the end of the book allows you to keep track of your progress. A considerable part of each unit is devoted to reading and writing Thai. The script is presented in manageable chunks in **àhn láir kěe-un** (*Reading and writing*) and tested in the reading exercises (**bàirp fèuk àhn**). The later units include an additional reading passage (**bòt àhn**).

A cassette has been produced to accompany this course. You are strongly advised to purchase this to gain a clear idea of how Thai should sound.

## How to use the book

Individuals will have their own preferred way of working through the course. If you have the cassette, you might like to start each unit by listening to the dialogue on tape a number of times with your book closed, simply to get your ear attuned to the language. Alternatively, you may prefer to work out what the dialogue means before you consider listening to it. It does not really matter what approach you adopt as long as you are happy with it and you are prepared to follow it regularly. Whatever approach you adopt however, you are ultimately faced with the task of memorising and accurately reproducing unfamiliar combinations of sounds. It is probably best to memorise words in meaningful phrases rather than in isolation and your pronunciation and intonation will obviously be greatly aided if you have the cassette to use as a model. Frequent review of earlier lessons and exercises is essential if the language in them is to become almost second nature.

People learning a language which is written in an unfamiliar script will often say, 'I only want to learn to speak it, I'm not bothered about writing.' They usually imagine that learning a new script will be extremely difficult and time-consuming, and that they will be able to steam ahead much more quickly if they just concentrate on the spoken language. You can, if you choose, work through this book in that fashion, simply ignoring the sections on script. But if you do, you won't be getting your money's worth from the course and you'll be adopting a short-sighted and self-limiting view. Just think how ridiculous you would think it if a Thai told you he was studying English conversation from this dialogue because he couldn't read western script ...*

A    กุดมอร์นิง ไมเนมอิสจอห์น

B    กุดมอร์นิง มิสเตอร์จอห์น เฮาอาร์ยูทูเด?

* (When you have reached Unit 11 you will see how silly it is!)

The familiar Thai script would encourage him to pronounce these English words with a Thai accent and he certainly wouldn't be able to get English speakers to write down new words for him if he was trying to expand his vocabulary; in short, he would never progress beyond the one or two books where English is written phonetically in Thai letters.

You may not intend to write letters in Thai nor read newspapers and novels; but if you want to build upon what you can learn from a book such as this, becoming literate in Thai is an absolute must!

Now that you have decided that you do want to learn to read Thai, here is the good news. The Thai script is presented in this course in such a way as to persuade you that it is neither extremely difficult nor time-consuming, and that even if you are one of the least gifted language learners, you can, with regular practice, learn to read and write Thai. All it really requires is the patience to copy out letters, words and then phrases a sufficient number of times until it becomes almost second nature. Eventually, copying out whole passages will improve not only your reading and writing skills but will also reinforce everything else you have learned about the language, including pronunciation and grammar. Keep going back over earlier lessons, because by reading material that is familiar, you will begin to read more quickly and develop the ability to recognise words instantly without having to laboriously identify individual letters each time.

Remember that when learning a foreign language, 'a little and often' is much more effective than long but infrequent sessions. Ten to fifteen minutes every day is far more productive than one long session once a week.

## *Romanisation of Thai*

For westerners learning the language it is convenient to use romanised Thai at the beginning, but it must be stressed that this is no more than a learning aid. It is not an acceptable alternative to the Thai script and most Thais would not be able to read Thai written in romanised form. There are a number of different systems of romanising Thai, each with their advantages and disadvantages. As with all systems, the one used in this book can offer only an approximate representation of the Thai sound. The most effective strategy is to learn pronunciations from the tape and to memorise Thai script spellings rather than romanised spellings. You should treat the romanisation system simply as a crutch and aim to discard it as quickly as possible.

# —PRONUNCIATION—

There are a few sounds in Thai that do not exist in English and which can cause some problems. But generally speaking, the vast majority of Thai sounds have a reasonably close equivalent in English.

## Consonants

At the beginning of a word, consonants are generally pronounced as in English. A few sounds, however, need further clarification:

**g** as in *get* (not *gin*)

**ng** A single sound which we are familiar with in English at the end of words like *wrong* and *song* but which also occurs at the beginning of words in Thai:

> **ngahn**       **ngâi**       **ngahm ngoo**

**bp** A single sound which is somewhere between a **b** sound and a **p** sound in English. Many learners find it hard to both produce this sound accurately and to distinguish it from **b**. Don't be discouraged if you do have problems; you will probably find that over a period of time you will gradually master it.

> **bpai**       **bpen**       **bpoo**       **bplào**

**dt** A single sound which is somewhere between a **d** sound and a **t** sound in English. Again, many learners find it difficult to distinguish from **t** at first, although usually such problems are short-lived.

**dtàir**           **dtìt**                **dtorn**                **dtrong**

At the end of a word the sounds **k**, **p**, and **t** are not 'released'. An example of an 'unreleased' **t** in English is the final letter in *rat* when *rat trap* is said quickly. At first you may feel that words ending in **k**, **p**, **t** all sound the same, but within a very short time you will find that you can hear a distinct difference.

**bpàhk**           **bàhp**                **bàht**

**yâhk**            **yâht**                **yâhp**

Many Thais have difficulty pronouncing an **r** sound and will substitute an l sound instead. Thus, **a-rai?** *(what?)* becomes **a-lai?** In words that begin with two consonants, you might also hear some Thais omit the second consonant sound. **krai?** *(who?)* becomes **kai?** and **bplah** *(fish)* becomes **bpah**. An even more bewildering change is when **kw** at the beginning of a word becomes **f**, so that **kwǎh** *(right)* is pronounced **fǎa!**

## Vowels

Most Thai vowels have near equivalents in English. In the romanisation system used in this book, vowels are pronounced as follows:

**a**    as in a*go*
**e**    as in p*e*n
**i**    as in b*i*t
**o**    as in c*o*t
**u**    as in f*u*n
**ah** as in f*a*ther
**ai**  as in Th*ai*
**air** as in f*air*
**ao**  as in L*ao*
**ay**  as in m*ay*
**ee**  as in f*ee*
**er**  as in numb*er*
**ew** as in f*ew*
**oh**  as in g*o*
**oo**  as in b*oo*k

**oo** as in *book*
**oo** as in *food*
**oy** as in *boy*

Other sounds, however, have no near equivalent in English, and you need to listen to the cassette to gain a proper idea of how they should be pronounced:

| eu | meu | séu | keu |
|----|-----|-----|-----|
| eu-a | mêu-a | sêu-a | něu-a |
| air-o | láir-o | gâir-o | tair-o |
| er-ee | ler-ee | ker-ee | ner-ee |

#  Tones

There are five tones in Thai: mid tone, low tone, high tone, rising tone and falling tone. These are represented in the romanisation system by the following accents: mid tone (no mark), low tone ( ` ), high tone ( ´ ), rising tone (   ) and falling tone ( ^ ). To help attune your ears to the sound of the different tones, the cassette begins with a Thai speaker saying the following words. Don't worry about meaning at this stage – simply concentrate on listening!

| **mid tone:** | kOOn | krai | mah | bpai |
|---------------|------|------|-----|------|
| | pairng | mee | dairng | bpen |
| **low tone:** | jàhk | bpàirt | sìp | bàht |
| | yài | jòrt | èek | nèung |
| **high tone:** | mái | káo | lót | lék |
| | róo | rót | náhm | púk |
| **rising tone:** | sǒo-ay | pǒm | sǒrng | kǒr |
| | sěe-a | kǒrng | nǎi | děe-o |
| **falling tone:** | mâi | châi | dâi | têe |
| | gâo | mâhk | chôrp | pôot |

It is obviously important to be able to both hear and reproduce tones correctly if you are going to make yourself understood. But don't let a fear of getting a tone wrong inhibit you from practising. Surprisingly, wrong tones are seldom the cause of misunderstandings and communication breakdowns. Indeed, many non-Thais operate confidently and effectively in the language with far from perfect accuracy in their tones.

# 1

## kOOn chêu a-rai?

### *What's your name?*

## คุณชื่ออะไร

## In this unit you will learn

- how to state your name, nationality and occupation
- how to ask someone else for the same information
- how to ask for confirmation
- the most frequently occurring consonants and six vowel symbols
- numbers 1–10
- to read some simple words and sentences

## ▶ — bòt sǒn-ta-nah  บทสนทนา *(Dialogue)* —

Peter is spending some time working at his company's Bangkok branch. The first person he meets at the office is Malee.

| Malee | sa-wùt dee kâ. | สวัสดีค่ะ |
| | kOOn chêu a-rai ká? | คุณชื่ออะไรคะ |
| Peter | chêu Peter krúp. | ชื่อ ปีเตอร์ ครับ |
| Malee | bpen kon a-may-ri-gun, châi mái? | เป็นคนอเมริกันใช่ไหม |
| Peter | mâi châi krúp. | ไม่ใช่ครับ |
| | bpen kon ung-grìt krúp. | เป็นคนอังกฤษครับ |

| | | |
|---|---|---|
| | mah jàhk Manchester. | มาจากแมนเช็สเตอร์ |
| | kǒr-tôht krúp, | ขอโทษครับ |
| | kOOn chêu a-rai krúp? | คุณชื่ออะไรครับ |

| | | |
|---|---|---|
| **sa-wùt dee** | *good morning / afternoon /* | สวัสดี |
| | *evening ; hello ; goodbye* | |
| **kâ, ká, krúp** | *(see* **pa-sǎh láir sǔng-kom***)* | ค่ะ, คะ, ครับ |
| **kOOn** | *you* | คุณ |
| **chêu** | *first name ;* | ชื่อ |
| | *to have the first name ...* | |
| **a-rai?** | *what?* | อะไร |
| **bpen** | *to be* | เป็น |
| **kon** | *person* | คน |
| **a-may-ri-gun** | *American* | อเมริกัน |
| **châi mái?** | *isn't that so?* | ใช่ไหม |
| **mâi châi** | *no (to ...* **châi mái?** *questions)* | ไม่ใช่ |
| **ung-grìt** | *English* | อังกฤษ |
| **mah** | *to come* | มา |
| **jàhk** | *from* | จาก |
| **kǒr-tôht** | *excuse me* | ขอโทษ |

Malee has taken Peter down to the Labour Department to sort out his work permit. An official is asking her for the information he needs to fill in his form.

| | | |
|---|---|---|
| **Official** | káo chêu a-rai krúp? | เขาชื่ออะไรครับ |
| **Malee** | chêu Peter kâ. | ชื่อ ปีเตอร์ ค่ะ |
| **Official** | nahm sa-gOOn a-rai? | นามสกุลอะไร |

| | | |
|---|---|---|
| **Malee** | nahm sa-gOOn Green kâ. | นามสกุล กรีน ค่ะ |
| **Official** | bpen kon châht a-rai krúp? | เป็นคนชาติอะไรครับ |
| **Malee** | bpen kon ung-grìt kâ. | เป็นคนอังกฤษค่ะ |
| **Official** | kon ung-grìt, châi mái? | คนอังกฤษใช่ไหม |
| **Malee** | châi kâ. | ใช่ค่ะ |
| **Official** | tum-ngahn a-rai? | ทำงานอะไร |
| **Malee** | bpen núk tÓO-rá-gìt kâ. | เป็นนักธุรกิจค่ะ |
| | tum ngahn gùp bor-ri-sùt AIG. | ทำงานกับบริษัท เอ ไอ จี |

| | | |
|---|---|---|
| **káo** | *he; she; they* | เขา |
| **nahm sa-gOOn** | *surname;* | นามสกุล |
| | *to have the surname ...* | |
| **châht** | *nation* | ชาติ |
| **tum-ngahn** | *to work* | ทำงาน |
| **núk tÓO-rá-gìt** | *businessman* | นักธุรกิจ |
| **gùp** | *with* | กับ |
| **bor-ri-sùt AIG** | *AIG Company* | บริษัท เอ ไอ จี |

## Comprehension

1  What nationality does Malee assume Peter is?
2  What is Peter's real nationality and where does he come from?
3  What is Peter's occupation?
4  Who are his employers?

# — pah-sǎh láir sǔng-kom  ภาษาและสังคม —
## (Language and culture)

First names are used in both formal and informal situations in Thailand. Thais, both male and female, should normally be addressed by their first name preceded by the title **kOOn** (คุณ) – usually spelt *khun* in romanised letters. Thus, Mrs. Patcharee Saibua, Mr. Sompong Tongkum and Miss Araya Jaroenwong should be addressed as *Khun* Patcharee, *Khun* Sompong and *Khun* Araya respectively. Thais dealing with westerners in a formal professional context will often prefer to use *khun* with the westerner's surname, Charles Phillips being addressed as *Khun Phillips* rather than *Khun Charles*. Surnames have only come into general usage in Thailand within the last hundred years and their usage is restricted to written documents.

# —————— sǔm-noo-un  สำนวน ——————
## (Key phrases and expressions)

 How to:

- greet someone

  sa-wùt dee krúp *(male speaking)*   สวัสดีครับ
  sa-wùt dee kâ *(female speaking)*   สวัสดีค่ะ

- ask somebody's name and say your own

  kOOn chêu a-rai?   คุณชื่ออะไร
  pǒm (dee-chún) chêu ...   ผม (ดิฉัน) ชื่อ ...

- ask somebody's surname and say your own

  kOOn nahm sa-gOOn a-rai?   คุณนามสกุลอะไร
  pǒm (dee-chún) nahm sa-gOOn ...   ผม (ดิฉัน) นามสกุล ...

- ask somebody's nationality and state your own

  kOOn bpen kon châht a-rai?  คุณเป็นคนชาติอะไร

  pŏm (dee-chún) bpen kon ung-grìt  ผม (ดิฉัน) เป็นคน
  อังกฤษ

- ask somebody's occupation and state your own

  kOOn tum ngahn a-rai?  คุณทำงานอะไร

  pŏm (dee-chún) bpen ...  ผม (ดิฉัน) เป็น ...

  pŏm (dee-chún) tum ngahn gùp ...  ผม (ดิฉัน) ทำงานกับ...

## kum ùt-tí-bai  คำอธิบาย
### (Language notes)

## 1  sa-wùt dee krúp/kâ  สวัสดีครับ/ค่ะ

This is a general greeting which can be used regardless of the time
of day. In informal spoken Thai it is often abbreviated to 'wùt dee.
The expression is also used when saying goodbye.

## 2  krúp, kâ, ká  ครับ ค่ะ คะ

There are a number of words in Thai which are extremely difficult
to translate into English. Among these are the 'polite particles' **krúp**,
**kâ** and **ká**, which are added to the end of statements and questions to
make the speaker's words sound more polite. Male speakers use
**krúp** at the end of both statements and questions, while females use
**kâ** at the end of statements and **ká** after questions. It is not necessary
to use these particles after every sentence in a conversation, although for the western learner it is probably best to risk sounding
too polite; to get a real 'feel' for using particles, however, it is
necessary to interact with Thais.

## 3 Pronouns

There are many more pronouns in Thai than in English; the correct choice will depend on such factors as the relative status and degree of intimacy between speakers. For the western learner, however, it is quite possible to use Thai effectively with a limited number of pronouns, the most common of which are :

| | | |
|---|---|---|
| **pǒm** | *I* (male) | ผม |
| **dee-chún/chún** | *I* (female) | ดิฉัน/ฉัน |
| **kOO n** | *you* (sing. and plur.) | คุณ |
| **káo** | *he, she, they* | เขา |
| **rao** | *we* | เรา |

Unlike western languages, the word for *I* varies according to the gender of the speaker; of the two female forms, **chún** is the less formal. However, Thais frequently omit pronouns altogether when it is clear from the context who is speaking, being addressed or being referred to. In many of the examples in this course, you will find that the pronoun has been omitted in Thai to make it sound more natural and that an arbitrary choice of pronoun has been included in the English translation:

| | |
|---|---|
| chêu a-rai? | *What's* **your** *name?* |
| chêu Peter. | **His** *name is Peter.* |

The first example could just as correctly have been translated as *What's* **his/her** *name?* and the second as **My** *name is Peter.* If you study the conversation, you will notice that **bpen kon ung-grìt** in the first dialogue means **I'm** *English* and in the second, **He's** *English.*

## 4 ... châi mái? ...ใช่ไหม *questions*

The words ... **châi mái?** can be tagged on to the end of a statement to transform it into a question, rather like ... *isn't it, ... don't they?*, etc. in English. It is a very useful question form for checking that you have heard or understood correctly what has just been said, for example, when you are told somebody's name ... **châi mái?** questions are answered either **châi** (ใช่) *yes* or **mâi châi** (ไม่ใช่) *no.*

| | |
|---|---|
| chêu Peter, châi mái? | *His name is Peter, isn't it?* |
| – **châi** | – Yes. |
| bpen kon a-may-ri-gun, châi mái? | *He's American, isn't he?* |
| – **mâi châi** | – No. |

## 5 'What?' questions

The Thai word for *what?* is **a-rai** (อะไร). It normally occurs at the end of a sentence:

| | |
|---|---|
| káo chêu a-rai? | *What's his name?* |
| káo nahm sa-gOOn a-rai? | *What's his surname?* |
| káo bpen kon châht a-rai? | *What nationality is he?* |
| káo tum ngahn a-rai? | *What (job) does he do?* |

To answer such questions, substitute **a-rai** with the appropriate word; an exception is the question **káo tum ngahn a-rai?** to which the normal response is **káo bpen ...** *(He is a ...)* followed by the name of the occupation:

| | |
|---|---|
| káo chêu a-rai? | |
| – káo chêu Sǒm-chai | *His name is Somchai.* |
| | |
| káo bpen kon châht a-rai? | |
| – káo bpen kon tai | *He is Thai.* |
| | |
| but | |
| | |
| káo tum ngahn a-rai? | |
| – káo bpen mǒr | *He is a doctor.* |

☑ — **bàirp fèuk hùt** แบบฝึกหัด *(Exercises)* —

1 Answer the following questions.

   (*a*)  káo chêu a-rai?
   (*b*)  káo nahm sa-gOOn a-rai?
   (*c*)  káo bpen kon châht a-rai?
   (*d*)  káo tum-ngahn a-rai?

(e) káo chêu a-rai?
(f) káo bpen kon châht a-rai?
(g) káo tum ngahn gùp bor-ri-sùt
   AIG, châi mái?

**2** How would you answer if a Thai
asked you these questions?

(a) kOOn chêu a-rai?
(b) kOOn nahm sa-gOOn a-rai?
(c) kOOn bpen kon châht a-rai?
(d) kOOn tum ngahn a-rai?

**3** Applying for a visa

Chantana, a Thai student (*student:* **núk-sèuk-săh**) is applying for a visa to study in England. Match the questions she was asked when she went to the British Embassy with the answers she gave.

*Questions*

(a) bpen kon tai, châi mái?
(b) tum-ngahn a-rai?
(c) nahm sa-gOOn a-rai?

(d) kOOn chêu a-rai?

*Answers*

(i) nahm sa-gOOn BOOn-dee.
(ii) châi kâ.
(iii) dee-chún cheu Chŭn-ta-nah kâ.
(iv) bpen núk-sèuk-săh kâ.

**4** How would you introduce these people?

|  | (a) | (b) | (c) | (d) |
|---|---|---|---|---|
| *name:* | Somchai | John | Makoto | Paula |
| *surname:* | Torngkum | Stevens | Iwasaki | Besson |
| *nationality:* | Thai | American | Japanese | French |
| *home town:* | Chiangmai | Florida | Tokyo | Paris |
| *occupation:* | doctor | student | businessman | teacher |

*Example:*

káo chêu Sŏm-chai
nahm sa-gOOn torng-kum
bpen kon tai
mah jàhk chee-ung-mài
bpen mŏr

Here are some of the words you will need:

| *French* | fa-rùng-sàyt |
| *Japanese* | yêe-bpÒOn |
| *doctor* | mŏr |
| *teacher* | ah-jahn |

**5** How would you ask the following questions?

(a) Excuse me, what's your name?
(b) His name is Somchai isn't it?

(c) What is his surname?
(d) He's Thai, isn't he?
(e) He's a teacher, isn't he?

## 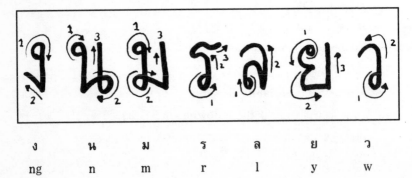 ——— àhn láir kĕe-un อ่านและเขียน ———
(Reading and writing)

### 1 Consonants

Consonants in Thai are divided into three groups or 'classes' called low class, mid class and high class. It is important to remember which class a consonant belongs to as the class of the initial consonant in a word will partly determine the tone of that word. The consonants in this unit are all *low class* consonants.

Thai consonants are all pronounced with an inherent '-*or*' sound; thus we can say at the end of this unit that we know the letters '**nor**', '**mor**', '**ngor**', '**ror**' and so on. Each Thai consonant also has a 'name' – '**nor**' is known as **nor nŏo** (**nŏo** means *mouse*) and then there is **mor máh** (**máh** means *horse*), **ngor ngoo** (**ngoo** means *snake*) and so on. When Thais learn their alphabet at school, they always learn the name of the letter but it is not necessary for the foreigner to know these names in order to be able to read.

Look carefully at the letters below. They are all written with a single stroke starting from the inside of the loop and moving outwards.

| ง | น | ม | ร | ล | ย | ว |
|---|---|---|---|---|---|---|
| ng | n | m | r | l | y | w |

In letters where there are two loops, the starting point is the top loop on the left hand side. Copy each letter a number of times until you can reproduce it accurately and naturally; say the name of the letter (e.g. **mor**) each time you write it to help you memorise it.

## 2 Vowels

Vowels are classified as either 'long' or 'short'. In English, an example of a short vowel sound is the *i* in *bin*, while the vowel sound in *seen* is long. As each vowel symbol is introduced you will need to remember whether it is a long or short vowel, as vowel length plays a part in determining the tone of a word.

The vowel symbols in this unit, with the exception of *-u-*, are written after a consonant symbol, the dash representing the position of a consonant. In subsequent units, however, you will see that certain vowel symbols are written above the consonant, others below and some in front.

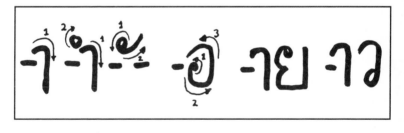

| -า | -ํา | - ̆- | -อ | -าย | -าว |
|------|------|------|------|------|------|
| -ah | -um | -u- | -or | -ai | -ao |
| (long) | (short + 'm') | (short) | (long) | (long) | (long) |

## 3 Words

Here are some simple words combining the consonants and vowels you have met in this unit. If you have the cassette that accompanies the course listen to them on cassette and then copy out each word a few times. The first two words occurred in the dialogue at the beginning of the unit . Go back to this section and see if you can identify them in the Thai script.

| มา | งาน | นาน | นาย | ลาว |
|------|--------|------|------|------|
| mah | ngahn | nahn | nai | lao |
| *to come* | *work* | *a long time* | *Mr* | *Lao* |

| นำ | มัน | รอ | ยอม |
|------|------|------|------|
| num | mun | ror | yorm |
| *to lead* | *it* | *to wait* | *to agree* |

## 4  Numbers

Although Arabic numerals are widely used in Thailand it is useful to be familiar with the Thai system of writing the numbers 1–10. These numbers are, incidentally, written the same way in the Lao and Cambodian scripts.

| ๑ | ๒ | ๓ | ๔ | ๕ |
|------|-------|------|------|------|
| nèung | sǒrng | sǎhm | sèe | hâh |
| 1 | 2 | 3 | 4 | 5 |

| ๖ | ๗ | ๘ | ๙ | ๑๐ |
|------|------|--------|------|------|
| hòk | jèt | bpàirt | gâo | sìp |
| 6 | 7 | 8 | 9 | 10 |

☑ ——— **bàirp fèuk àhn** แบบฝึกอ่าน ———
*(Reading exercises)*

**1** How many letters can you identify in this sample of Thai? Put a
faint pencil stroke through every letter you can recognise.

ตลาดทางด้านยุโรปของเราในตอนนี้พูดได้ว่าไปได้สวย โดยเฉพาะ
ที่อังกฤษตอนนี้การไปเที่ยวเมืองไทยเป็นที่นิยมกันมากเหมือนกับ
เป็นแฟชั่นอีกอย่างหนึ่ง   เดิมเขาจะไปฮ่องกงกันมากกว่าเพราะ
ฮ่องกงเป็นเมืองขึ้นของเขาและคนพูดภาษาอังกฤษกันได้เป็นส่วน
มาก

Perhaps learning to read Thai isn't quite as daunting as you
thought! You probably found, however, that it required quite an
effort of concentration to scan through these few lines. As you
become more accustomed to the Thai script, you will find that
you can pick out letters and words quickly and effortlessly.

**2** Read the words in the table several times until you can read
both rows and columns quickly and accurately. When you can
do this, pick words at random and see how quickly you can read
them. As a further test, listen to the exercise on cassette and
write down the words as dictation. Don't worry about what the
words mean at this stage.

| | | | |
|---|---|---|---|
| มา | ยา | นาม | งาน |
| วัน | นำ | รำ | รอ |
| นอน | ราย | นาย | ยาย |
| ลาว | ยาว | ราว | ยอม |

WATERFORD
NO

— 21 —

**3** In Thai writing there are no spaces between words. Spaces are used rather for punctuation purposes and tend to occur where there would be a full stop or comma in English. For the western learner, this means that there is the added complication of having to recognise where one word ends and another begins. In fact this is not nearly such a formidable task as it may at first seem. Try to work out where one word ends and the next begins in the sentences below. If it helps, draw a faint pencil line to indicate the boundary. Note that all of the vowel symbols in the sentences must occur after a consonant; they cannot occur as the first letter of a word. You can check your answers in the Key.

ยามลาวมา

นายรอนาน

นางลานาย

ยายรำนาน

**4** How would you dial these Bangkok telephone numbers?

(a) ๒๓๖-๔๘๙๐

(b) ๕๘๐-๗๓๕๙

(c) ๒๒๕-๗๓๘๑

(d) ๖๙๓-๒๑๔๕

(e) ๓๗๑-๙๕๔๘

# Learning a new script

You can only learn to read and write Thai by regular practice. Ten to fifteen minutes practice every day is much more effective than one hour twice a week, and as long as you stick to daily practice you should find that you make rapid progress. You might, for example, try some of the following 'learning strategies': copy each letter and each word a dozen or so times until you can write it quickly and accurately; look at the dialogues in Thai script and see how many letters, and how many parts of words you can recognise; and get into the habit of doodling in Thai so as to improve your handwriting , or making up sentences with the Thai words you can spell.

# 2

## — nêe tâo-rài ká? *How much is this?* —
## นี่เท่าไรคะ

### *In this unit you will learn*

- how to ask the price of something
- how to negotiate a discount
- how to find out the names of things
- some more numbers: 20, 30, 40 ... 100
- the main mid class consonants
- some new vowels

### bòt sŏn-ta-nah   บทสนทนา

Peter's wife, Sue is admiring the shirts at one of the pavement stalls along Sukhumwit Road in central Bangkok.

| Sue | nêe tâo-rài ká? | นี่เท่าไรคะ |
|-----|-----------------|-------------|
| Vendor | bpàirt-sìp bàht kâ. | แปดสิบบาทค่ะ |
| Sue | bpàirt-sìp bàht lěr ká? | แปดสิบบาทหรือคะ |
| | pairng bpai nòy. | แพงไปหน่อย |
| | hòk-sìp bàht dâi mái? | หกสิบบาทได้ไหม |
| Vendor | mâi dâi kâ. | ไม่ได้ค่ะ |

|        | mâi pairng.                        | ไม่แพง                      |
|--------|------------------------------------|-----------------------------|
|        | sǒo-ay ná.                         | สวยนะ                       |
| Sue    | sěe dairng mee mái?                | สีแดงมีไหม                   |
| Vendor | mee kâ.                            | มีค่ะ                        |
|        | sěe dairng sǒo-ay mâhk ná ká.      | สีแดงสวยมากนะคะ              |
| Sue    | hòk-sìp bàht mâi dâi lěr ká?       | หกสิบบาทไม่ได้หรือคะ         |
| Vendor | jèt-sìp bàht gôr láir-o gun.       | เจ็ดสิบบาทก็แล้วกัน          |
|        | mâi pairng ná.                     | ไม่แพงนะ                     |
| Sue    | oh kay.                            | โอ เค                        |
|        | dtòk long jèt-sip bàht.            | ตกลงเจ็ดสิบบาท               |

| nêe | this | นี่ |
|---|---|---|
| **tâo-rài?** | *how much?* | เท่าไร |
| **bpàirt-sip** | *eighty* | แปดสิบ |
| **bàht** | *baht* (unit of currency) | บาท |
| **lěr?** (spelt **rěu** ) | *(question word)* | หรือ |
| **pairng** | *expensive* | แพง |
| **... bpai nòy** | *a little too ...* | ... ไปหน่อย |
| **hòk-sìp** | *sixty* | หกสิบ |
| **dâi** | *can* | ได้ |
| **... dâi mái?** | *can you ...?* | ได้ไหม |
| **mâi** | *not* | ไม่ |
| **mâi dâi** | *can't; no* (in ... **dâi mái?** questions) | ไม่ได้ |
| **sǒo-ay** | *beautiful, pretty* | สวย |
| **ná** | (see **kum ùt-tí-bai 10**) | นะ |
| **sěe dairng** | *red* | สีแดง |

| mee | have | มี |
|---|---|---|
| ... **mái?** | (question word) | ไหม |
| **mâhk** | very, much | มาก |
| **jèt-sìp** | seventy | เจ็ดสิบ |
| ... **gôr láir-o gun** | I'll settle for ... | ... ก็แล้วกัน |
| **oh kay** | O.K. | โอ เค |
| **dtòk long** | agree(d) | ตกลง |

Peter, meanwhile, has gone to a market, where he spots some unfamiliar fruits.

| Peter | nêe a-rai krúp? | นี่อะไรครับ |
|---|---|---|
| Vendor | nóy-nàh kâ. | น้อยหน่าค่ะ |
| Peter | a-rai ná krúp? | อะไรนะครับ |
| Vendor | rêe-uk wâh nóy-nàh kâ. | เรียกว่าน้อยหน่าค่ะ |
| Peter | nóy-nàh, châi mái? | น้อยหน่าใช่ไหม |
| Vendor | châi kâ. | ใช่ค่ะ |
| | a-ròy ná. wǎhn. | อร่อยนะ หวาน |
| | lorng chim mái? | ลองชิมไหม |
| | . . . a-ròy mái? | . . .อร่อยไหม |
| Peter | a-ròy krúp. loh la tâo-rài? | อร่อยครับ โลละเท่าไร |
| Vendor | loh la sèe-sìp bàht kâ. | โลละสี่สิบบาทค่ะ |
| Peter | lót nòy, dâi mái krúp. | ลดหน่อยได้ไหมครับ |
| Vendor | sèe-sìp mâi pairng kâ. | สี่สิบไม่แพงค่ะ |
| | kít sǒrng loh jèt-sìp-hâh | คิดสองโลเจ็ดสิบห้า |
| | gôr láir-o gun. | ก็แล้วกัน |
| Peter | krúp . . . | ครับ . . . |
| | láir-o glôo-ay wěe la tâo-rài? | แล้วกล้วยหวีละเท่าไร |
| Vendor | wěe la yêe-sìp kâ. | หวีละยี่สิบค่ะ |

| nóy-nàh | custard apple | น้อยหน่า |
| a-rai ná? | pardon? | อะไรนะ? |
| rêe-uk wâh ... | (it's) called ... | เรียกว่า ... |
| a-ròy | to be tasty | อร่อย |
| wǎhn | to be sweet | หวาน |
| lorng chim | to taste; try out | ลองชิม |
| loh | kilo | โล |
| loh la tâo-rài? | how much a kilo? | โลละเท่าไร |
| lót | to reduce | ลด |
| nòy | a bit | หน่อย |
| kít | to think; charge | คิด |
| glôo-ay | banana | กล้วย |
| wěe la ... | ... per bunch | หวีละ ... |

## Comprehension

1  What colour shirt does Sue want?
2  How much does the vendor ask?
3  What price do they finally agree on?
4  Does Peter like the custard apple he tries?
5  How many kilos does he buy and how much does he pay?
6  How much are the bananas?

## — pah-sǎh láir sǔng-kom ภาษาและสังคม —

Most financial transactions in Thailand, whether shopping, booking hotel rooms or taking a taxi, have traditionally been open to bargaining. While there are now areas of Bangkok life where this practice has disappeared (e.g. fixed prices in department stores, the recently introduced meter-taxis), the ability to haggle *politely* over prices is a must for the foreigner in Thailand. The best thing to do is to try to get some idea in advance of a reasonable price for the goods or services you are trying to purchase so that your bargaining shows some credibility: to assume that all prices have been marked up by a certain percentage is too simplistic. Above all else, the bargaining should be carried out in a relaxed and easy-going manner; a smile and a sense of humour are far more likely to secure a satisfactory deal than an angry and aggressive approach.

The best place to practise bargaining is in the markets. Even in central Bangkok there are still traditional-style markets selling fresh foodstuffs, household goods and cheap toiletries. If you want to watch Thais haggling over the prices, the best time to go is early in the morning, at about 7 a.m. By mid-morning, when things have quietened down, it is worth returning to practise your own language skills. Like Peter, in the second dialogue, you can ask what unfamiliar (and familiar) fruits are called in Thai (**nêe a-rai?** or **nêe rêe-uk wâh a-rai?**), ask the vendor to repeat what she said (**a-rai ná?**), confirm that you have heard it correctly (**rêe-uk wâh ... châi mái?**), ask her the price of her produce and try to knock the price down a little. If you have the same conversation with three different vendors, you will find that within a matter of days it becomes second nature.

Bangkok's largest market is at Chatuchak Park opposite the northern bus terminal. Once a weekend market, it is now open every day. The vast range of goods on sale includes plants, pets, books, tapes, clothes, material, furniture, antiques, electrical goods – in fact, just about everything.

───────── **sŭm-noo-un** สำนวน ─────────

How to:

- ask the price of something

  nêe tâo-rài?  นี่เท่าไร

- say that something is too expensive
  pairng bpai nòy
  
  แพงไปหน่อย

- suggest a price
  jèt-sìp bàht dâi mái?
  
  เจ็ดสิบบาทได้ไหม

- ask for a discount
  lót nòy dâi mái?
  
  ลดหน่อยได้ไหม

- ask what something is called
  nêe a-rai?
  
  นี่อะไร
  
  nêe rêe-uk wâh a-rai?
  
  นี่เรียกว่าอะไร

- ask how much something costs per kilo
  X loh la tâo-rài?
  
  X โลละเท่าไร

## kum ùt-tí-bai คำอธิบาย

### 1 'How much?' questions

The Thai word for *how much?* is **tâo-rài?** (เท่าไร). It always occurs at the end of a sentence:

| | |
|---|---|
| nûn tâo-rài? | *How much is that?* |
| séu *(buy)* tâo-rài? | *How much did you buy it for?* |
| séu rót *(car)* tâo-rài? | *How much did you buy the car for?* |

### 2 Numbers

In the first unit you learned the numbers 1–10. This unit adds the multiples of ten up to 100. These are formed in a regular way with the exception of twenty.

| *twenty* | yêe-sìp | ๒๐ |
|---|---|---|
| *thirty* | săhm-sìp | ๓๐ |

| forty | sèe-sìp | ๔๐ |
| fifty | hâh-sìp | ๕๐ |
| sixty | hòk-sìp | ๖๐ |
| seventy | jèt-sìp | ๗๐ |
| eighty | bpàirt-sìp | ๘๐ |
| ninety | gâo-sìp | ๙๐ |
| one hundred | (nèung) róy | ๑๐๐ |

## 3 ... lěr? หรือ

This is another question word, similar in use to ... **châi mái?** in that it is seeking confirmation. It is rather like the English ..., *eh?* Notice that in the conversation, Sue makes a second – and rather half-hearted – attempt to knock the price down to sixty using ... **mâi dâi lěr?** which might be translated as *You can't ..., then?* baht, You will often hear **lěr?** as a single word response to a statement; in such situations it can be translated as *Really?*

## 4 Adjectives as verbs

Adjectives in Thai occur after the noun. They do not require the verb *is/are* in front of them; a word like **pairng** can be thought of as meaning both *expensive* and *to be expensive*, or even *it is expensive*.

| sêu-a sǒo-ay | *A beautiful shirt / The shirt is beautiful.* |
| glôo-ay a-ròy | *A tasty banana / The banana is tasty.* |

## 5 Negative sentences

The negative is formed by adding the word **mâi** (ไม่) in front of the main verb or adjective:

| mâi pairng | *It's not expensive.** |
| mâi sǒo-ay | *It's not beautiful.* |
| mâi bpai *(go)* | *I'm not going.* |

\* Remember that the pronoun *(I, you, he, she, we, you, they, it)* is often omitted in Thai when it is clear what is being referred to. This is especially so in the case of the Thai word for *it*, **mun** (มัน) which Thais avoid in formal speech because it is regarded as impolite.

## 6 dâi ได้

The most common meaning of the verb **dâi** is *can*. It occurs after the main verb:

| | |
|---|---|
| pǒm bpai dâi | *I can go. (I-go-can)* |
| káo pôot tai dâi | *He can speak Thai. (He-speak-Thai-can)* |

In negative sentences, the word **mâi** occurs immediately before **dâi**:

| | |
|---|---|
| pǒm bpai mâi dâi | *I can't go.* |
| káo pôot tai mâi dâi | *He can't speak Thai.* |

The question formula ... **dâi mái?** (... ได้ไหม) *can you / he / I etc. ...?* likewise comes at the end of a sentence:

| | | |
|---|---|---|
| pǒm bpai dâi mái? | *Can I go?* | (I-go-can-question word) |
| káo pôot tai dâi mái? | *Can he speak Thai?* | (He-speak-Thai-can-question word) |

## 7 Colours

The word **sěe** (สี) is both a noun – *colour* – and a verb, *to be the colour x*. **sěe** is normally used in front of the specific colour word when describing the colour of something.

| | |
|---|---|
| sěe a-rai? | *What colour is it?* |
| sěe dairng | *(It is) red.* |
| sêu-a sěe a-rai? | *What colour is the shirt?* |
| sêu-a sěe dairng mee mái? | *Do you have a red shirt?* |

The most common colour words are:

| | | |
|---|---|---|
| sěe dairng | *red* | สีแดง |
| sěe kěe-o | *green* | สีเขียว |
| sěe lěu-ung | *yellow* | สีเหลือง |

| | | |
|---|---|---|
| sěe núm ngern | *blue* | สีน้ำเงิน |
| sěe dum | *black* | สีดำ |
| sěe núm dtahn | *brown* | สีน้ำตาล |
| sěe kǎo | *white* | สีขาว |

## 8  ... mái?  ... ไหม *questions*

You have already met the question forms **... châi mái?** *(isn't that so?)* and **... dâi mái?** *(can you ...?).* The question word **mái** can also be used on its own to make simple questions:

| | |
|---|---|
| sǒo-ay mái? | *Is it pretty?* |
| nóy-nàh a-ròy mái? | *Is the custard apple tasty?* |
| glôo-ay pairng mái? | *Are bananas expensive?* |

If you want to say *yes* to a **... mái?** question you simply repeat the main verb in the question:

| | |
|---|---|
| sǒo-ay mái? | *Is it pretty?* |
| – sǒo-ay | *– Yes.* |
| pairng mái? | *Is it expensive?* |
| – pairng | *– Yes.* |

To say *no*, use the negative word **mâi** in front of the verb.

| | |
|---|---|
| pairng mái? | *Is it expensive?* |
| – mâi pairng | *– No.* |
| a-ròy mái? | *Is it tasty?* |
| mâi a-ròy | *– No.* |

Be careful not to confuse the question word **... mái?** (... ไหม), pronounced with a high tone, and negative **mâi** (ไม่) pronounced with a falling tone!

## 9  *Word order*

Normal word order in Thai is *subject + verb + object.* Notice how Sue puts **sěe dairng** at the beginning of the sentence when she is asking if the vendor has any red T-shirts. This strategy of putting the topic at the beginning of the sentence is very common in Thai. It would also have been perfectly correct for her to have said **mee sěe dairng mái?**

## 10 ná นะ

You will hear Thais use the word **ná** very frequently. There is no single adequate English translation but it means something like *Right?, O.K?* or *... you know*. It is the kind of word that you will get a feel for by listening to Thais.

## 11 loh la tâo-rài? โลละเท่าไร

**la** (ละ) can be translated as *per*. Notice that the word order in Thai is quite different from English when asking and stating the price of things per kilo:

| | | | |
|---|---|---|---|
| nóy-nàh | loh | **la** | tâo-rài? |
| *custard apple* | *kilo* | per | *how much?* |
| sôm | loh | **la** | sèe-sìp bàht |
| *orange* | *kilo* | per | *forty baht* |

However, not all fruits are bought by the kilo. Bananas are bought by the bunch, while large fruit, such as water melons **(dtairng moh)**, papayas **(ma-la-gor)**, pineapples **(sùp-bpa-rót)** and mangoes **(ma-môo-ung)** are bought individually. When asking about the price of these, substitute the word **loh** with **wěe** (which literally means *comb*) for bananas and **bai** for individual fruit.

| | |
|---|---|
| glôo-ay **wěe** la tâo-rài? | *How much are bananas per* bunch? |
| ma-la-gor **bai** la tâo-rài? | *How much are papayas per* fruit? |

 —————— **bàirp fèuk hùt** แบบฝึกหัด ——————

1 How well can you bargain? Imagine that you have been quoted the prices below. Say that it is a little too expensive and suggest a price twenty baht cheaper. The first one has been done for you.

(*a*) gâo-sìp bàht
pairng bpai nòy krúp/kâ
jèt-sìp bàht dâi mái?

    (b)  jèt-sìp bàht
    (c)  bpàirt-sìp bàht
    (d)  sèe-sìp bàht
    (e)  hâh-sìp bàht

2  How would you say:

    (a)  How much is this?
    (b)  That's a bit expensive.
    (c)  Can you lower the price a little?
    (d)  How about fifty baht?
    (e)  The red (one) isn't pretty.
    (f)  Do you have green?

3  How would you ask the price of the different kinds of fruit below?

    (a)  sùp-bpa-rót    (b)  sôm    (c)  glôo-ay    (d)  ma-la-gor
    (e)  ma-môo-ung    (f)  dtairng-moh    (g)  nóy-nàh

**4** Complete the dialogue. Peter is trying to find out the Thai word for 'mango'. This is what the vendor said to him. But what were his questions?

| | |
|---|---|
| **Peter** | ....................................? |
| **Vendor** | rêe-uk wâh ma-môo-ung kâ. |
| **Peter** | ....................................? |
| **Vendor** | ma-môo-ung kâ. |
| **Peter** | ....................................? |
| **Vendor** | châi kâ. |
| **Peter** | ....................................? |
| **Vendor** | bai la yêe-sìp bàht kâ. |
| **Peter** | ....................................? |
| **Vendor** | lót mâi dâi kâ. |

 —————— **àhn láir kěe-un** อ่านและเขียน ——————

## 1 Consonants

In the first unit you learned the most common low class consonants. In this unit you meet the main *mid class* consonants.

| ก | จ | ด | ต | บ | ป | อ |
|---|---|---|---|---|---|---|
| g | j | d | dt | b | bp | ('zero') |

## 2 'Zero' consonant

Notice that the final symbol of this group is identical in appearance to the vowel -or you learned in the first lesson. When the symbol occurs at the beginning of a word, however, it is a consonant, which we can call 'zero consonant' because it has no sound of its own. It is used when writing words which begin with a vowel *sound*.

| | | | |
|---|---|---|---|
| ahng | อาง | ao | อาว |
| um | อำ | ai | อาย |

## 3 Vowels

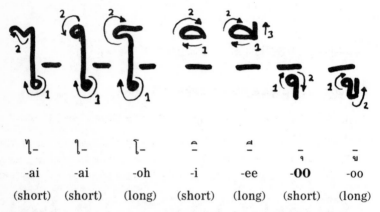

| ไ- | ใ- | โ- | ◌ิ | ◌ี | ◌ุ | ◌ู |
|---|---|---|---|---|---|---|
| -ai | -ai | -oh | -i | -ee | **-oo** | -oo |
| (short) | (short) | (long) | (short) | (long) | (short) | (long) |

The first three vowels are written in front of the consonant, even though the consonant is pronounced first. Although the first two vowels are pronounced exactly the same, when it comes to writing, they are not interchangeable and you have to memorise the correct spelling of a word.

☑——— **bàirp fèuk àhn** แบบฝึกอ่าน ———

1 Here is the same sample of Thai script that you met in the first unit. Again, put a faint pencil stroke through all the letters you can now recognise.

ตลาดทางด้านยุโรปของเราในตอนนี้พูดได้ว่าไปได้สวย โดยเฉพาะ
ที่อังกฤษตอนนี้การไปเที่ยวเมืองไทยเป็นที่นิยมกันมากเหมือน
กับเป็นแฟชั่นอีกอย่างหนึ่งเดิมเขาจะไปฮ่องกงกันมากกว่าเพราะ
ฮ่องกงเป็นเมืองขึ้นของเขา   และคนพูดภาษาอังกฤษกันได้เป็น
ส่วนมาก

2  Try to read these words before listening to them on the cassette.
Don't worry if you find it difficult to hear the difference
between ด  and ต  at this stage. It will come with practice!

| | | | |
|---|---|---|---|
| กิน | กัน | ใจ | ดู |
| ดี | ตา | ตี | บิน |
| ใบ | ไป | ปี | โมง |
| ปู | โรง | ยุง | อัน |

3  Look out for these words in the dialogue.

| | | | | | |
|---|---|---|---|---|---|
| ไป | มี | กัน | โอ | ลอง | โล |

You should now be able to read all of the above words.  While
this may seem a fairly small number, you will notice that
there are many other words that you can *almost* read, such as
the following:

| | | | | | |
|---|---|---|---|---|---|
| นี่ | ว่า | น้อย | ได้ | ไม่ | ยี่ |

But they all have a little mark at  the top which you have not
met yet.

4  These sentences all have five words. Check where the word
boundaries occur and read the sentences aloud. (All of the words
that you are reading atthe moment are pronounced with a
mid tone.)

๑    ยุงบินไปบินมา
๒    ลุงยินดีมาดู
๓    ในนามีปูดำ

๔ ยามลาวตีงูตาย

๕ รอดูนางงามดัง

5 Match the dates. In Thailand, the year is normally counted according to B.E.(Buddhist Era) which is 543 years ahead of the A.D. year. 2500 B.E. is thus 1957 A.D.

| | | | |
|---|---|---|---|
| (*a*) | 19 July 1981 | (i) | ๕/๑/๒๔๙๗ |
| (*b*) | 8 November 1948 | (ii) | ๒๕/๑๒/๒๕๓๙ |
| (*c*) | 5 January 1954 | (iii) | ๑๙/๖/๒๕๒๔ |
| (*d*) | 25 December 1996 | (iv) | ๓/๙/๒๕๓๗ |
| (*e*) | 3 September 1994 | (v) | ๘/๑๑/๒๔๙๑ |

Floating market at Damnoen Saduak in Rachburi Province.

# 3

## bpai rohng rairm ree-noh tâo-rài?

—— *How much to the Reno Hotel?* ——

ไปโรงแรมรีโนเท่าไร

## *In this unit you will learn*

- the language of taxi transactions
- numbers 20 – 100
- **láir-o** as a past time marker
- verbs of *knowing*
- reduplication of adjectives and adverbs
- **mâi ... ròrk** in simple contradictions
- 'live' syllables and 'dead' syllables

## bòt sǒn-ta-nah   บทสนทนา

Sue has flagged down a meter-taxi and before getting into the vehicle asks the driver if he will take her to Sukhumwit Road Soi 33, where she is staying

| Sue | bpai ta-nǒn sÒO-kǑOm-wít | ไปถนนสุขุมวิท |
| | soy sǎhm-sìp sǎhm mái ká? | ซอยสามสิบสามไหมคะ |
| Taxi | bpai krúp . . . | ไปครับ . . . |

—— **39** ——

As they approach their destination, the taxi driver asks Sue if she wants him to drive into the *soi* (*lane*).

| | | |
|---|---|---|
| **Taxi** | kâo soy mái krúp? | เข้าซอยไหมครับ |
| **Sue** | kâo kâ. | เข้าค่ะ |
| | bpai sÒOt soy. | ไปสุดซอย |
| | tĕung sèe-yâirk láir-o | ถึงสี่แยกแล้ว |
| | lée-o kwǎh. | เลี้ยวขวา |
| **Taxi** | lée-o kwǎh têe-nêe châi mái krúp? | เลี้ยวขวาที่นี่ใช่ไหมครับ |
| **Sue** | kâ. láir-o lée-o sái têe-nôhn. | ค่ะ แล้วเลี้ยวซ้ายที่โน่น |
| | ... ler-ee bpai èek nít nèung | ... เลยไปอีกนิดหนึ่ง |
| | ... jòrt têe-nêe kâ. | ... จอดที่นี่ค่ะ |
| **Taxi** | dtrong-née châi mái krúp? | ตรงนี้ใช่ไหมครับ |
| **Sue** | kâ. tâo-rài ká? | ค่ะ เท่าไรคะ |
| **Taxi** | hâh-sìp jèt bàht krúp. | ห้าสิบเจ็ดบาทครับ |
| **Sue** | kít hòk-sìp gôr láir-o gun. | คิดหกสิบก็แล้วกัน |
| **Taxi** | kòrp-kOOn krúp. | ขอบคุณครับ |
| | chôhk dee krúp. | โชคดีครับ |
| **Sue** | chôhk dee kâ. | โชคดีค่ะ |

| | | |
|---|---|---|
| **bpai** | *to go* | ไป |
| **ta-nǒn** | *road* | ถนน |
| **ta-nǒn sÒO-kǑOm-wít** | *Sukhumwit Road* | ถนนสุขุมวิท |
| **soy** | *soi, lane* | ซอย |
| **sǎhm-sìp sǎhm** | *thirty-three* | สามสิบสาม |
| **kâo** | *to enter* | เข้า |
| **sÒOt soy** | *end of the soi* | สุดซอย |
| **tĕung** | *to reach* | ถึง |

| | | |
|---|---|---|
| **sèe-yâirk** | *crossroads* | สี่แยก |
| **láir-o** | *and then; already* | แล้ว |
| **lée-o** | *to turn* | เลี้ยว |
| **kwǎh ...** | *right* | ขวา |
| **têe-nêe** | *here* | ที่นี่ |
| **kâ** | *yes* | ค่ะ |
| **sái** | *left* | ซ้าย |
| **têe-nôhn** | *over there* | ที่โน่น |
| **ler-ee bpai** | *carry on, go on* | เลยไป |
| **èek** | *again; further* | อีก |
| **nít nèung** | *a little bit* | นิดหนึ่ง |
| **jòrt** | *park* (verb) | จอด |
| **dtrong-née** | *right here* | ตรงนี้ |
| **hâh-sìp jèt** | *fifty-seven* | ห้าสิบเจ็ด |
| **kòrp-kOOn** | *thank you* | ขอบคุณ |
| **chôhk dee** | *good luck* | โชคดี |

Peter, meanwhile, is taking a 'tuk-tuk' to meet a friend at a small hotel in central Bangkok. Before getting into the vehicle, he checks that the driver knows where it is.

## RENO HOTEL

NO.40 SOI KASEMSON 1 RAMA 1 ROAD.    40 ซ.เกษมสันต์ 1 ตรงข้ามสนามกีฬา
OPP. NATIONAL STADIUM BANGKOK    ถ. พระราม 1 กรุงเทพฯ
TEL. 2150026 - 2150027    โทร. 2150026 - 2150027

**Peter**   róo-jùk rohng rairm ree-noh mái?   รู้จักโรงแรมรีโนไหม
**tuk-tuk**   rohng rairm ree-noh lěr?   โรงแรมรีโนหรือ

| Peter | krúp. yòo soy ga-sǎym-sǔn | ครับ อยู่ซอยเกษมสันต์ |
| | glâi glâi sa-nǎhm gee-lah | ใกล้ๆ สนามกีฬา |
| | hàirng châht. | แห่งชาติ |
| tuk-tuk | oh sa-nǎhm gee-lah hàirng châht | โอ สนามกีฬาแห่งชาติ |
| | châi mái? | ใช่ไหม |
| | róo-jùk. | รู้จัก |
| Peter | bpai tâo-rài krúp? | ไปเท่าไรครับ |
| tuk-tuk | bpàirt-sìp bàht krúp | แปดสิบบาทครับ |
| Peter | pairng bpai nòy krúp. | แพงไปหน่อยครับ |
| tuk-tuk | mâi pairng ròrk krúp. | ไม่แพงหรอกครับ |
| | rót dtìt mâhk na. | รถติดมากนะ |
| Peter | hòk-sìp dâi mái? | หกสิบได้ไหม |
| tuk-tuk | mâi dâi krúp. | ไม่ได้ครับ |
| | kít jèt-sìp gôr láir-o gun. | คิดเจ็ดสิบก็แล้วกัน |
| Peter | oh kay. bpai. | โอ เค ไป |

| róo-jùk | *to know* | รู้จัก |
| rohng rairm | *hotel* | โรงแรม |
| rohng rairm ree-noh | *Reno Hotel* | โรงแรมรีโน |
| yòo | *to be situated at* | อยู่ |
| soy ga-sǎym-sǔn | *Soi Kasemsan* | ซอยเกษมสันต์ |
| glâi glâi | *near* | ใกล้ๆ |
| sa-nǎhm gee-lah hàirng châht | *National Stadium* | สนามกีฬาแห่งชาติ |
| bpàirt-sìp | *eighty* | แปดสิบ |
| mâi ... ròrk | *not ... at all* | ไม่...หรอก |
| rót dtìt | *traffic jam* | รถติด |

## Comprehension

1  Does Sue want to go into the **soi**?
2  Which way does she want to go once they have reached the crossroads?
3  How much is her taxi fare?
4  What **soi** is the Reno Hotel situated in?
5  What is the nearest major landmark?
6  How much does the 'tuk-tuk' driver want to charge?
7  What fare does Peter finally negotiate?

# — pah-sǎh láir sǔng-kom    ภาษาและสังคม —

You can travel around Bangkok by ordinary bus, air-conditioned bus, **samlor** or 'tuk-tuk' (a three-wheeled motorised pedi-cab) or taxi. On ordinary buses there is a fixed fare within the city centre, while on air-conditioned buses, fares are calculated according to the distance travelled. Street maps with full details of all the bus routes are readily available from bookshops and hotels in Bangkok, while route maps in English are also now posted at many bus-stops. Buses are frequent although nearly always overcrowded, fares are cheap, and with exclusive bus lanes on some busy roads, the public transport system somehow manages to run reasonably efficiently amid the general chaos of Bangkok traffic.

Taxis offer a less stressful way of travelling around. To hail a taxi you should raise your hand and signal to the driver with a beckoning motion with the fingers pointing *downwards*. All taxis in central Bangkok are now air-conditioned and the vast majority have recently installed meters, thus making it unnecessary to haggle over the price. Before getting into a vehicle, you do, however, need to enquire whether the driver is prepared to take you to your destination (he may decide that the traffic is just too bad to go that way). It is not a bad idea to also check that he knows the place that you want to go to: he, too, may be a newcomer to the city. Although tipping is not customary, many passengers seem to round-up the meter price. As your Thai improves, you may find that a taxi journey offers an excellent opportunity for a spot of conversation practice. Polite conversation is out of the question if you go by **samlor** (literally, 'three-wheels') or 'tuk-tuk', so-named because of the spluttering sound of its engine. You will also have to negotiate the price with the driver *before* getting into the vehicle. Beware of causing offence by placing your feet against the rail behind the driver's seat; to do so is extremely bad manners and is likely to disturb your driver's concentration – with potentially disastrous consequences.

Many of the major roads in Bangkok have small roads or lanes – called **soy** (spelt *soi* in English) – leading off them. These are usually residential areas with a few small shops and vary in length from a couple of hundred metres to a kilometre or more. If you are nego tiating a price with a taxi driver or 'tuk-tuk' driver it can obviously make some difference as to whether you intend to get off at the entrance to the soi (**bpàhk soy**), the middle (**glahng soy**) or the end (**sÒOt soy**).

─────────── **sŭm-noo-un**   สำนวน ───────────

How to ask a taxi driver:

- if he knows *X*

    róo-jùk *X* mái?                  รู้จัก *X* ไหม

- if he will take you to *X*

    bpai *X* mái?                     ไป *X* ไหม

- how much he will charge to go to *X*

    bpai *X* tâo-rài?                 ไป *X* เท่าไร

How to tell a taxi driver:

- the fare is too expensive and suggest an alternative

    pairng bpai nòy *X* (bàht) dâi mái?   แพงไปหน่อย *X* (บาท)
                                      ได้ไหม

- to go into the *soi*

    kâo soy                          เข้าซอย

- to go to the entrance / middle / end of the *soi*
  bpai bpàhk / glahng / sòOt soy　　ไปปาก/กลาง/สุดซอย
- to turn left / right
  lée-o sái / kwǎh　　เลี้ยวซ้าย / ขวา
- to go straight on
  ler-ee bpai èek　　เลยไปอีก
- to stop here / over there
  jòrt têe-nêe / têe-nôhn　　จอดที่นี่ / ที่โน่น

## kum ùt-tí-bai　คำอธิบาย

## 1 Numbers

The numbers 11 - 20 are as follws:

| | | | |
|---|---|---|---|
| *11* | sìp-èt | *16* | sìp-hòk |
| *12* | sìp-sǒrng | *17* | sìp-jèt |
| *13* | sìp-sǎhm | *18* | sìp-bpàirt |
| *14* | sìp-sèe | *19* | sìp-gâo |
| *15* | sìp-hâh | *20* | yêe-sìp |

The remaining numbers between 10 and 100 are formed in a regular way with the exception of 21, 31, 41, etc. where the word for *one* is **èt** and not **nèung**. (Remember that *twenty* is **yêe-sìp**.)

| | | | |
|---|---|---|---|
| *21* | yêe-sìp-èt | *41* | sèe-sìp-èt |
| *22* | yêe-sìp-sǒrng | *42* | sèe-sìp-sǒrng |
| *23* | yêe-sìp-sǎhm | *51* | hâh-sìp-èt |
| *24* | yêe-sìp-sèe | *52* | hâh-sìp-sǒrng |
| *25* | yêe-sìp-hâh | *61* | hôk-sìp-èt |
| *26* | yêe-sìp-hòk | *62* | hôk-sìp-sǒrng |
| *27* | yêe-sìp-jèt | *71* | jèt-sìp-èt |
| *28* | yêe-sìp-bpàirt | *72* | jèt-sìp-sǒrng |
| *29* | yêe-sìp-gâo | *81* | bpàirt-sìp-èt |
| *31* | sǎhm-sìp-èt | *82* | bpàirt-sìp-sǒrng |
| *32* | sǎhm-sìp-sǒrng | *91* | gâo-sìp-èt |
| *33* | sǎhm-sìp-sǎhm | *92* | gâo-sìp-sǒrng |

## 2 láir-o แล้ว

The word **láir-o** has already occurred in the idiomatic expression **gôr láir-o gun**. It occurs most frequently, however, after a verb to show that the action of the verb has been completed.

| | |
|---|---|
| káo bpai láir-o | *They have gone.* |
| pǒm dtòk long láir-o | *I have agreed.* |

In the dialogue **láir-o** joins two simple sentences together and might be translated as *and then*.

## 3 'Here' and 'there'

The basic words for *here* and *there* are **têe-nêe** (ที่นี่) and **têe-nûn** (ที่นั่น) respectively. **têe-nôhn** (ที่โน่น) suggests something further away – *over there* – while **dtrong-née** (ตรงนี้) is a more emphatic *right here*.

## 4 kâ and krúp ค่ะ and ครับ

In the first unit you met the particles **kâ** and **krúp** which are tagged onto the end of a sentence to make it sound more polite. When these particles occur on their own, they simply mean *yes*. If you listen to a Thai man on a telephone you may hear him saying little more than **krúp ... krúp ... krúp ... krúp.**

## 5 róo-jùk รู้จัก

The word **róo-jùk** means *to know* in the sense of being acquainted with people, places or things. A different word, **róo** (รู้) or more politely, **sâhp** (ทราบ), is used for knowing facts.

| | |
|---|---|
| róo-jùk mái? | *Do you know him?* |
| mâi róo-jùk | *No.* |

| bpai mái? | *Are you going?* |
|---|---|
| mâi sâhp / mâi róo | *I don't know.* |

## 6 Reduplication

A common feature of spoken Thai is the repetition (linguists call it reduplication) of an adjective or adverb. Thus in the second part of the Dialogue, Peter tells the 'tuk-tuk' driver that his destination is **glâi glâi** *(near, near)* the National Stadium. Reduplication scarcely changes the meaning; it simply sounds nicer to the Thai ear in certain situations. You will sometimes find Thai market vendors transferring the process to English as they assure you that two items are 'same, same' in either quality or price.

## 7 mâi ... ròrk ไม่ ... หรอก

When **mâi** is used with **ròrk**, for example in statements like **mâi pairng ròrk** or **mâi sǒo-ay ròrk**, the word **ròrk** conveys the sense that the speaker is contradicting an opinion or assumption held by the person he or she is speaking to. Thus, a wife complaining about her husband's latest purchase might say **pairng** in a disapproving tone of voice, only for him to retort, **mâi pairng ròrk**.

☑ ———— **bàirp fèuk hùt**   แบบฝึกหัด ————

1 How would you ask a taxi driver if he would take you to the following places?

(a) Siam Square (**sa-yǎhm sa-kwair**)
(b) Sukhumwit Road, Soi 39
(c) Wat Phra Kaeo (The Temple of the Emerald Buddha) (**wút prá gâir-o**)
(d) Don Muang Airport (**sa-nǎhm bin dorn meu-ung**)
(e) Regent Hotel

2 Match the numbers in the three columns.

| (a) | 56 | (i) | jèt-sìp-sèe | A | ๓๘ |
|---|---|---|---|---|---|
| (b) | 97 | (ii) | sèe-sìp-sǒrng | B | ๕๖ |

| | | | | | |
|---|---|---|---|---|---|
| (c) | 38 | (iii) | gâo-sìp-jèt | C | ๓๘ |
| (d) | 74 | (iv) | sǎhm-sìp-bpàirt | D | ๔๒ |
| (e) | 42 | (v) | hâh-sìp-hòk | E | ๗๔ |

**3** Complete the dialogue.

Peter is taking a taxi to a friend's house at the end of Sukhumwit Road, Soi 53. The 'tuk-tuk' driver's words are given below. What did Peter say?

| | |
|---|---|
| **Peter** | ..................................... |
| **tuk-tuk** | kâo soy mái krúp? |
| **Peter** | ..................................... |
| **tuk-tuk** | bpai sÒOt soy châi mái krúp? |
| **Peter** | ..................................... |
| **tuk-tuk** | jèt-sìp bàht krúp. |
| **Peter** | ..................................... |
| **tuk-tuk** | mâi pairng ròrk krúp. |
| **Peter** | ..................................... |
| **tuk-tuk** | kít hòk-sìp bàht gôr láir-o gun. |

**4** How would you say:

(a) Turn left at the crossroads.
(b) Park over there.
(c) Go on a bit.
(d) Go to the end of the soi.
(e) Turn right just here.

🎙 ——— **àhn láir kĕe-un** อ่านและเขียน ———

The words that you learned to read in the first two units were all pronounced with a mid tone. Now it is time to start learning how to read words pronounced with some other tones. By the end of this section you will have begun to read words with high tones, falling tones and low tones. In order to do this, you will have to bear three things in mind when reading a Thai word or syllable: (1) whether the initial consonant is a low class, mid class or high class consonant;

(2) whether the vowel is a long vowel or a short vowel; and (3) whether the syllable is a 'dead' syllable or a 'live' syllable.

# 1 'Live' syllables and 'dead' syllables

The terms 'live' and 'dead' refer to the way a syllable ends. A 'live' syllable can be prolonged in a droning voice, whereas it is physically impossible to do this with a 'dead' syllable.

*Live syllables* end either with long vowels (e.g. **ah, ai, ao, ee, oo** etc.), a '*m*', '*n*' or '*ng*' sound or the short vowel **ai**. All the words in the script exercises in Unit 1 and Unit 2 are live syllables. Here are some examples to remind you:

| มา | งาน | ไป | ดู | ลาว |
|-----|-------|------|-----|-----|
| mah | ngahn | bpai | doo | lao |

Notice that they are all pronounced with a mid tone.

*Dead syllables* end with either a short vowel (e.g. **i**, **u**) or a '*p*', '*t*' or '*k*' sound. Here are some examples:

| ติ | ดุ | รีบ | นิด | มาก |
|-----|------|------|-----|------|
| dtì | dÒO | rêep | nít | mâhk |

Firstly, you will see that these words are pronounced with different tones; the remainder of this section on the script will explain how the tone of a dead syllable is determined by the class of the initial consonant and the length of the vowel.

Secondly, notice that in our transcription, บ (b) and ด (d) have been written as **p** and **t**. This is because the sounds that can occur at the end of Thai words are quite limited and so certain letters change their pronunciation when they occur at the end of a word.

Here are the consonants you learned in Unit 2 once more, indicating how they are pronounced when they occur as an initial consonant and as a final consonant:

| | ก | จ | ด | ต | บ | ป | อ |
|---|---|---|---|---|---|---|---|
| initial | g | j | d | dt | b | bp | (zero) |
| final | k | t | t | t | p | p | – |

A full list of initial and final consonant sounds appears in the Appendix on page 235.

## 2 Dead syllables with low class initial consonants

If the initial consonant in a dead syllable is low class, the tone will be either high or falling: if the vowel is *short* (e.g. ◌ั, ◌ิ, ◌ุ ) the tone is *high*:

| นิด | รับ | ลุก |
|---|---|---|
| nít | rúp | lóok |

If the vowel is *long* (e.g. –อ, –า, ◌ี, ◌ู ) the tone is *falling*:

| มาก | ยอด | รีบ | ลูบ |
|---|---|---|---|
| mâhk | yôrt | rêep | lôop |

## 3 Dead syllables with mid class initial consonants

If the initial consonant in a dead syllable is mid class, the tone will always be *low,* regardless of whether the vowel is long or short.

| กับ | จาก | ติด | ดีด | จุด | จอด |
|---|---|---|---|---|---|
| gùp | jàhk | dtìt | dèet | jòot | jòrt |

## 4 Summary of tone rules

The tone rules you have just met can be summarised in the following chart. You may find it helpful to make a copy of it to use for reference and checking until you feel completely confident about the rules.

| consonant class | LIVE SYLLABLE | DEAD SYLLABLE | |
|---|---|---|---|
| | | Short Vowel | Long Vowel |
| LOW CLASS | **MID TONE** | **HIGH TONE** | **FALLING TONE** |
| MID CLASS | **MID TONE** | **LOW TONE** | **LOW TONE** |

☑ ———— **bàirp fèuk àhn** แบบฝึกอ่าน ————

Use the summary chart above to help you work through these exercises. Don't worry if it takes you some time; if you understand the principles at this stage, you will find that your reading speed will quickly improve. It is well worth taking the time to work through this lesson two or three times, rather than pushing on to the next with a rather wobbly grasp of how tone rules operate!

1   Dead or (a)live? The words below occur in the dialogue. How many 'live' syllables are there? When you can read all these words, turn back to the dialogues and try to pick them out in the Thai script.

| ไป | อีก | นิด | จอด | มาก |
|---|---|---|---|---|
| กัน | ดี | รีโน | ติด | โรง |

2   What tone? The tone mark has been deliberately omitted in the transcription of these Thai words. What tone should they be pronounced with?

| บีบ | นาง | กัด | จุด | นัด |
|------|-------|------|-------|------|
| beep | nahng | gut | joot | nut |

| ปี | ดาบ | จาน | จาก | ตาย |
|------|------|------|------|------|
| bpee | daap | jahn | jahk | dtai |

| ลาบ | ราว | มีด | รอบ | ปาก |
|------|------|------|------|-------|
| lahp | rao | meet | rorp | bpahk |

3  Practise reading the words in the table, taking your time to make sure you get the tone correct. Do the exercise several times until you can read through from right to left and top to bottom at a reasonable speed. You can give yourself further practice by using the cassette recording of the exercise for dictation practice.

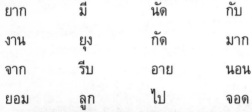

| ยาก | มี | นัด | กับ |
|------|------|------|------|
| งาน | ยุง | กัด | มาก |
| จาก | รีบ | อาย | นอน |
| ยอม | ลูก | ไป | จอด |

A 'tuk-tuk' in Bangkok

# 4

## ao kâo pùt gài

*——— I'll have chicken fried rice ———*

## เอาข้าวผัดไก่

### In this unit you will learn

- how to order drinks and simple meals
- classifiers and counting
- more low class consonants and four new vowel symbols
- how to read words with no written vowel symbol

## bòt sǒn-ta-nah    บทสนทนา

Peter is taking his three children out for lunch in a coffee shop.

| | | |
|---|---|---|
| **Waitress** | ao a-rai ká? | เอาอะไรคะ |
| **Peter** | kǒr doo may-noo nòy krúp. | ขอดูเมนูหน่อยครับ |
| **Waitress** | nêe kâ. | นี่ค่ะ |
| **Peter** | ao kâo pùt gài sǒrng jahn | เอาข้าวผัดไก่สองจาน |
| | kâo pùt gÔOng jahn nèung | ข้าวผัดกุ้งจานหนึ่ง |
| | láir-o gôr ba-mèe náhm | แล้วก็บะหมี่น้ำ |
| | chahm nèung. | ชามหนึ่ง |
| **Waitress** | láir-o ao náhm a-rai ká? | แล้วเอาน้ำอะไรคะ |

| Peter | kǒr bpép-sêe sǒrng gâir-o | ขอเป๊ปซี่สองแก้ว |
|---|---|---|
| | núm ma-náo gâir-o nèung | น้ำมะนาวแก้วหนึ่ง |
| | láir-o bee-a sǐng kòo-ut nèung. | แล้วเบียร์สิงห์ขวดหนึ่ง |
| | ao núm kǎirng bplào | เอาน้ำแข็งเปล่า |
| | gâir-o nèung dôo-ay. | แก้วหนึ่งด้วย |
| **Waitress** | bpép-sêe mâi mee. | เป๊ปซี่ไม่มี |
| | koh-lâh dâi mái? | โคล่าได้ไหม |
| **Peter** | dâi krúp. | ได้ครับ |
| **Waitress** | ao bee-a kòo-ut yài | เอาเบียร์ขวดใหญ่ |
| | rěu kòo-ut lék? | หรือขวดเล็ก |
| **Peter** | kòo-ut yài krúp. | ขวดใหญ่ครับ |

| ao | *want* (verb) | เอา |
|---|---|---|
| **kǒr ... (nòy)** | *I'd like ...* | ขอ |
| **doo** | *to look at* | ดู |
| **may-noo (4)** | *menu* | เมนู |
| **nêe kâ** | *here you are* | นี่ค่ะ |
| **kâo** | *rice* | ข้าว |
| **pùt** | *fry; fried* | ผัด |
| **gài** | *chicken* | ไก่ |
| **sǒrng** | *two* | สอง |
| **jahn** | *plate* | จาน |
| **nèung** | *one* | หนึ่ง |
| **gÔOng** | *shrimp* | กุ้ง |
| **láir-o gôr** | *and* | แล้วก็ |
| **ba-mèe** | *egg noodles* | บะหมี่ |
| **ba-mèe náhm** | *egg noodle soup* | บะหมี่น้ำ |

| chahm | bowl | ชาม |
|---|---|---|
| **náhm** | water | น้ำ |
| **bpép-sêe** | Pepsi | เป๊ปซี่ |
| **gâir-o** | glass | แก้ว |
| **núm ma-náo** | lemonade | น้ำมะนาว |
| **kòo-ut** | bottle | ขวด |
| **bee-a sǐng** | Singha beer | เบียร์สิงห์ |
| **núm kǎirng bplào** | iced water | น้ำแข็งเปล่า |
| **dôo-ay** | too; also | ด้วย |
| **koh-lâh** | Coca-Cola | โคล่า |
| **yài** | large | ใหญ่ |
| **reu** | or | หรือ |
| **lék** | small | เล็ก |

Malee has been having lunch with three friends at the noodle shop on the corner.

| | | | |
|---|---|---|---|
| **Malee** | nǒo, nǒo gèp dtung. | หนู หนู เก็บสตางค์ |
| **Waitress** | nêe ba-mèe náhm châi mái? | นี่บะหมี่น้ำใช่ไหม |
| **Malee** | châi kâ. láir-o gôr | ใช่ค่ะ แล้วก็ |
| | mee gée-o náhm chahm nèung | มีเกี๊ยวน้ำชามหนึ่ง |
| | kâo nâh bpèt sǒrng jahn | ข้าวหน้าเป็ดสองจาน |
| | láir-o gôr bpép-sêe kòo-ut nèung | แล้วก็เป๊ปซี่ขวดหนึ่ง |
| | núm kǎirng bplào gâir-o nèung | น้ำแข็งเปล่าแก้วหนึ่ง |
| | láir-o gôr say-wen up sǒrng kòo-ut. | แล้วก็เซเวนอัพสองขวด |
| **Waitress** | túng mòt bpàirt-sìp-hòk bàht kâ. | ทั้งหมดแปดสิบหกบาทค่ะ |

| | |
|---|---|
| ข้าวหน้าไก่ | *chicken rice* |
| kâo nâh gài | |
| ข้าวหน้าเป็ด | *duck rice* |
| kâo nâh bpèt | |
| ข้าวหมูแดง | *red pork rice* |
| kâo mǒo dairng | |
| ข้าวผัด ไก่ กุ้ง หมู | *fried rice – chicken shrimp* |
| kâo pùt gài gÔOng mǒo | *pork* |
| บะหมี่น้ำ | *egg noodle soup* |
| ba-mèe náhm | |
| บะหมี่แห้ง | *egg noodles* |
| ba-mèe hâirng | |
| เกี๊ยวน้ำ | *won ton soup* |
| gée-o náhm | |

| nǒo | (way of addressing young waitresses) | หนู |
| gèp | *to collect, keep* | เก็บ |
| dtung | *money; satang* | สตางค์ |
| gée-o náhm | *won ton soup* | เกี๊ยวน้ำ |
| bpèt | *duck* | เป็ด |
| kâo nâh bpèt | *duck rice* | ข้าวหน้าเป็ด |
| say-wen up | *Seven-Up* | เซเวนอัพ |
| túng mòt | *altogether* | ทั้งหมด |

## *Comprehension*

1  How many plates of fried rice did Peter order?
2  What did he and his children have to drink?
3  How many people in Malee's group had duck rice?
4  What had been in the empty bowls on Malee's table?
5  What did Malee's final bill come to?

# pah-sǎh láir sǔng-kom
## ภาษาและสังคม

Most Thais eat three meals a day although many will supplement this with snacks throughout the day. Traditionally rice formed the basis of all three meals and would be accompanied by various side dishes such as fried or pickled vegetables, curry, soup, and meat and fish dishes.

Thais living in towns and cities tend to eat out a lot. There are eating places to suit nearly every pocket, ranging from road-side stalls and noodle shops to air-conditioned coffee shops and restaurants. In recent years western fast-food restaurants have become increasingly popular in Bangkok.

When you go into a restaurant you will usually find someone waiting attentively to serve you. But if you do need to attract a waiter's attention beckon with your fingers pointing *downwards* (as when calling a taxi). If the waiter or waitress is a child, then you can call out, **nǒo, nǒo** (literally 'mouse, mouse' – but also an affectionate way of addressing children!); otherwise it is more appropriate to say **kOOn krúp (kâ)**. When you want to pay, you can say either **chék bin** or **gèp dtung;** although there are no strict rules, the former is more appropriate in air-conditioned restaurants – where tipping is customary – and the latter in noodle shops, where it is unnecessary to tip.

# sǔm-ɲoo-un สำนวน

How to:

● attract a waiter's or waitress's attention

kOOn krúp (kâ) คุณครับ (ค่ะ)

- ask for the menu

  kŏr doo may-noo nòy          ขอดูเมนูหน่อย

- ask for a glass of water

  ao núm kǎirng bplào gâir-o nèung   เอาน้ำแข็งเปล่าแก้วหนึ่ง

- ask for the bill

  gèp dtung krúp (kâ)          เก็บสตางค์ครับ (ค่ะ)

  chéck bin krúp (kâ)          เช็คบิล ครับ (ค่ะ)

 ——————— **kum ùt-tí-bai**  คำอธิบาย ———————

## 1 *Polite requests: asking for things*

When asking for something the most polite word to use is **kŏr** ... (ขอ ...) *I'd like* ... The word **nòy** (หน่อย), which literally means *a little* is added at the end of the phrase to make it sound a little more polite. if, however the actual amount of the thing requested is specified (i.e. *two* plates of fried rice, *one* bottle of beer), the word **nòy** is dropped. In restaurants it is perfectly acceptable to use **ao** (เอา) *I want* ... when ordering.

## 2 *Classifiers*

In English, *uncountable nouns*, such as coffee, rice and milk are usually counted by the container in which they are purchased. The word *bread* is quite unusual in having its own special 'count word', *loaf*. In Thai, however, every noun has to be counted using a 'count word' or *classifier*. The classifiers for nouns in this unit have exact equivalents in English; in later units you will meet classifiers that cannot be readily translated. Study the examples carefully. Notice that if the number is *one* it comes after the classifier, but otherwise, the word order is *noun + number + classifier*. you will meet more common classifiers in subsequent units.

| noun | number | classifier | |
|------|--------|-----------|---|
| koh-lâh | **sǒrng** | kòo-ut | *two (bottles of) Coke* |
| kâo pùt | **sǎhm** | jahn | *three (plates of) fried rice* |
| gah-fair | **bpàirt** | tôo-ay | *eight (cups of) coffee* |
| ba-mèe náhm | **sèe** | chahm | *four (bowls of) noodle soup* |

but

| noun | classifier | number | |
|------|-----------|--------|---|
| koh-lâh | kòo-ut | nèung | *a (or 'one') bottle of Coke* |
| gah-fair | tôo-ay | nèung | *a cup of coffee* |
| pêu-un | kon | nèung | *a friend* |

## 3 dtung สตางค์

**dtung** is a shortened form of 'satang'. It has the more general meaning, *money* in the expressions **gèp dtung** (literally, *collect the money*) and **mâi mee dtung** (*I haven't any money*). The satang is the smallest unit of Thai currency. There are 100 satang in one baht, although today, it exists only in the 25-satang and 50-satang coins.

# ☑ ——— bàirp fèuk hùt แบบฝึกหัด ———

**1** Match the following orders with the right drinks.

(a) bpép-sêe hâh kòo-ut
(b) núm ma-náo sèe gâir-o
(c) bee-a sǐng sǎhm kòo-ut
(d) núm kǎirng bplào sǒrng gâir-o
(e) gah-fair sǒrng tôo-ay

**2** How would you ask the waiter for the following items?

(a) the menu
(b) two bowls of noodle soup
(c) three plates of chicken fried rice
(d) five glasses of water
(e) the bill

**3** Peter and a friend have stopped off for lunch at a small noodle shop. What did they want to eat? And what did they eat in the end?

| Waitress | ao a-rai ká? |
| Peter | kǒr kâo pùt gÔOng sǒrng jahn krúp. |
| Waitress | kâo pùt gÔOng mâi mee kâ. |
| | mee kâo pùt gài láir-o gôr kâo pùt mǒo. |
| Peter | ao kâo pùt gài jahn nèung láir-o gôr |
| | kâo pùt mǒo jahn nèung. |
| Waitress | kâ. láir-o ao náhm a-rai ká? |
| Peter | ao bpép-sêe kòo-ut nèung |
| | láir-o bee-a sǐng kòo-ut yài. |
| Waitress | bpép-sêe mâi yen ('cold') kâ. |
| | koh-lâh dâi mái? |
| Peter | dâi krúp. |
| Waitress | láir-o bee-a sǐng kòo-ut yài |
| | mâi mee kâ. |
| | kòo-ut lék dâi mái? |
| Peter | dâi krúp. |

# 📷 —— àhn láir kěe-un อ่านและเขียน ——

## 1 Consonants

The new consonants in this unit are all *low clasos* consonants (like those in Unit 1). Be careful not to confuse ค *(k)* with ด *(d)* which you learned in Unit 2; ช *(ch)* and ซ *(s)* also look very similar, although the latter has an additional 'notch' on its left 'arm'.

| ค | ช | ซ | ท | พ | ฟ |
| --- | --- | --- | --- | --- | --- |
| k | ch | s | t | p | f |

## 2 Vowels

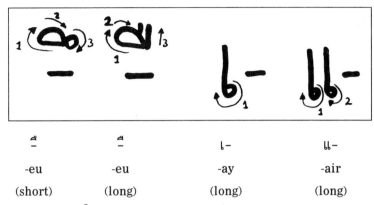

| ◌ื | ◌ื | เ- | แ- |
|----|----|----|----|
| -eu | -eu | -ay | -air |
| (short) | (long) | (long) | (long) |

The symbol ◌ื is unusual in that if there is no final consonant (i.e. if the word ends with an '-eu' sound) the zero consonant symbol must be added:

| with final consonant | | no final consonant (add -อ) | |
|---|---|---|---|
| คืน | keun | คือ | keu |
| มืด | mêut | มือ | meu |

The symbol เ- changes from an -*ay* sound to **er-ee** when it occurs with the consonant ย at the end of the word:

| เลย | เคย |
|---|---|
| ler-ee | ker-ee |

(You may remember the word เลย in the expression เลยไปอีก in Unit 3.)

## 3 Vowel shortener symbol: ◌็

When this symbol, which is identical to the number eight, appears above a consonant and in conjunction with the vowel symbols เ- and แ- the vowels change from long vowels to short vowels:

| เป็น | เล็ก | เก็บ | แซ็ก |
|---|---|---|---|
| bpen | lék | gèp | cháirk |

There is one special case where the symbol appears on top of a consonant with no accompanying written vowel. This is the word ก็ pronounced **gor**.

## 4 Words with no vowel symbol

When a word consists of two consonant symbols with no written vowel symbol, a short **o** vowel must be supplied:

| คน | มด | จน | กด |
|-----|-----|-----|-----|
| kon | mót | jon | gòt |

Note that both **kon** and **mót** begin with a low class consonant but that **mót** has a high tone because it is a dead syllable and the vowel is short, **gòt** has a mid class initial consonant and thus is pronounced with a low tone.

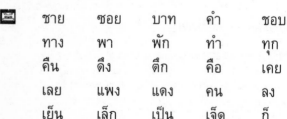

✔ ——— **bàirp fèuk àhn**   แบบฝึกอ่าน ———

1 This exercise give you practice in reading words containing some of the new letters you have learned in this unit. Don't forget to distinguish between 'live' and 'dead' syllables'! Look back to your tone rules chart in Unit 3. Better still, make a copy of it so that you can keep referring to it when reading Thai words. This will ease some of the burden of memorisation and you will find that you gradually absorb the rules through practice.

| ชาย | ซอย | บาท | คำ | ชอบ |
|------|------|------|------|------|
| ทาง | พา | พัก | ทำ | ทุก |
| คืน | ดึง | ตึก | คือ | เคย |
| เลย | แพง | แดง | คน | ลง |
| เย็น | เล็ก | เป็น | เจ็ด | ก็ |

**2** Spot the word. All of these words occur in the Dialogue section. When you can read them, turn back to the beginning of the unit, cover up  the romanised part of the dialogue and scan through the Thai  script until you can locate them.

| | | | | |
|---|---|---|---|---|
| ดู | เมนู | จาน | ก็ | ชาม |
| มี | เล็ก | แดง | เก็บ | เป็ด |
| เซเวนอัพ | แปด | บาท | | |

**3** You may not be able to read very much Thai yet, but already you can make practical use of what you do know. You can, for example,

(*a*) choose the cheapest bottle of beer:

(i)  ๔๙ บาท  (ii)  ๗๓ บาท  (iii)  ๖๕ บาท

(*b*) find your way to your friend's house on Soi 19:

(i) ซอย ๑๕  (ii) ซอย ๑๗  (iii) ซอย ๑๙

(*c*) go through the correct door at public conveniences (if you know that **chai** means *men*)

(i) ชาย  (ii) หญิง

# How are you progressing?

One of the potentially frustrating things about learning to read and write Thai is that you have to absorb so many rules initially before you can read even the simplest dialogues or passages. One good piece of news, however, is that once you have learned these rules, you will find that in Thai there is a much closer match between the spelling of a word and the way it is pronounced than there is in English. Another good piece of news is that you are nearly half-way there. By the end of Unit 8 you should be able to read most of the dialogues in the book and by Unit 10 you will be attempting special reading passages. So keep working through the script sections, retracing your steps if necessary, reviewing earlier material until it becomes second nature, and 'doodling' until your writing becomes quite elegant.

# 5

## hôrng kǒrng kOOn Sǒm-chai yòo têe-nǎi?
## —— *Where's Khun Somchai's room?* ——
## ห้องของคุณสมชายอยู่ที่ไหน

## *In this unit you will learn*

- how to ask where things are
- how to describe the location of things
- how to express possession
- how to say *thank you*
- the main high class consonants
- silent **ห** at the beginning of a word

## —— **bòt sǒn-ta-nah**   บทสนทนา ——

Peter has come to visit Somchai at his office. He stops to ask a secretary where Somchai's room is.

| Peter | kǒr-tôht krúp | ขอโทษครับ |
|---|---|---|
|  | hôrng kǒrng kOOn Sǒm-chai | ห้องของคุณสมชาย |
|  | yòo têe-nǎi? | อยู่ที่ไหน |
| Secretary | yòo kâhng bon kâ. | อยู่ข้างบนค่ะ |

|          |                      |                  |
|----------|----------------------|------------------|
|          | chún sahm.           | ชั้นสาม          |
| Peter    | kòrp-kOOn mâhk krúp. | ขอบคุณมากครับ    |
| Secretary| mâi bpen rai kâ.     | ไม่เป็นไรค่ะ     |

| hôrng        | *room*                  | ห้อง          |
|--------------|-------------------------|---------------|
| kǒrng        | *of*                    | ของ           |
| têe-nǎi?     | *where*                 | ที่ไหน        |
| kâhng bon    | *upstairs*              | ข้างบน        |
| chún         | *floor, level; class*   | ชั้น          |
| mâi bpen rai | *never mind*            | ไม่เป็นไร     |

Meanwhile, Sue is trying to find out if there is a post office nearby ...

| Sue       | kǒr-tôht ká                        | ขอโทษค่ะ                  |
|-----------|-------------------------------------|--------------------------|
|           | tǎir-o née mee bprai-sa-nee mái?    | แถวนี้มีไปรษณีย์ไหม      |
| Passer-by | bprai-sa-nee lěr?                   | ไปรษณีย์หรือ             |
|           | mee kâ.                             | มีค่ะ                    |
|           | yòo soy nèung                       | อยู่ซอย ๑                |
|           | glâi glâi ta-na-kahn grOOng-tâyp.   | ใกล้ๆ ธนาคารกรุงเทพ     |
| Sue       | glai mái ká?                        | ไกลไหมคะ                 |
| Passer-by | mâi glai kâ.                        | ไม่ไกลค่ะ                |
|           | dern bpai tahng née                 | เดินไปทางนี้             |
|           | bpra-mahn hâh nah-tee               | ประมาณห้านาที            |
|           | láir-o gôr těung.                   | แล้วก็ถึง                |

| tǎir-o née    | *this vicinity* | แถวนี้     |
|---------------|-----------------|------------|
| bprai-sa-nee  | *post office*   | ไปรษณีย์   |
| ta-na-kahn    | *bank*          | ธนาคาร     |

| grOOng-tâyp | Bangkok | กรุงเทพฯ |
| --- | --- | --- |
| **glai** | *far* | ไกล |
| **dern** | *walk* | เดิน |
| **tahng née** | *this way* | ทางนี้ |
| **bpra-mahn** | *about* | ประมาณ |
| **nah-tee** | *minute* | นาที |

And now Peter is asking the way to a restaurant.

| Peter | kŏr-tôht krúp | ขอโทษครับ |
| --- | --- | --- |
| | bpai ráhn ah-hǎhn kwǔn jai | ไปร้านอาหารขวัญใจ |
| | bpai tahng nǎi krúp? | ไปทางไหนครับ |
| **Passer-by** | těung fai sǔn-yahn láir-o | ถึงไฟสัญญาณแล้ว |
| | lée-o kwǎh kâo soy sǎhm-sìp-sèe | เลี้ยวขวาเข้าซอย ๓๔ |
| | ráhn ah-hǎhn yòo tahng sái. | ร้านอาหารอยู่ทางซ้าย |
| **Peter** | kòrp-kOOn mâhk krúp. | ขอบคุณมากครับ |
| | glai mái krúp? | ไกลไหมครับ |
| **Passer-by** | mâi glai ròrk. | ไม่ไกลหรอก |
| | dern bpai sùk sŏrng sǎhm | เดินไปสักสองสาม |
| | nah-tee tâo-nún. | นาทีเท่านั้น |

| **ráhn-ah-hǎhn** | *restaurant* | ร้านอาหาร |
| --- | --- | --- |
| **ráhn-ah-hǎhn kwǔn jai** | *Khwan Jai Restaurant* | ร้านอาหารขวัญใจ |
| **... bpai tahng nái?** | *which way is it to ...?* | ... ไปทางไหน |
| **fai sǔn-yahn** | *traffic lights* | ไฟสัญญาณ |
| **sùk** | *(see Grammar 8, on page 73 )* | สัก |
| **sŏrng sǎhm** | *two or three; a few* | สองสาม |
| **tâo-nún** | *only* | เท่านั้น |

## *Comprehension*

1  On which floor is Somchai's office?
2  Where is the nearest post office for Sue?
3  What is near the post office?
4  How long will it take Sue to walk there?
5  What soi is Khwan Jai Restaurant in?
6  Which way does Peter have to go when he reaches the traffic lights?
7  How far away is the restaurant?

## — **pah-sǎh láir sǔng-kom** ภาษาและสังคม —

It is unrealistic at this stage to expect to be able to understand complicated directions given in Thai. Asking directions, however, is an excellent way of practising speaking Thai with strangers, even if you don't always catch the answer. You can always start by asking the way to somewhere you know, so that you can say 'thank you' and walk off confidently in the right direction even if you actually understood very little. Repeat the exercise a number of times, however, and you will find your listening skills steadily improve.

## ———— **sǔm-noo-un** สำนวน ————

How to:

- ask and state the location of something

  ... yòo têe-nǎi?          ... อยู่ที่ไหน

  ... yòo ...               ... อยู่ ...

- ask if there is ... in the vicinity

  tǎir-o née mee ... mái?   แถวนี้มี ... ไหม

- express and acknowledge thanks

  kòrp-kOOn (mâhk)          ขอบคุณ (มาก)

mâi bpen rai                    ไม่เป็นไร

● ask the way to somewhere
bpai ... bpai tahng nái?        ไป ... ไปทางไหน

🔊 ——————— **kum ùt-tí-bai** คำอธิบาย ———————

## 1 'where?' questions

**têe-nǎi?** (ที่ไหน?) *where?* always occurs at the end of a sentence in Thai. The word **têe** is dropped when the main verb is **bpai** *(to go)*.

| | |
|---|---|
| kOOn púk yòo têe-nǎi? | *Where are you staying?* |
| káo séu têe-nǎi? | *Where did he buy it?* |
| kOOn bpai nǎi? | *Where are you going?* |

## 2 Possession

There are no special words for *his, hers, my, yours* etc. in Thai. Ownership or possession is indicated using the word **kǒrng** (ของ) *of* in the order *object + **kǒrng** (of) + owner:*

| | |
|---|---|
| hôrng kǒrng kOOn Sǒm-chai | *Khun Somchai's room.* |
| bâan kǒrng chún | *my house* (house-of-I) |
| bpép-sêe kǒrng krai? | *Whose Pepsi?* (Pepsi-of-who?) |

The word **kǒrng** is optional and frequently omitted:

| | |
|---|---|
| bâhn chún yòo glai. | *My house is a long way away.* |
| rót kOOn Sǒm-chai yòo têe-nǎi? | *Where's Khun Somchai's car?* |

## 3 kâhng ข้าง

**kâhng**, which basically means *side*, occurs commonly in the following phrases:

kâhng bon          *on top, upstairs*          ข้างบน

— **71** —

| kâhng lâhng | *below, underneath, downstairs* | ข้างล่าง |
| kâhng nai | *inside* | ข้างใน |
| kâhng nôrk | *outside* | ข้างนอก |
| kâhng lǔng | *behind* | ข้างหลัง |
| kâhng nâh | *in front* | ข้างหน้า |

# 4 chún ชั้น

British people sometimes find themselves on the wrong floor because Thais call the ground floor **chún nèung** and what the British call the *first floor* is **chún sǒrng**. Note that although the Thai word for *floor* is pronounced the same as the informal female word for *I*, they are spelt differently.

| ชั้น | chun | *floor, storey* |
| ฉัน | chun | *I* |

# 5 tǎir-o แถว

You will quite often hear the word **tǎir-o** reduplicated when people are making fairly vague statements about the location of something.

| bâhn káo yòo tǎir-o tǎir-o bpra-dtoo náhm | *His house is in the Pratu Nam area.* |
| dtǎir-o dtǎir-o bahng lum-poo mee rohng rairm tòok | *In the Banglampu area there are cheap hotels.* |

# 6 'Near' and 'far'

To any westerner learning Thai it seems particularly perverse that two words with opposite meanings should sound almost identical. To a Thai, of course, there is a world of difference between **glâi** (ใกล้) *near* and **glai** (ไกล) *far*. But if you have difficulty hearing the difference between mid tones and falling tones, don't despair; you will often find that **glâi** *(near)* is reduplicated and becomes **glâi glâi.**

## 7  Bangkok

The Thai word for *Bangkok* is **grOOng-tâyp** (กรุงเทพฯ) which can be translated as 'City of Angels'. In fact, this is a hugely abbreviated form of the full name of the city, which is recorded in the Guiness Book of Records as the world's longest place-name. 'Bangkok' was the name of a small village on the Chao Phya River which became Thailand's capital after 1782.

## 8  sùk สัก

You will very often hear the word **sùk** used in front of numbers in Thai. It generally conveys the idea of 'just' or 'as little as' but it usually does not need to be translated at all in English.

| | |
|---|---|
| sùk sŏrng săhm nah-tee | *(just) two or three minutes* |
| sùk tâo-rài? | *how much?* |

## ☑ ——— bàirp fèuk hùt  แบบฝึกหัด ———

1  Where are they? Use the picture on the following page to make up sentences describing where these people are.

*Example:* Peter, Sue láir-o gôr Tom yòo kâhng nai

(a)  ... yòo kâhng nai

(b)  ... yòo kâhng nôrk

(c)  ... yòo kâhng bon

(d)  ... yòo kâhng lâhng

(e)  ... yòo kâhng nâh

(f)  ... yòo kâhng lŭng

2 How would you ask if there was one of the following nearby:

(a) telephone box      (dtôo toh-ra-sùp)

(b) photocopy service   (bor-ri-gahn tài àyk-ga-săhn)

(c) toilet            (hôrng náhm)

(d) hospital         (rohng pa-yah-bahn)

(e) bank            (ta-nah-kahn)

**3** These were some directions Peter was given. Follow them on the map. What was he looking for?

(*a*) tĕung sèe-yâirk láir-o lée-o kwǎh láir-o lée-o sái kâo soy nèung. dern bpai bpra-mahn hâh nah-tee. yòo sÒOt soy.

(*b*) dern bpai tĕung fai sǔn-yahn láir-o lée-o sái. ler-ee bpai èek nít nèung láir-o lée-o kwǎh. yòo bpàhk soy lék lék.

(*c*) tĕung sèe-yâirk láir-o lée-o sái láir-o lée-o sái èek kâo soy nèung. yòo glâi glâi ta-nah-kahn grOOng-tâyp.

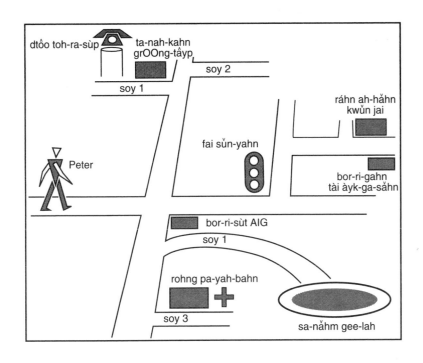

# àhn láir kĕe-un อ่านและเขียน

## 1 Consonants

All of the new consonants in this unit are *high class* consonants. High class consonants are pronounced with an inherent *rising* tone; so when reading the letters below, we would say **kŏr, chŏr, tŏr, pŏr**, etc. You will notice that there are three different high class 's' symbols. Of these, the most common is the first, with the other two appearing mainly in words of foreign origin.

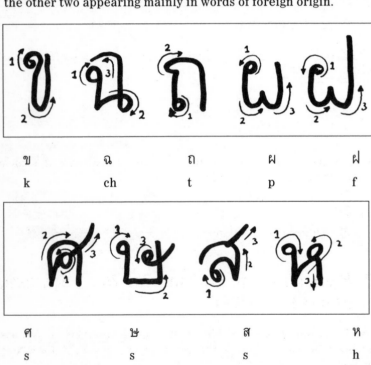

| ข | ฉ | ถ | ผ | ฝ |
|---|---|---|---|---|
| k | ch | t | p | f |

| ศ | ษ | ส | ห |
|---|---|---|---|
| s | s | s | h |

If you compare the consonants in this unit with the low class consonants you met in Unit 4, you will see that they can be paired up. The basic consonant sound is the same with only the inherent rising tone distinguishing the high class consonants from the low class consonants.

| low class | ค | ช | ท | พ | ฟ | ซ |
|---|---|---|---|---|---|---|
| | kor | chor | tor | por | for | sor |
| high class | ข | ฉ | ถ | ผ | ฝ | ส,ศ,ษ |
| | kŏr | chŏr | tŏr | pŏr | fŏr | sŏr |

## 2 High class consonants at the beginning of live syllables

Live syllables with an initial high class consonant are pronounced with a *rising* tone.

| ขาย | ผม | สอง |
|---|---|---|
| kăi | pŏm | sŏrng |

A rare exception is the female word for *I*, **dee-chún** and **chún** where the tone on **chún** is high.

| ดิฉัน | ฉัน |
|---|---|
| dee-chún | chún |

## 3 High class consonants at the beginning of dead syllables

Dead syllables that begin with a high class consonant are always pronounced with a *low* tone, regardless of whether the vowel is long or short.

| หก | สิบ | ถูก | ขาด |
|---|---|---|---|
| hòk | sìp | tòok | kàht |

# 4 Silent ห at the beginning of a word

There are a number of words in Thai that are spelt with an initial ห which is not pronounced. The function of this 'silent h' is to convert the consonant that follows into a high class consonant. All such words then follow the tone rules of words with an initial high class consonant.

| ไหน | หยุด | หลอด |
|-----|------|------|
| nǎi | yòOt | lòrt |

An important exception to note is the question word **mái?** which is spelt as if it should have a rising tone, although in normal speech it is pronounced with a high tone.

| ไหม | mái? |
|-----|------|

# 5 Summary of tone rules

The tone rules for syllables and words with initial high class consonants can be summarised as follows:

| consonant class | LIVE SYLLABLE | DEAD SYLLABLE | |
|-----------------|---------------|-----------------------|-----------------------|
| | | *Short Vowel* | *Long Vowel* |
| HIGH CLASS | **RISING TONE** | **LOW TONE** | **LOW TONE** |

─────── **bàirp fèuk àhn** แบบฝึกอ่าน ───────

1  On the next page are some common words that begin with a high class consonant. The live syllables will have a rising tone and dead syllables will have a low tone. Read through the exercise several times until you can do it quickly and accurately.

| ขาย | ขอ | ขับ | ฉีด |
|------|------|------|------|
| ถาม | ถูก | ผิด | ฝาก |
| สี | สุด | สอน | สาว |
| สัก | สิบ | หัก | หา |
| หลัง | หวัด | หลาย | หนู |

2 Spot the word. You should now be able to read all these words from the dialogue. Turn back to the beginning of this unit and try to find each one without referring to the romanised section.

| ขอโทษ | ของ | สมชาย | ไหน | บน |
|--------|------|--------|------|------|
| มาก | เป็นไร | แถว | มี | ไหม* |
| ซอย | ทาง | นาที | ก็ | ถึง |
| อาหาร** | ใจ | ไป | ไฟ | สัก |
| สอง | สาม | | | |

   \* Remember, this is pronounced with a high tone in normal speech.
 \*\* The letter ร at the end of a word is pronounced as if it were an '*n*'.

3 Match the figure with the word.

| | | | |
|------|------|------|------|
| (i) | ๒ | (a) | แปด |
| (ii) | ๓ | (b) | หก |
| (iii) | ๖ | (c) | สิบ |
| (iv) | ๗ | (d) | สาม |
| (v) | ๘ | (e) | เจ็ด |
| (vi) | ๑๐ | (f) | สอง |

— 79 —

# 6

## sòng bpai ung-grìt tâo-rài?
*—— How much does it cost to send to ——*
*England?* ส่งไปอังกฤษเท่าไร

### *In this unit you will*

- learn how to carry out basic transactions at the post office
- learn how to change money
- learn how to ask people to do something
- learn three different words for *want*
- learn two new classifiers
- review the major points you have learned of the Thai script
- read a short passage of simple Thai

## —— bòt sǒn-ta-nah    บทสนทนา ——

Sue is at the post office to send some postcards and a package.

| | | |
|---|---|---|
| Sue | sòng bpóht-gáht bpai ung-grìt | ส่งโปสการ์ดไปอังกฤษ |
| | tâo-rài ká? | เท่าไรคะ |
| Clerk | gâo bàht krúp. | เก้าบาทครับ |
| Sue | ao sèe doo-ung kâ. | เอาสี่ดวงค่ะ |

| Clerk | sǎhm-sìp-hòk bàht krúp. | สามสิบหกบาทครับ |
|---|---|---|
| Sue | láir-o nêe sòng bpai a-may-ri-gah | แล้วนี่ส่งไปอเมริกา |
| | tâo-rài ká? | เท่าไรคะ |
| Clerk | sòng bpai tahng ah-gàht rěu | ส่งไปทางอากาศหรือ |
| | tahng reu-a krúp? | ทางเรือครับ |
| Sue | tahng ah-gàht kâ. | ทางอากาศค่ะ |
| | yàhk ja long ta-bee-un dôo-ay | อยากจะลงทะเบียนด้วย |
| Clerk | hòk-sìp bàht krúp ... | หกสิบบาทครับ ... |
| | túng mòt gâo-sìp-hòk bàht krúp. | ทั้งหมดเก้าสิบหกบาทครับ |
| Sue | děe-o ... | เดี๋ยว ... |
| | dtôrng-gahn jòt-mǎi ah-gàht | ต้องการจดหมายอากาศ |
| | sǒrng pàirn láir-o gôr sa-dtairm | สองแผ่น แล้วก็แสตมป์ |
| | sǎhm bàht sèe doo-ung dôo-ay kâ. | สามบาทสี่ดวงด้วยค่ะ |

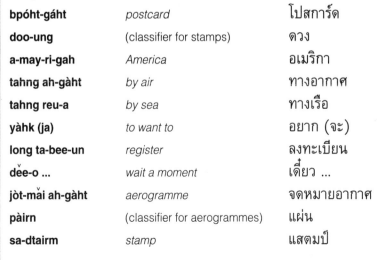

| **sòng** | send | ส่ง |
|---|---|---|
| **bpóht-gáht** | postcard | โปสการ์ด |
| **doo-ung** | (classifier for stamps) | ดวง |
| **a-may-ri-gah** | America | อเมริกา |
| **tahng ah-gàht** | by air | ทางอากาศ |
| **tahng reu-a** | by sea | ทางเรือ |
| **yàhk (ja)** | to want to | อยาก (จะ) |
| **long ta-bee-un** | register | ลงทะเบียน |
| **děe-o ...** | wait a moment | เดี๋ยว ... |
| **jòt-mǎi ah-gàht** | aerogramme | จดหมายอากาศ |
| **pàirn** | (classifier for aerogrammes) | แผ่น |
| **sa-dtairm** | stamp | แสตมป์ |

Peter wants to change some traveller's cheques at the bank.

**Peter**    yàhk ja lâirk bplèe-un chék    อยากจะแลกเปลี่ยนเช็ค
dern-tahng dâi mái?    เดินทางได้ไหม

**Clerk**    dâi krúp    ได้ครับ
kǒr doo núng-sěu dern-tahng láir    ขอดูหนังสือเดินทางและ
chék dern-tahng krúp.    เช็คเดินทางครับ

**Peter**    nêe krúp.    นี่ครับ

**Clerk**    ja lâirk bplèe-un sǒrng róy    จะแลกเปลี่ยนสองร้อย
bporn, châi mái krúp?    ปอนด์ใช่ไหมครับ

**Peter**    châi krúp.    ใช่ครับ

**Clerk**    ùt-dtrah lâirk bplèe-un wun née    อัตราแลกเปลี่ยนวันนี้
sèe-sìp-hâh bàht dtòr nèung bporn    สี่สิบห้าบาทต่อหนึ่งปอนด์
chôo-ay sen chêu têe-nêe krúp.    ช่วยเซ็นชื่อที่นี่ครับ

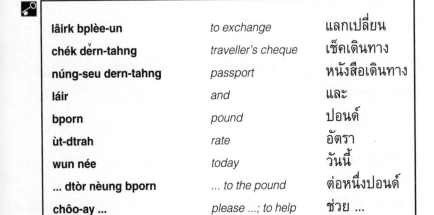

| | | |
|---|---|---|
| **lâirk bplèe-un** | *to exchange* | แลกเปลี่ยน |
| **chék děrn-tahng** | *traveller's cheque* | เช็คเดินทาง |
| **núng-seu dern-tahng** | *passport* | หนังสือเดินทาง |
| **láir** | *and* | และ |
| **bporn** | *pound* | ปอนด์ |
| **ùt-dtrah** | *rate* | อัตรา |
| **wun née** | *today* | วันนี้ |
| **... dtòr nèung bporn** | *... to the pound* | ต่อหนึ่งปอนด์ |
| **chôo-ay ...** | *please ...; to help* | ช่วย ... |
| **sen chêu** | *to sign* | เซ็นชื่อ |

## Comprehension

1  How many postcards is Sue going to send to England?
2  Does she plan to send the package to America by air-mail or sea mail?
3  How much do the stamps and package come to?
4  What does Sue nearly forget to buy?
5  How much money does Peter want to change?
6  What is the exchange rate?

## —pah-sǎh láir sǔng-kom   ภาษาและสังคม—

Post offices in Thailand are open from 8.30 a.m. to 4.30 p.m. on weekdays but are closed at weekends. In Bangkok, the Central Post Office, located on New Road, is however open on both Saturday and Sunday, and offers, in addition to normal post office services, a 24-hour telegram service. Post office facilities are also available in many of the larger Bangkok hotels and on university campuses.

Banks are open from 8.30 a.m. to 3.30 p.m. on weekdays and are closed at the weekend. In Bangkok, many of the major banks have currency exchange kiosks outside the main building, some of which are open until 8 p.m. seven days a week.

## ———— sǔm-noo-un   สำนวน ————

How to say:

● How much is it to send to England?

sòng bpai ung-grìt tâo-rài?   ส่งไปอังกฤษเท่าไร

● How much is it to send it by air?

sòng bpai tahng ah-gàht tâo-rài?   ส่งไปทางอากาศเท่าไร

● I'd like to register it

yàhk ja long ta-bee-un   อยากจะลงทะเบียน

- I need four nine-baht stamps

  dtôrng-gahn sa-dtairm gâo bàht
  sèe doo-ung

  ต้องการแสตมป์เก้าบาท
  สี่ดวง

 ——————— **kum ùt-tí-bai** คำอธิบาย ———————

## 1 Classifiers

In Unit 4 you learned that classifiers have to be used when counting things in Thai. In this unit the classifiers **doo-ung** (for counting stamps) and **pàirn** (for counting aerogrammes and flat-shaped objects such as sheets of paper or slices of ham) are introduced. Notice that when Sue asks for four nine-baht stamps in the Dialogue, she uses only the classifier without mentioning the word for *stamp* because it is quite clear from the context what she is referring to.

## 2 'want'

The verb **yàhk (ja)** (อยาก (จะ)) *want to, would like to* is always followed by another verb:

| | |
|---|---|
| yàhk bpai dôo-ay | *I want to go too.* |
| mâi yàhk mah | *He doesn't want to come.* |

The verb **ao** (เอา) *want* is always followed by a noun:

| | |
|---|---|
| ao bpép-sêe sŏrng kòo-ut | *We want two Pepsis.* |
| ao jòt-măi ah-gàht pàirn nèung | *I want an aerogramme.* |

The verb **dtôrng-gahn** (ต้องการ) *want (to), need (to)* can be followed by either a verb or a noun:

| | |
|---|---|
| dtôrng-gahn long ta-bee-un | *I need to register it.* |
| dtôrng-gahn bee-a kòo-ut nèung | *I need a bottle of beer.* |

## 3  chôo-ay ช่วย

**chôo-ay** is used to indicate politeness when asking someone to do something. Like **kŏr** (see Unit 4), which is used when asking for something, it is often used in conjunction with **nòy**.

chôo-ay sen chêu têe-nêe (nòy)  *Please sign here.*

chôo-ay bpìt bpra-dtoo nòy  *Please shut the door.*

chôo-ay bpèrt nâh-dtàhng nòy  *Please open the window.*

**chôo-ay** also occurs as a verb meaning *to help.*

## ☑ ———— bàirp fèuk hùt  แบบฝึกหัด ————

1  At the post office.
   Read the short dialogues. What did the people want and how much did it cost?

   (a)  **A** nêe sòng bpai yêe-bpÒOn tâo-rài ká?
       **B** sòng bpai tahng ah-gàht châi mái krúp?
       **A** châi kâ. yàhk ja long ta-bee-un dôo-ay.
       **B** gâo-sìp-hâh bàht krúp.

   (b)  **A** jòt-mǎi ah-gàht tâo-rài krúp?
       **B** pàirn la sìp-sŏrng bàht kâ.
       **A** ao sǎhm pàirn láir-o gôr sa-dtairm hâh bàht sèe doo-ung. túng mòt tâo-rài krúp?

   (c)  **A** sòng bpóht-gáht bpai fa-rùng-sàyt tâo-rài ká?
       **B** gâo bàht krúp.
       **A** ao sǎhm doo-ung kâ láir-o gôr jòt-mǎi ah-gàht pàirn nèung. túng mòt tâo-rài ká?

2  How would you ask:

   (a)  how much it costs to send a postcard to America?
   (b)  how much it costs to send something by airmail?
   (c)  for five nine-baht stamps?
   (d)  for four aerogrammes?
   (e)  how much all that comes to?

**3** Supply the correct classifier in these phrases.

- (a) sa-dtairm gâo bàht hâh ...
- (b) ga-fair sǒrng ...
- (c) pêu-un ... nèung
- (d) ba-mèe náhm sǎhm ...
- (e) koh-lâh sèe ...
- (f) jòt-mǎi ah-gàht ... nèung
- (g) kâo pùt gÔOng sǒrng ...

📖 ——————àhn láir kěe-un    อ่านและเขียน——————

At this stage it is worth pausing to review the key points that you have learned so far.

## 1 Consonants

You have learned the following consonants: (note that the consonant sound of each letter is given when it occurs both as an initial and as a final consonant).

| Low class | น | ม | ง | ร | ล | ย | ว |
|---|---|---|---|---|---|---|---|
| *initial* | n | m | ng | r | l | y | w |
| *final* | n | m | ng | n | n | | |
| | ค | ช | ซ | ท | พ | ฟ | |
| *initial* | k | ch | s | t | p | f | |
| *final* | k | t | t | t | p | p | |
| **Mid class** | ก | จ | ด | ต | บ | ป | อ |
| *initial* | g | j | d | dt | b | bp | zero |
| *final* | k | t | t | t | p | p | |

| High class | ข | ฉ | ถ | ผ | ฝ | ศ,ส,ษ | ห |
|---|---|---|---|---|---|---|---|
| *initial* | k | ch | t | p | f | s | h |
| *final* | k | t | t | p | p | t | |

# 2 Vowels

You have learned the following vowels:

| *Long vowels* | –า | –อ | โ– | ◌ี | ◌ู | ◌ื | เ– | แ– |
|---|---|---|---|---|---|---|---|---|
| | -ah | -or | -oh | -ee | -oo | -eu | -ay | -air |

| *Short vowels* | ◌ั | ไ– | ใ– | ◌ิ | ◌ุ | ◌ึ | เ◌ะ | แ◌ะ |
|---|---|---|---|---|---|---|---|---|
| | -u | -ai | -ai | -i | **-OO** | eu | -e | -air |

# 3 Live syllables and dead syllables

You have learned the difference between live syllables and dead syllables:

| *Live syllables* | syllables that end with a *long vowel* or a *m, n, ng* sound, or the short vowel *ai*. |
|---|---|
| | e.g.  มี    รอ    ดู    ปี    จาน  ดำ   ยัง |
| *Dead syllables* | syllables that end with a *short vowels* or a *p, t, k* sound. |
| | e.g.  ดุ    ติ    กด    ดับ   สิบ   จาก  หมด |

# 4 Summary of tone rules

| consonant | LIVE | DEAD SYLLABLE | |
| class | SYLLABLE | Short Vowel | Long Vowel |
| LOW CLASS | **MID TONE** | **HIGH TONE** | **FALLING TONE** |
| MID CLASS | **MID TONE** | **LOW TONE** | **LOW TONE** |
| HIGH CLASS | **RISING TONE** | **LOW TONE** | **LOW TONE** |

# 5 Reading words

By now, whenever you read a Thai word or syllable, you will have learned to ask yourself three questions: (i) is it a live or dead syllable? (ii) what class is the initial consonant? and (iii) is the vowel long or short? Once you have answered these questions you should be able to identify the tone of a word correctly. At this stage, don't worry if you are finding it difficult to memorise the tone rules: simply copy the chart above and keep it handy for subsequent lessons (the act of copying itself will help you to memorise it). After a while, you will soon find you need to refer to it less and less and when you feel ready, you can dispense with it altogether.

☑ ——————— **bàirp fèuk àhn**    แบบฝึกอ่าน ———————

🖳 1   When you have worked through the table on the following page , test yourself by picking words at random and seeing how quickly you can read them. Many of the words in this exercise will now be familiar to you. Remember that regular practice over the same exercises in this and previous units can greatly improve your speed of reading. Copying out the words will also help greatly.

| | | | |
|---|---|---|---|
| ใจ | พูด | ไทย | นาน |
| ทำ | ไป | พัก | แถว |
| ไหม | ขอโทษ | จาก | ของ |
| เป็น | แปด | บาท | แพง |
| หก | จอด | มี | หมู |
| เล็ก | หนาว | เย็น | สี |

2  Spot the word.

Here are some words from the dialogue which you should be able to read now.

| | | | |
|---|---|---|---|
| ไป | บาท | สามสิบ | หก |
| อเมริกา* | ทาง | อากาศ | หรือ |
| ลง | หกสิบ | หมด | จดหมาย |
| สอง | | | |

*' Zero consonant' at the beginning of the word is pronounced 'a'.

## —— **bòt àhn**   บทอ่าน   *(Reading passage)* ——

Now you are nicely warmed-up for your first passage of Thai which is all about Khun Yupha's family. By the time you have read it, you should know where she comes from, her husband's name, his home province and occupation and how many sons and daughters the couple have.

ยุพาเป็นคนไทย  มาจากจังหวัดเลย  สมชายเป็นสามีของยุพา  สมชาย
มาจากจังหวัดตาก ยุพากับสมชายมีลูก ๕ คน มีลูกชาย ๒ คน มีลูกสาว
๓ คน

| สามี | husband |
| จังหวัด | province |
| ตาก | (name of a province in northern Thailand) |
| เลย | (name of a province in northern Thailand) |
| กับ | and, with |
| ลูกชาย | son |
| ลูกสาว | daughter |

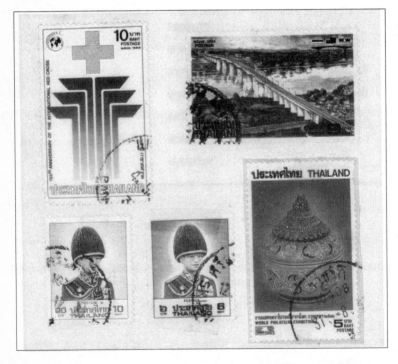

A Selection of Thai stamps

# 7

## kǒr pôot gùp ... nòy, dâi mái?
### —— *Could I speak to ..., please?* ——
## ขอพูดกับ ... หน่อย ได้ไหม

### *In this unit you will learn*

- the language of telephone transactions
- *who?* and *when?* questions
- talking about the future
- direct and indirect speech
- parts of the day
- tone marks (i): **mái àyk**
- silent อ at the beginning of a word

## —— bòt sǒn-ta-nah    บทสนทนา ——

Sue is telephoning Malee, but her maid answers the call.

| Sue | hun-loh | ฮันโล |
|------|---------|-------|
|  | kǒr pôot gùp kOOn Mah-lee nòy | ขอพูดกับคุณมาลีหน่อย |
|  | dâi mái ká? | ได้ไหมคะ |
| **Maid** | krai pôot ká? | ใครพูดคะ |

| | | |
|---|---|---|
| **Sue** | chún Sue pôot kâ. | ฉัน Sue พูดค่ะ |
| **Maid** | krai ká? | ใครคะ |
| | chôo-ay pôot dung dung nòy dâi mái? sǎi mâi dee. | ช่วยพูดดังๆ หน่อยได้ไหม สายไม่ดี |
| **Sue** | kâ. chún Sue pôot kâ. bpen pêu-un fa-rùng. | ค่ะ ฉัน Sue พูดค่ะ เป็นเพื่อนฝรั่ง |
| **Maid** | ror sùk kroo ná ká ... kOOn Mah-lee mâi yòo kâ. òrk bpai kâhng nôrk. | รอสักครู่นะคะ ... คุณมาลีไม่อยู่ค่ะ ออกไปข้างนอก |
| **Sue** | lěr ká? ja glùp mêu-rai ká? | หรือคะ จะกลับเมื่อไรคะ |
| **Maid** | mâi sâhp kâ. kít wâh ja glùp dtorn bài. dtorn bài toh mah mài ná ká. | ไม่ทราบค่ะ คิดว่าจะกลับตอนบ่าย ตอนบ่ายโทรมาใหม่ นะคะ |
| **Sue** | kâ. kòrp-kOOn kâ. sa-wùt dee kâ. | ค่ะ ขอบคุณค่ะ สวัสดีค่ะ |

| | | |
|---|---|---|
| **hun-loh** | *hello* (on telephone) | ฮันโล |
| **pôot** | *speak* | พูด |
| **krai** | *who?* | ใคร |
| **dung** | *loud* | ดัง |
| **sǎi** | *(telephone) line* | สาย |
| **dee** | *good* | ดี |
| **mâi dee** | *bad* | ไม่ดี |
| **pêu-un** | *friend* | เพื่อน |

| | | |
|---|---|---|
| **fa-rùng** | *westerner* | ฝรั่ง |
| **ror** | *wait* | รอ |
| **krôo** | *a moment* | ครู่ |
| **òrk** | *to go out* | ออก |
| **kâhng nôrk** | *outside* | ข้างนอก |
| **ja** | *(future time marker)* | จะ |
| **glùp** | *return* | กลับ |
| **mêu-rai?** | *when?* | เมื่อไร |
| **sâhp** | *to know* | ทราบ |
| **kít** | *to think* | คิด |
| **wâh** | *... that;* (see **kum ùt-tí-bai** (i)) | ว่า |
| **dtorn** | *period of time* | ตอน |
| **bài** | *afternoon* | บ่าย |
| **dtorn bài** | *afternoon* | ตอนบ่าย |
| **toh** | *to telephone* | โทร |
| **mài** | *again; new* | ใหม่ |

Peter is trying to call a friend at the British Embassy.

| | | |
|---|---|---|
| **Peter** | hun-loh | ฮันโล |
| | têe-nôhn sa-tǎhn tôot ung-grìt | ที่โน่นสถานทูตอังกฤษ |
| | châi mái krúp? | ใช่ไหมครับ |
| **Embassy** | châi kâ. | ใช่ค่ะ |
| **Peter** | kǒr dtòr ber sǎhm-sǒon-sèe | ขอต่อเบอร์สาม ศูนย์ สี่ |
| | dâi mái krúp? | ได้ไหมครับ |
| **Embassy** | ror sùk krôo ná ká ... | รอสักครู่นะคะ ... |
| | sǎi mâi wâhng ná ká. | สายไม่ว่างนะคะ |

— 93 —

|        |                       |                         |
|--------|-----------------------|-------------------------|
|        | ja koy gòrn mái?      | จะคอยก่อนไหม            |
| Peter  | a-rai ná krúp?        | อะไรนะครับ              |
| Embassy| sǎi mâi wâhng kâ.     | สายไม่ว่างค่ะ           |
|        | ja koy gòrn mái?      | จะคอยก่อนไหม            |
| Peter  | mâi bpen rai.         | ไม่เป็นไร               |
|        | děe-o ja toh mah mài. | เดี๋ยวจะโทรมาใหม่        |

| sa-tǎhn tôot     | embassy          | สถานทูต      |
|------------------|------------------|--------------|
| kǒr dtòr ...     | could I have     |              |
|                  | extension...     | ขอต่อ        |
| bĕr              | number           | เบอร์        |
| soon             | zero             | ศูนย์        |
| wâhng            | free, vacant     | ว่าง         |
| koy              | to wait          | คอย          |
| gòrn             | before, first    | ก่อน         |
| ja koy gòrn mái? | will you hold?   | จะคอยก่อนไหม |
| děe-o            | in a minute      | เดี๋ยว       |

## Comprehension

1 Why does the maid have problems understanding Sue?
2 How does Sue describe herself to the maid?
3 Where is Malee?
4 When does the maid think she will be back?
5 What does she advise Sue to do?
6 What extension does Peter want?
7 Why can't he get through?
8 What does he decide to do?

# —pah-sǎh láir sǔng-kom   ภาษาและสังคม—

At this stage any telephone transactions you might need to make in Thai will probably be limited to asking to speak to someone, or asking an operator for an extension number. Stick to English for important transactions such as confirming flights or get a Thai to help you with the call.

The word **toh-ra-sùp** in Thai is both the noun *telephone* and the verb *to telephone*. As a verb it is often shortened to **toh**. You will see this abbreviated form at the end of newspaper advertisements – the equivalent of 'tel.'

When giving telephone numbers or extension numbers, Thais usually use the word **toh** for *two* instead of **sǒrng** as it is felt that **sǒrng** and **sǎhm** *(three)* might easily be confused over the phone. **toh** is a Sanskrit* word meaning *two*. Although it is pronounced the same way as the abbreviated word for 'to telephone' it is spelt differently.

โทร.                  โท

tel.                  two

(* Sanskrit is the language of classical India from which Thai has borrowed many words in the same way that English has borrowed from Latin.)

# —————— sǔm-noo-un   สำนวน ——————

How to say:

● Could I speak to ..., please?

kǒr pôot gùp kOOn ... nòy dâi mái?   ขอพูดกับคุณ ... หน่อยได้ไหม

● Who's speaking, please? / Is that ...?

krai pôot krúp (ká)   ใครพูดครับ (คะ)

têe-nôhn ... châi mái krúp (ká)?   ที่โน่น ...ใช่ไหมครับ (คะ)

- This is ... speaking

    pǒm (chún) ... pôot          ผม (ฉัน) ... พูด

- Could you speak up a little please?

    (chôo-ay) pôot dung dung nòy      (ช่วย) พูดดังๆ หน่อย
    dâi mái?          ได้ไหม

- The line is bad / busy

    sǎi mâi dee          สายไม่ดี

    sǎi mâi wâhng          สายไม่ว่าง

- Could you hold on a moment, please?

    ror sùk krôo          รอสักครู่

- Could I have extension ..., please?

    kǒr dtòr ber ...          ขอต่อเบอร์ ...

- I'll ring back later

    děe-o ja toh mah mài          เดี๋ยวจะโทรมาใหม่

- Sorry, I've got the wrong number

    kǒr-tôht toh pìt ber          ขอโทษ โทรผิดเบอร์

---

📖    ## kum ùt-tí-bai    คำอธิบาย ————

## 1 *Telephone calls*

The English word *hello* is used at the beginning of phone calls and the
Thai greeting / farewell **sa-wùt dee** at the end.

## 2 'Who?' questions

The question word **krai** (ใคร) *who?* can occur either at the beginning or at the end of a sentence depending on its function. It occurs with **kŏrng** (*of*) to mean *whose?* although the word **kŏrng** is often omitted.

| | |
|---|---|
| krai bpai? | *Who is going?* |
| krai tum? | *Who did it?* |
| kOOn bpai gùp krai? | *Who are you going with?* |
| káo tum ngahn gùp krai? | *Who does he work with?* |
| rót (kŏrng) krai? | *Whose car?* |

## 3 lĕr? หรือ

You met the question word **lĕr?** (spelt **rĕu**) in Unit 2 where it occurred at the end of a sentence. When it occurs on its own, it means *really?* and can be used both as a genuine expression of surprise and as a bland conversational rejoinder to assure the speaker that you are still listening!

## 4 Talking about the future

As we have already mentioned, Thai verbs do not change their endings to indicate tense in the same way as verbs in European languages. Often it is only from the context that you can tell whether a Thai is talking about events in the future or the past. When you want to be quite specific about referring to the future, however, add the word **ja** (จะ) in front of the main verb.

| | |
|---|---|
| kOOn ja bpai mêu-rai? | *When will you go?* |
| káo ja glùp dtorn bài | *He will return in the afternoon.* |

## 5 'When?' questions

**mêu-rai** (เมื่อไร) *when?* normally occurs at the end of a sentence.

| | |
|---|---|
| káo mah mêu-rai? | *When is he coming?* |
| kOOn séu mêu-rai? | *When did you buy it?* |

# 6 'Know'

**sâhp** (ทราบ) is a polite, formal word for *to know* which you would use when speaking to strangers or people of obviously higher social status. In less formal situations **róo** (รู้) is widely used. In Unit 3, you met the word **róo-jùk** (รู้จัก) which also means *to know* but in the sense of being acquainted with a person or place.

# 7 wâh ว่า

**wâh** follows verbs like **kít** (คิด) *to think* and **bòrk** (บอก) *to say, tell* and introduces either direct speech – the exact words spoken by the person – or indirect or reported speech. It can often be conveniently translated as *that*.

> pǒm kít wâh mâi bpai      *I think (that) I won't go.*
> káo bòrk wâh glùp dtorn bài    *He said (that) he would be back in the afternoon* or *He said, 'I'll be back in the afternoon'.*

As a verb, **wâh** means *to say* or *to think* and is often used when asking someone's opinion:

> kOOn wâh yung-ngai?      *What do you think?*

# 8 dtorn ตอน

**dtorn** means *section* or *period of time*. It occurs commonly with the words for 'morning', 'afternoon', 'evening', etc. Note that when referring to the time when an action takes place, Thai does not need the word for *in*.

| | | |
|---|---|---|
| **dtorn cháo** | *(in the) morning* | ตอนเช้า |
| **dtorn bài** | *(in the) afternoon* | ตอนบ่าย |
| **dtorn yen** | *(in the) evening* | ตอนเย็น |
| **dtorn glahng wun** | *(in the) daytime* | ตอนกลางวัน |

| **dtorn glahng keun** | *night time, at night* | ตอนกลางคืน |

☑ ————— **bàirp fèuk hùt** แบบฝึกหัด ———————

1  Here is part of a telephone conversation between Sue and Malee.
You know Malee's answers, but what was Sue saying?

| **Sue** | ..................................... |
| **Malee** | kOOn Peter mâi yòo kâ |
| | òrk bpai kâhng nôrk |
| **Sue** | ..................................... |
| **Malee** | káo bòrk wâh ja glùp dtorn bài |
| | dtorn bài toh mah mài ná |
| **Sue** | ..................................... |
| **Malee** | sa-wùt dee kâ |

2  How would you ask:

(a)  to speak to Khun Marisa?
(b)  who is speaking?
(c)  for extension 359?
(d)  someone to hang on for a moment
(e)  When Khun Araya will return?
(f)  someone to speak a little louder?

3  Your colleagues are out of the office but have left messages
saying where they have gone and when they will be back. How
would you respond to someone asking to speak to them? The first
one is done for you as an example You will find the messages on
the next page.

*Example :*

(a) **A** kǒr pôot gùp k**OO**n Mah-lee nòy dâi mái ká?

    **B** k**OO**n Mah-lee mâi yòo krúp (kâ)

       òrk bpai kâhng nôrk

       kít wâh ja glùp dtorn bài

(b) **A** kǒr pôot gùp k**OO**n Cha-nít nòy dâi mái krúp?

    **B** ...................................

(c) **A** kǒr pôot gùp k**OO**n Wít-ta-yah nòy dâi mái ká?

    **B** ...................................

## 🔊———— àhn láir kěe-un    อ่านและเขียน ————

The chart summarising tone rules in Unit 6 will help you to read any dead syllable, but it only covers live syllables that are pronounced with a mid tone or rising tone.

As you will have realised, there are many live syllables that are pronounced with a falling, high or low tone – words such as **mâi**, **chêu**, **láir-o**, **yài**, **đtòr** and so on.

In words like these, the tone is represented by a tone mark which is written above the initial consonant. If the initial consonant has an ͘ or ͘ vowel above it, then the tone mark is written above the vowel. The two most common tone marks are **mái àyk**, which you are about to meet, and **mái toh** which will be introduced in the next unit.

## 1 mái àyk (ʾ): *tone rules*

This tone mark looks like a number one. It is written above the initial consonant and in line with the right-hand perpendicular stroke. Unfortunately for the learner, due to changes in the language that have occurred over hundreds of years, this one tone mark can represent two different tones! As with dead syllables, the determining factor is the class of the initial consonant. If **mái àyk** occurs on a low class initial consonant, the tone will be a *falling* tone:

| *Low class* | ไม่ | ที่ | ชื่อ |
|---|---|---|---|
| | mâi | têe | chêu |

If the initial consonant is either mid class or high class, then the tone is *low:*

| *Mid class* | ไก่ | ต่อ | จ่าย |
|---|---|---|---|
| | gài | dtòr | jài |
| *High class* | สี่ | หนึ่ง* | หน่อย* |
| | sèe | nèung | nòy |

*Remember that silent ห 'converts' the next consonant to high class.

## 2 Silent อ *at the beginning of a word*

In Unit 5 you met words that began with a silent ห. There are also a small number of words – only four in fact – that begin with a silent อ. These are all pronounced with a *low tone*. They are all very common words and it is well worth copying them down and memorising them at this stage. Two of them – **yòo** and **yàhk** – have already occurred in the Dialogues.

| อยู่ | อย่า | อย่าง | อยาก |
|------|------|-------|------|
| yòo | yàh | yàhng | yàhk |
| *to be situated at* | *don't* | *like, kind* | *to like to* |

☑ ———— **bàirp fèuk àhn**   แบบฝึกอ่าน ————

▣ 1  All of these words are written with **mái àyk**. This means they will
     be pronounced with either a falling tone or a low tone.

| ไม่ | นี่ | พ่อ | แม่ |
|------|------|------|------|
| ตื่น | คู่ | ไข่ | ไก่ |
| แต่ | สั่ง | ใส่ | ต่อ |
| ชื่อ | ใช่ | พี่ | ที่ |
| หนึ่ง | หล่อ | หน่อย | หมั่น |

2  Next, some short phrases from this and earlier units, using words
   with **mái àyk**.

| ใช่ไหม | ไม่ใช่ | นี่เท่าไร |
|--------|--------|-----------|
| แพงไปหน่อย | ไม่แพงหรอก | ยี่สิบบาท |
| ถึงสี่แยก | จอดที่นี่ | อยู่ที่โน่น |
| ไม่เป็นไร | ส่งไปทางอากาศ | จดหมายอากาศสองแผ่น |

3  And finally, here is Peter negotiating with a 'tuk-tuk' driver.

**Peter**   ไปซอยสามสิบสามเท่าไร
**tuk-tuk**  ซอยสามสิบสามหรือ
             คิดแปดสิบบาท

**Peter**   แปดสิบบาทหรือ
แพงไปหน่อย

**tuk-tuk**   ไม่แพงหรอก
รถติดมาก


(a)   Where does Peter want to go?
(b)   How much does the tuk-tuk driver ask for?
(c)   What is Peter's reaction?
(d)   What is the tuk-tuk driver's justification?

# 8

## chern kâhng nai ná ká

——————— *Do come in!* ———————

## เชิญข้างในนะคะ

### In this unit you will learn

- how to greet people and make introductions
- how to talk about your family
- kin terms: brothers and sisters, sons and daughters
- *how many?* questions
- *... yet?* questions
- tone marks (ii): **mái toh, mái dtree** and **mái jùt-dta-wah**

——————— **bòt sǒn-ta-nah**   บทสนทนา ———————

Sue and her husband Peter are visiting Sue's friend Chanida at her home.

| | | |
|---|---|---|
| **Chanida** | sa-wùt dee kâ kOOn Sue. | สวัสดีค่ะ คุณ Sue |
| | chern kâhng nai ná ká. | เชิญข้างในนะคะ |
| **Sue** | kòrp-kOOn kâ. | ขอบคุณค่ะ |
| | nêe Peter fairn chún gùp lôok. | นี่ Peter แฟนฉันกับลูก |

| | | |
|---|---|---|
| **Chanida** | sa-wùt dee kâ. | สวัสดีค่ะ |
| | kOOn Peter sa-bai dee lěr ká? | คุณPeterสบายดีหรือคะ |
| **Peter** | sa-bai dee krúp. | สบายดีครับ |
| | láir-o kOOn Chanida lâ krúp? | แล้วคุณชนิดาล่ะครับ |
| **Chanida** | sa-bai dee měu-un gun kâ. | สบายดีเหมือนกันค่ะ |
| | kOOn Peter pôot tai gèng ná | คุณ Peter พูดไทยเก่งนะ |
| | yòo meu-ung tai nahn mái? | อยู่เมืองไทยนานไหม |
| **Peter** | mâi nahn krúp. | ไม่นานครับ |
| | sùk sǒrng sǎhm deu-un tâo-nún. | สักสองสามเดือนเท่านั้น |
| **Chanida** | sǒrng sǎhm deu-un tâo-nún lěr? | สองสามเดือนเท่านั้นหรือ |
| | gèng ná. | เก่งนะ |
| | pôot tai chút. | พูดไทยชัด |
| **Peter** | bplào krúp. | เปล่าครับ |
| | mâi gèng. | ไม่เก่ง |
| | pôot dâi nít-nòy tâo-nún. | พูดได้นิดหน่อยเท่านั้น |
| **Chanida** | láir-o lôok lâ. | แล้วลูกล่ะ |
| | pôot pah-sǎh tai bpen mái? | พูดภาษาไทยเป็นไหม |
| **Sue** | bpen nít-nòy kâ. | เป็นนิดหน่อยค่ะ |

| | | |
|---|---|---|
| **chern** | *please; to invite* | เชิญ |
| **kâhng nai** | *inside* | ข้างใน |
| **fairn** | *boy / girlfriend; spouse* | แฟน |
| **lôok** | *child, children* | ลูก |
| **sa-bai** | *to be well, comfortable* | สบาย |
| **sa-bai dee lěr?** | *how are you?* | สบายดีหรือ |
| **láir-o ... lâ?** | *and how about ...?* | แล้ว ... ล่ะ |

| | | |
|---|---|---|
| **měu-un gun** | *likewise* | เหมือนกัน |
| **gèng** | *to be good at something* | เก่ง |
| **yòo** | *to live (in, at)* | อยู่ |
| **meu-ung tai** | *Thailand* | เมืองไทย |
| **nahn** | *a long time* | นาน |
| **deu-un** | *month* | เดือน |
| **tâo-nún** | *only* | เท่านั้น |
| **pôot** | *to speak* | พูด |
| **chút** | *clear* | ชัด |
| **bplào** | *no* | เปล่า |
| **pah-sǎh** | *language* | ภาษา |
| **bpen** | *to be able to* | เป็น |
| **nít-nòy** | *a little bit* | นิดหน่อย |

Sue and Chanida are looking through some old family snaphots of Chanida's.

| | | |
|---|---|---|
| **Sue** | kOOn Chanida mee pêe-nórng gèe kon? | คุณชนิดามีพี่น้อง กี่คน |
| **Chanida** | mee sèe kon kâ. | มีสี่คนค่ะ |
| | mee pêe-chai kon nèung, | มีพี่ชายคนหนึ่ง |
| | pêe-sǎo kon nèung, nórng-chai | พี่สาวคนหนึ่ง น้องชาย |
| | kon nèung láir-o gôr | คนหนึ่งแล้วก็ |
| | nórng-sǎo kon nèung. | น้องสาวคนหนึ่ง |
| **Sue** | nêe pêe-chai, châi mái ká? | นี่พี่ชายใช่ไหม |
| **Chanida** | châi kâ. chêu Wít. | ใช่ค่ะ ชื่อวิท |
| **Sue** | ah-yÓO tâo-rài ká? | อายุเท่าไรค่ะ |
| **Chanida** | ah-yÓO sǎhm-sìp-sǒrng kâ. | อายุสามสิบสองค่ะ |

| Sue | dtàirng ngahn láir-o rěu yung? | แต่งงานแล้วหรือยัง |
|---|---|---|
| Chanida | dtàirng ngahn hâh bpee láir-o. | แต่งงานห้าปีแล้ว |
| Sue | mee lôok láir-o rěu yung ká? | มีลูกแล้วหรือยังคะ |
| Chanida | mee láir-o. mee sǒrng kon | มีแล้ว มีสองคน |
| | lôok chai ah-yÓO sǎhm kòo-up | ลูกชายอายุสามขวบ |
| | lôok sǎo ah-yÓO sǒrng kòo-up. | ลูกสาวอายุสองขวบ |
| | láir-o kOOn Sue lâ. | แล้วคุณ Sue ล่ะ |
| | mee pêe-nórng mái? | มีพี่น้องไหม |

| gèe | how many? | กี่ |
|---|---|---|
| pêe-nórng | brothers and sisters | พี่น้อง |
| pêe-chai | older brother | พี่ชาย |
| pêe-sǎo | older sister | พี่สาว |
| nórng-chai | younger brother | น้องชาย |
| nórng-sǎo | younger sister | น้องสาว |
| ah-yÓO | age | อายุ |
| dtàirng ngaan | to be married | แต่งงาน |
| ... láir-o rěu yung? | ... yet (or not)? | แล้วหรือยัง |
| lôok chai | son | ลูกชาย |
| kòo-up | year(s) old | ขวบ |
| lôok sǎo | daughter | ลูกสาว |

## Comprehension

1 How long has Peter been in Thailand?
2 What compliments does Chanida pay Peter?
3 Do Peter and Sue's children speak Thai?

4  How many brothers and sisters does Chanida have?
5  Who is Wit?
6  How old is he?
7  Is he married?
8  How old are his children?

# —pah-săh láir sŭng-kom ภาษาและสังคม—

If you are invited to a Thai home, you should normally remove your shoes before entering the house. The traditional Thai greeting is the **wâi** (ไหว้) , in which the head is bowed slightly and the hands are held in a prayer-like position in front of the face at approximately chin height. How low the head is bowed and the height at which the hands are held reflect the degree of respect conveyed by the person **wai**-ing. A child **wai**-ing an adult, for example, may hold their hands so that the tips of the fingers are close to the forehead, while an adult responding may keep their own fingertips well below their chin.

Thais also show respect for older people by trying to keep their head at a lower level when passing or talking to them. For very tall people this can be tricky, however; an obvious attempt to bend forward a little is quite sufficient. It should be mentioned that for Thais, the head is a taboo area: never attempt to ruffle a Thai's hair in jest or offer a friendly pat on the head. Beware, also, of sitting with one or both legs stretched out in front of you, for to point your feet directly towards someone is impolite. Keeping your feet firmly on the ground or demurely tucked to one side, as inconspicuous as possible!

## ──────── sǔm-noo-un สำนวน ────────

How to:

● ask how someone is

| | |
|---|---|
| sa-bai dee lěr krúp (ká) *(formal)* | สบายดีหรือครับ (คะ) |
| bpen yung-ngai bâhng? *(informal)* | เป็นอย่างไรบ้าง |

● ask how many brothers and sisters a person has

| | |
|---|---|
| mee pêe-nórng gèe kon? | มีพี่น้องกี่คน |

● Ask about a person's age

| | |
|---|---|
| ah-yÓO tâo-rài? | อายุเท่าไร |

● Ask whether a person is married

| | |
|---|---|
| dtàirng ngahn láir-o rěu yung? | แต่งงานแล้วหรือยัง |

● Ask whether a person has any children

| | |
|---|---|
| mee lôok láir-o rěu yung? | มีลูกแล้วหรือยัง |

## ൽ ──────── kum ùt-tí-bai คำอธิบาย ────────

### 1 *Polite commands*

The word **chern** (เชิญ) *to invite* is used to preface a polite command or invitation:

| | |
|---|---|
| chern kâhng nai | *Please come in.* |

| | |
|---|---|
| chern nûng | *Please sit down.* |

## 2  Introductions

The easiest way to introduce someone is simply, **nêe ...** *(This is ...)*. A more formal expression is **kǒr náir-num hâi róo-jùk gúp ...** (ขอแนะนำให้รู้จักกับ ...) *I'd like to introduce you to ...* When introduced to someone, you can simply greet them with **sa-wùt dee krúp (kâ)**, or more formally you could say, **yin dee têe dâi róo-jùk gun** (ยินดีที่ได้รู้จักกัน) *I'm pleased to meet you.*

## 3  fairn แฟน

The word **fairn** derives from the English *fan* (as in 'supporter', not 'cooling device') and is the normal word for boyfriend or girlfriend. Its meaning is extended to include *husband* and *wife* which can occasionally lead the westerner into unworthy speculation. Is that ultra-respectable, middle-aged lady with the nice husband telling you she went to the cinema with him last night ... or with a secret boyfriend?

## 4  'How are you?'

The question **sa-bai dee lěr?** (สบายดีหรือ) *Are you well?* is normally answered **sa-bai dee**. The same answer is appropriate for the more informal enquiry **bpen yung-ngai bâhng?** (เป็นอย่างไรบ้าง) *How are things?*

## 5  láir-o ... lâ แล้ว ... ล่ะ

When **láir-o** occurs at the beginning of a sentence, it can be translated as *and* or *and then*. When it occurs in combination with the final particle **lâ** it means *(and) how / what about ...?*

| | |
|---|---|
| láir-o kOOn lâ? | *And how about you?* |
| láir-o lôok lâ? | *And how about the children?* |
| láir-o pêu-un lâ? | *And what about your friend?* |

## 6 Countries

**meu-ung** (เมือง) is an informal word for *country* while **bpra-tâyt** (ประเทศ) is more formal. In spoken Thai you are more likely to hear Thailand referred to as **meu-ung tai** while **bpra-tâyt** is normally used in writing.

## 7 Children

The word **lôok** (ลูก) *child, children* refers only to children in the sense of *offspring*. Thais would use **lôok** in sentences like *How many children do you have?*, *Her children are lovely, Whose child is that?* and so on. When talking about children as an age category, in statements like *Thai children are very polite, Children under 12 not permitted* and so on, Thais use the word **dèk** (เด็ก).

## 8 bpen เป็น

You have previously met **bpen** meaning *to be*, when it occurred in front of a noun. When it occurs at the end of a sentence it means *can, to be able to* or *to know how to do something*. This use of **bpen** overlaps with the word **dâi** (see Unit 2); both **bpen** and **dâi** are used when talking about knowledge of foreign languages.

> pôot (pah-săh) ung-grìt bpen mái?    *Do you speak English?*
> pôot tai mâi bpen.    *I don't speak Thai.*

Note that if you want to say that you can speak a language a little, then **nít-nòy** *(a little)* occurs at the end of the statement, after **bpen** or **dâi**.

> chún pôot bpen nít-nòy.    *I can speak it a little.*
> káo pôot tai dâi nít-nòy.    *He can speak Thai a little.*

## 9 pêe-nórng พี่น้อง

The word for *brothers and sisters* – **pêe-nórng** – literally means *older siblings* and *younger siblings* and makes no reference to gender at all.

Sometimes you may hear someone referring to a member of their family as **pêe** and you will not know whether it is an older brother or older sister. When it is necessary to be specific, the word **chai** *(male)* or **săo** *(female)* is added after **pêe** or **nórng**. These same gender words are also used with **lôok** *(child)* to distinguish between sons and daughters.

Both **pêe** and **nórng** are also used to mean *you* in certain contexts. An older friend, classmate or work colleague might be addressed as **pêe** as a sign of both respect and friendship. The word **nórng** is often used in restaurants to summon a waiter or waitress; but it can also convey a relationship of closeness or intimacy between the two speakers.

## 10 'How many?' questions

The question word **gèe** (กี่) *how many?* is always followed by a classifier. Frequently it will be preceded by a noun.

| | |
|---|---|
| mee lôok gèe kon? | *How many children do you have?* |
| bpai gèe wun? | *How many days are you going for?* |
| ao koh-lâh gèe kòo-ut? | *How many Colas do you want?* |

## 11  ... láir-o rěu yung? แล้วหรือยัง *questions*

This expresion occurs at the end of a sentence and means *... yet (or not)?* **láir-o** is often omitted and the question abbreviated to *... rěu yung?*

| | |
|---|---|
| dtàirng ngahn láir-o rěu yung? | *Are you married (yet)?* |
| mee lôok láir-o rěu yung? | *Do you have any children (yet)?* |
| gin kâo rěu yung? | *Have you eaten yet?* |

To say *yes* to such questions, you repeat the verb and the word **láir-o**:

| | |
|---|---|
| dtàirng ngahn láir-o | *Yes (I'm married).* |
| mee láir-o | *Yes (I do have children).* |
| gin láir-o | *Yes (I have eaten).* |

To say *no*, you simply say **yung.**

## 12 Age

Age is stated using the verb **ah-yÓO** (อายุ) *to be aged* ... followed
the number and then the word **kòo-up** (ขวบ) or **bpee** (ปี), both of
which mean *years*. **kòo-up** is used when talking about children up to
the age of thirteen or fourteen; for people older than that, **bpee** is
used. **láir-o** *(already)* often occurs at the end of the expression.

ah-yÓO hòk kòo-up (láir-o)          *six years old*
ah-yÓO yêe-sìp-hâh bpee (láir-o)    *twenty-five years old*

If, as is almost inevitable, a Thai asks you how old you are, you can
try making your first bad joke in Thai by answering **yêe-sìp-hâh
kòo-up.** If you are solemnly corrected, console yourself that not
everyone shares the same sense of humour and keep working on your
delivery!

☑ ——————**bàirp fèuk hùt**    แบบฝึกหัด————

1   How would you respond to a Thai if they said the following to you?

   (*a*)   sa-bai dee lěr krúp?
   (*b*)   kOOn pôot pah-săh tai bpen mái?
   (*c*)   yòo meu-ung tai nahn mái?
   (*d*)   kOOn pôot tai gèng.
   (*e*)   chern kâhng nai ná krúp.
   (*f*)   mee pêe-nórng mái?
   (*g*)   kŏr-tôht, kOOn dtàirng ngahn láir-o rěu yung?

2   Complete the dialogue. Sue has gone to register at a local clinic.
    A receptionist is taking down details from the answers Sue gives.
    What questions did the receptionist ask?

   **Receptionist**      ......................................
   **Sue**               chêu Susan Ford kâ.
   **Receptionist**      ......................................
   **Sue**               ah-yÓO săhm-sìp-hâh bpee láir-o.

| Receptionist | yÓO ............................ |
| Sue | mâi nahn kâ. |
| | sŏrng sǎhm deu-un tâo-nún. |
| Receptionist | kŏr-tôht ..................... |
| Sue | kâ, dtàirng ngahn láir-o. |
| Receptionist | ..................................... |
| Sue | mee láir-o. |
| | mee lôok chai sŏrng kon |
| | láir-o gôr lôok sǎo kon nèung. |
| Receptionist | ..................................... |
| Sue | ah-yÓO sìp kòo-up, bpàirt kòo-up |
| | láir-o gôr hâh kòo-up. |

**3**   How would you say the following in Thai?

(a)   Hello, Khun Sunisa, how are you?
(b)   Please come in.
(c)   Have you been in England long?
(d)   Your older sister speaks English well.
(e)   How many brothers and sisters do you have?
(f)   How old is your younger brother?

## àhn láir kěe-un   อ่านและเขียน

In the last unit you met the tone mark **mái àyk**. The other main tone mark is **mái toh** which is introduced in this unit together with the much less common **mái dtree** and **mái jùt-dta-wah**. Scan through some of the earlier dialogues to see how frequently **mái àyk** and **mái toh** tone marks occur. Once you have mastered these, you are well on the way to being able to read the dialogues in Thai script.

# 1  mái toh (◌้): *tone rules*

This tone mark looks like a number two with an elongated tail and is written above the initial consonant. Like **mái àyk** which you met in the previous unit, this single tone mark also represents two different tones!

When **mái toh** occurs on a low class initial consonant, the tone will be *high*:

| Low class | นี้ | ร้าน | ซื้อ |
|---|---|---|---|
| | née | ráhn | séu |

If the initial consonant is either mid class or high class, then the tone is *falling*:

| Mid class | ได้ | บ้าน | กุ้ง |
|---|---|---|---|
| | dâi | bâhn | gÓOng |
| High class | ข้าว | ให้ | ถ้า |
| | kâo | hâi | tâh |

# 2  mái dtree (◌๊ ) and mái jùt-dta-wah (◌๋ ): *tone rules*

In addition to **mái àyk** and **mái toh** there are two other tone marks to learn. But these are much less frequently encountered than the tone marks you have already learned. **mái dtree** looks like a number seven: it always produces a *high* tone. The symbol for **mái jùt-dta-wah** is a cross; words with this mark are always pronounced with a *rising tone*.

| *mái dtree* | เป๊ปซี่ | ต๊อก | จุ๊บ |
|---|---|---|---|
| | bpép-sêe | dtórk | jÓOp |

| *mái jùt-dta-wah* | เดี๋ยว | ต๋อย | อู๋ |
|---|---|---|---|
| | dĕe-o | dtŏy | ŏo |

## 3 Summary of tone mark rules

Tone marks are used, where necessary, to indicate tones in 'live' syllables. (There are only a few exceptions where a tone mark is used in a dead syllable.) The chart below summarises these rules:

| *initial* *consonant* *class* | mái àyk (-́) | mái toh (-̈) | mái dtree (-̃) | mái jùt-dta-wah (-̇) |
|---|---|---|---|---|
| LOW CLASS | **FALLING** | **HIGH** | **HIGH** | **RISING** |
| MID CLASS | **LOW** | **FALLING** | **HIGH** | **RISING** |
| HIGH CLASS | **LOW** | **FALLING** | **HIGH** | **RISING** |

Again, as a learning aid, you might find it helpful to make your own copy of this chart and keep it handy for reference rather than trying to memorise everything immediately.

☑──────── **bàirp fèuk àhn** แบบฝึกอ่าน ────────

1 All of these words are written with **mái toh** and are therefore pronounced with either a falling tone or a high tone.

| ต้อง | ทิ้ง | บ้าน | ให้ |
|---|---|---|---|
| รู้ | ขึ้น | นี้ | ถ้า |
| เก้า | น้ำ | แล้ว | กุ้ง |

ร้อน      ห้อง      ซื้อ      ป้าย
โน่น      แก้ว      หน้า      ได้

2 And now some phrases from this and earlier units, using words with **mái toh.**

ได้ไหม      ไม่ได้      สามสิบห้า      เข้าซอยไหม
รู้จักไหม      ก็แล้วกัน          ข้าวผัดกุ้ง
แก้วหนึ่ง      ข้าวหน้าไก่     แถวนี้      ร้านอาหาร
ทั้งหมดห้าสิบบาท           สองร้อยบาท

3 Now that you know **mái toh** you can begin to read some common prohibition notices. The Thai word for *forbidden* is **hâhm.**

ห้ามเข้า          *No entry*

ห้ามจอด          *No parking*

ห้ามสูบบุหรี่        *No smoking*

You will also commonly see the words **kâo** *(to enter)* and **òrk** *(to go out).* Often the word **tahng** *(way)* is tagged to the front of these words.

เข้า          *Entry*          ทางเข้า

ออก          *Exit*           ทางออก

4 And finally, here is Somchai with a couple of friends ordering lunch in a noodle shop. You can check up on the names of different food dishes in Unit 4.

| | |
|---|---|
| **Somchai** | ขอข้าวผัดกุ้งสองจาน |
| | แล้วก็ข้าวหน้าเป็ด |
| **Waiter** | ข้าวหน้าเป็ดไม่มี |
| | มีข้าวหน้าไก่แล้วก็ข้าวหมูแดง |

| Somchai | ขอข้าวหมูแดงก็แล้วกัน |  |
|---|---|---|
|  | แล้วก็น้ำส้มสามแก้ว | (น้ำส้ม  *orange juice*) |
| **Waiter** | น้ำส้มไม่มี |  |
|  | มีเป๊ปซี่เท่านั้น |  |

(*a*)   What did Somchai order?
(*b*)   Which food dish did the restaurant not have?
(*c*)   What did Somchai choose instead?
(*d*)   What is the only drink that the restaurant has?
(*e*)   What drinks did Somchai originally order?

# 9

## ngahn dtorn née bpen yung-ngai?

### *How's work these days?*
### งานตอนนี้เป็นอย่างไร

## *In this unit you will learn*

- how to talk about working and living in Bangkok
- how to express opinions and preferences
- the comparative form of adjectives
- some ways of intensifying adjectives and adverbs
- *not very ...*
- names of the regions of Thailand
- six important vowels and some less common consonants

## bòt sǒn-ta-nah    บทสนทนา

Peter is asking Khun Somchai about his job ...

| Peter | ngahn dtorn née bpen yung-ngai? | งานตอนนี้เป็นอย่างไร |
|---|---|---|
| Somchai | gôr ... dee měu-un gun. | ก็ ... ดีเหมือนกัน |
| | ngern deu-un gôr chái dâi. | เงินเดือนก็ใช้ได้ |
| | dtàir bahng krúng kít wâh nâh bèu-a | แต่บางครั้งคิดว่าน่าเบื่อ |

|            | dtôrng dtèun dtàir cháo | ต้องตื่นแต่เช้า |
|            | láir-o glùp bâhn dèuk. | แล้วกลับบ้านดึก |
|            | rót mun dtìt jung ler-ee. | รถมันติดจังเลย |
|            | tÓOk wun glùp bâhn sěe-a way-lah | ทุกวันกลับบ้านเสียเวลา |
|            | sǒrng chôo-a-mohng gwàh. | สองชั่วโมงกว่า |
|            | róo-sèuk wâh yâir ná. | รู้สึกว่าแย่นะ |
| Peter      | châi. yâir jing jing. | ใช่ แย่จริงๆ |
| Somchai    | láir-o ah-gàht mun mâi dee. | แล้วอากาศมันไม่ดี |
|            | bahng krúng kít wâh yàhk ja | บางครั้งคิดว่าอยากจะ |
|            | yái bpai yòo dtàhng jung-wùt. | ย้ายไปอยู่ต่างจังหวัด |
|            | ah-gàht mun dee gwàh, sa-àht | อากาศมันดีกว่า สะอาด |
|            | gwàh. rót mâi dtìt, kon mâi nâirn | กว่ารถไม่ติด คนไม่แน่น |
|            | měu-un têe grOOng-tâyp. | เหมือนที่กรุงเทพฯ |

| ngahn | work | งาน |
| dtorn née | now | ตอนนี้ |
| bpen yung-ngai? | how is it? | เป็นอย่างไร |
| gôr ... | well ... | ก็ ... |
| ... měu-un gun | fairly ... | เหมือนกัน |
| ngern deu-un | salary | เงินเดือน |
| chái dâi | reasonable, acceptable | ใช้ได้ |
| dtàir | but | แต่ |
| bahng | some | บาง |
| krúng | time(s) | ครั้ง |
| nâh bèu-a | boring | น่าเบื่อ |
| dtôrng | have to, must | ต้อง |
| dtèun | to wake up | ตื่น |

| | | |
|---|---|---|
| **(dtàir) cháo** | *(from) early morning* | (แต่) เช้า |
| **bâhn** | *house, home* | บ้าน |
| **dèuk** | *late at night* | ดึก |
| **rót** | *car* | รถ |
| **mun** | *it* | มัน |
| **dtìt** | *to stick, be stuck* | ติด |
| **jung ler-ee** | *(intensifier)* | จังเลย |
| **tÓOk** | *every* | ทุก |
| **wun** | *day* | วัน |
| **sěe-a** | *to spend, waste* | เสีย |
| **way-lah** | *time* | เวลา |
| **chôo-a-mohng** | *hour* | ชั่วโมง |
| **... gwàh** | *more than ...* | กว่า |
| **róo-sèuk** | *to feel* | รู้สึก |
| **yâir** | *to be a nuisance, a hassle* | แย่ |
| **jing** | *true, truly* | จริง |
| **ah-gàht** | *air, weather, climate* | อากาศ |
| **yái** | *to move* | ย้าย |
| **dtàhng jung-wùt** | *up-country, outside Bangkok* | ต่างจังหวัด |
| **sa-àht** | *clean* | สะอาด |
| **nâirn** | *to be crowded* | แน่น |
| **měu-un** | *like, similar, as* | เหมือน |

Chanida, meanwhile, asks Sue how she likes living in Bangkok.

| | | |
|---|---|---|
| **Chanida** | kOOn Sue chôrp yòo grOOng-tâyp mái? | คุณ Sue ชอบอยู่ กรุงเทพฯ ไหม |
| **Sue** | chôrp kâ. nâh sǒn jai. | ชอบค่ะ น่าสนใจ |

| | | |
|---|---|---|
| **Chanida** | jing lěr ká? | จริงหรือคะ |
| | chún wâh grOOng-tâyp dtorn née | ฉันว่ากรุงเทพฯ ตอนนี้ |
| | mâi nâh yòo ler-ee. pôr mâir bòrk | ไม่น่าอยู่เลย พ่อแม่บอก |
| | wâh mêu-a gòrn rót mâi kôy mee, | ว่า เมื่อก่อนรถไม่ค่อยมี |
| | dtèuk sǒong sǒong gôr mâi kôy mee. | ตึกสูงๆ ก็ไม่ค่อยมี |
| | dtorn nún mee klorng mee dtôn-mái | ตอนนั้นมีคลองมีต้นไม้ |
| | sǒo-ay láir-o ah-gàht sa-àht. | สวยแล้วอากาศสะอาด |
| **Sue** | kOOn Cha-ní-dah bpen kon | คุณชนิดาเป็นคน |
| | grOOng-tâyp châi mái ká? | กรุงเทพฯ ใช่ไหมคะ |
| **Chanida** | mâi châi kâ. | ไม่ใช่ค่ะ |
| | pôr mâir yái mah yòo têe-nêe | พ่อแม่ย้ายมาอยู่ที่นี่ |
| | mêu-a chún yung dèk. | เมื่อฉันยังเด็ก |
| | mêu-a gòrn chún yòo pâhk dtâi. | เมื่อก่อนฉันอยู่ภาคใต้ |
| | gèrt têe jung-wùt poo-gèt. | เกิดที่จังหวัดภูเก็ต |

| | | |
|---|---|---|
| **chôrp** | to like | ชอบ |
| **wâh** | to think, say | ว่า |
| **mâi ... ler-ee** | not at all | ไม่ ... เลย |
| **nâh yòo** | habitable | น่าอยู่ |
| **pôr** | father | พ่อ |
| **mâir** | mother | แม่ |
| **bòrk (wâh)** | to say, tell (that) | บอก (ว่า) |
| **mêu-a gòrn** | formerly | เมื่อก่อน |
| **mâi kôy ...** | hardly, scarcely | ไม่ค่อย ... |
| **dtèuk** | concrete building | ตึก |
| **sǒong** | high | สูง |
| **klorng** | canal | คลอง |

| | | |
|---|---|---|
| **dtôn-mái** | *tree* | ต้นไม้ |
| **mêu-a** | *when* | เมื่อ |
| **mêu-a chún yung dèk** | *when I was still a child* | เมื่อฉันยังเด็ก |
| **pâhk dtâi** | *the South* | ภาคใต้ |
| **gèrt** | *to be born* | เกิด |
| **poo-gèt** | *Phuket* | ภูเก็ต |

## Comprehension

1 How does Somchai feel about his salary?
2 How long does it take Somchai to get home from work?
3 What advantages does Somchai believe that working up-country has over Bangkok?
4 Does Chanida like Bangkok?
5 Where does she come from?
6 When did she move to Bangkok?
7 How does she describe the Bangkok of 'the good old days'?

## pah-sǎh láir sǔng-kom
### ภาษาและสังคม

Bangkok justifiably has the reputation of having one of the world's worst traffic congestion problems. Almost 90% of the country's automobiles are registered there and during the rush hour they nearly all seem to be out on the streets, grid-locked and spewing noxious fumes. The first day of the school term is invariably the worst, with horror stories each year of school children getting stuck in jams for up to six hours. Many people who live in the suburbs will leave home before 6 a.m. in order to beat the morning rush and they will quite likely leave work later than necessary to try to escape some of the late afternoon chaos.

Attempts to solve the problem have included special bus lanes, elaborate one-way detours, wide-scale construction of flyovers and elevated by-passes; ambitious politicians pledge their commitment to resolving the problem and the local press carry regular reports about the (distant) prospect of a new public transport system, either underground or an above street level monorail.

Bangkok residents appear to bear all this with remarkable resignation and few would consider foregoing the economic opportunies afforded by the capital in favour of a better living environment up-country. In fact, while every Bangkok resident complains that the traffic is getting worse each year, the vast majority of the city's population has grown up knowing little else. An unprecedented building boom in the last decade has added to the environmental nightmare, with multi-storey office blocks, shopping centres and condominiums springing up chaotically almost overnight. Despite this, many people, both Thais and foreigners, feel that Bangkok has a richness and vitality that are quite unique.

# ———— sǔm-noo-un  สำนวน ————

How to:

- ask someone's opinion of something

  ... bpen yung-ngai?                ... เป็นอย่างไร

- give your opinion

  kít wâh ...                        คิดว่า ...

  róo-sèuk wâh ...                   รู้สึกว่า ...

- compare things

  ... dee gwàh                       ... ดีกว่า

  ... sa-àht gwàh                    ... สะอาดกว่า

- emphasise something

| ... jing jing | ... จริงๆ |
| ... jung ler-ee | ... จังเลย |
| mâi ... ler-ee | ไม่ ... เลย |

 ———— **kum ùt-tí-bai** คำอธิบาย ————

## 1 gôr ก็

**gôr** is used in several different ways. One common use is at the beginning of a sentence when it serves as a hesitation device, rather like English, *Well, ....* In other contexts it can mean *too, also;* there is an example of this when chanida says, **rót mâi kôy mee, dteuk sŏong sŏong gôr mâi kôy mee.** Another common meaning is, *so, therefore.*

## 2 mĕu-un gun เหมือนกัน

**mĕu-un gun** literally means *likewise, similarly* and is often used in this way. The phrase also has an idiomatic usage, indicating a qualified or lukewarm *yes* response.

| dee mái? | *Is it good?* |
| dee mĕu-un gun | *Quite good* |
| chôrp mái? | *Do you like it?* |
| chôrp mĕu-un gun | *Yes, I quite like it.* |

## 3 nâh น่า

When **nâh** occurs in front of a verb it forms an adjective meaning *worthy of ... .*

| bèu-a | *to be bored* | nâh bèu-a | *boring* |
| sŏn jai | *to be interested in* | nâh sŏn jai | *interesting* |
| yòo | *to live* | nâh yòo | *habitable, nice to live in* |

| | | | |
|---|---|---|---|
| rúk | *to love* | nâh rúk | *lovable, sweet, cute* |
| gin | *to eat* | nâh gin | *tasty* |

## 4 Noun + pronoun + verb

This is a very common pattern in spoken Thai. You may hear some Thais carry the construction across to English, with statements like *My teacher, he is not nice.*

| | | |
|---|---|---|
| rót mun dtìt | *The traffic is jammed.* | (traffic-it-stuck) |
| ah-gàht mun mâi dee | *The air is bad.* | (air-it-not-good) |
| Sǒm-chai káo mâi mah | *Somchai's not coming.* | (Somchai-he-not-come) |

## 5 Intensification

The easiest way to emphasise or 'intensify' an adjective or adverb is simply to add **mâhk** (มาก) *very, much* after it. In this unit, two additional ways of intensification are introduced, adding **jung ler-ee** (จังเลย) or **jing jing** (จริง ๆ) after the adjective, both of which can be translated as *really ...* or *ever so ... .* You can also use **mâhk** in front of **jung ler-ee** although very often this is abbreviated in speech to ... **mâhk ler-ee.**

dee mâhk jung ler-ee        *very good*
or
dee mâhk ler-ee

**ler-ee** is also used with **mâi** to intensify negative statements. The pattern **mâi ... ler-ee** (ไม่ ... เลย), with **ler-ee** occurring at the end of the sentence, can be translated as *not ... at all.*

| | |
|---|---|
| mâi nâh yòo ler-ee | *not very nice to live in at all* |
| mâi mee ler-ee | *There aren't any at all.* |
| mâi pairng ler-ee | *not at all expensive* |

It is important to distinguish between **mâi ... ler-ee** and **mâi ... ròrk** (see Unit 3), for both can be translated as *not ... at all.* **mâi ... ler-ee** is essentially a statement of fact, whereas **mâi ... ròrk** is a statement of contradiction.

| | |
|---|---|
| – pairng jung ler-ee | *It's ever so expensive.* |
| – mâi pairng ròrk | *No, it isn't (at all).* |

## *6* gwàh กว่า

The comparative form of adjectives is formed by adding **gwàh**
*(more than)*:

| dee | *good* | dee gwàh | *better* |
|-----|--------|----------|----------|
| sa-àht | *clean* | sa-àht gwàh | *cleaner* |
| lék | *small* | lék gwàh | *smaller* |

Note also the use of **gwàh** in the expression **sŏrng chôo-a-mohng
gwàh** *(more than two hours)*.

## *7* chôrp ชอบ

**chôrp** means *to like*. It is important not to confuse it with **yàhk (ja)**
(อยาก (จะ)) *to want to, would like to* which you met in Unit 6. **chôrp**
can be followed by either a verb or a noun, but **yàhk ja** is
always followed by a verb.

| chôrp yòo têe-nêe | *I like living here.* |
|-------------------|------------------------|
| yàhk ja yòo têe-nêe | *I would like to live here.* |
| chôrp (gin) ah-hǎhn tai | *I like (eating) Thai food.* |
| yàhk ja gin ah-hǎhn tai | *I would like to eat Thai food.* |

## *8* mâi kôy ... ไม่ค่อย ...

**mâi kôy ...** *(not very ..., hardly, scarcely)* is an extremely useful way
of 'modifying' or toning down negative responses. The word
**tâo-rài** (เท่าไร) often occurs at the end of the phrase, but does not
change the meaning.

| mâi kôy chôrp (tâo-rài) | *I don't like it very much.* |
|-------------------------|-------------------------------|
| mâi kôy sǒo-ay (tâo-rài) | *It's not very nice.* |
| mâi kôy pairng (tâo-rài) | *It's not very expensive.* |

## *9* mêu-a เมื่อ

**mêu-a** means *when* and is used when you are talking about things
that happened in the past.

| | |
|---|---|
| mêu-a chún yung dèk | *when I was still a child* |
| mêu-a chún ah-yÓO hâh kòo-up | *when I was five years old* |
| mêu-a gòrn | *formerly, in the past* |
| mêu-a sǎhm bpee gòrn | *three years ago* |

## 10 pâhk ภาค

Thailand is divided into four **pâhk** (regions), each of which has its own distinct dialect and traditional customs.

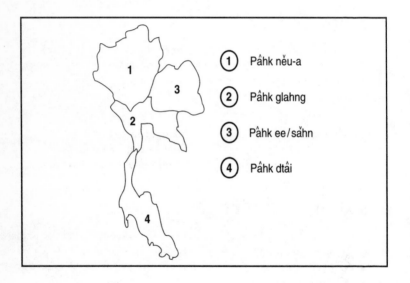

(1) Pâhk něu-a

(2) Pâhk glahng

(3) Pâhk ee/sǎhn

(4) Pâhk dtâi

| | | |
|---|---|---|
| pâhk něu-a | *the North* | ภาคเหนือ |
| pâhk dtâi | *the South* | ภาคใต้ |
| pâhk glahng | *the Central* | ภาคกลาง |
| pâhk ee-sǎhn | *the North East* | ภาคอีสาน |

——— **bàirp fèuk hùt** แบบฝึกหัด ———

**1** bèu-a ...

Here are some people grumbling about their job and wishing they had their neighbour's. What does each one say? (The first one is done for you.)

*Example:*
(a)  bèu-a.
mâi kôy chôrp bpen **dtum-ròo-ut.**
yàhk bpen **ta-hǎhn** mâhk gwàh.

(a)  dtum-ròo-ut  *(policeman)*
(b)  ta-hǎhn  *(soldier)*
(c)  kroo  *(teacher)*
(d)  mǒr  *(doctor)*
(e)  lay-kǎh-nÓO-gahn  *(secretary)*
(f)  núk tÓO-rá-gìt  *(businessman)*
(g)  núk núng-sěu pim  *(journalist)*
(h)  mâir bâhn  *(housewife)*
(i)  sàyt-těe *(millionaire)*

**2** Somchai is weighing up the advantages and disadvantages of living in Bangkok or outside the capital. Which statements do you think he would list under each heading?

(*a*)  yòo gr**OO**ng-tâyp ...
(*b*)  yòo dtàhng jung-wùt ...

(i)  ah-gàht sa-àht gwàh
(ii)  ngern deu-un gôr chái dâi
(iii)  kon nâirn
(iv)  dtôrng dtèun dtàir cháo láir-o glùp bâhn dèuk
(v)  rót mâi dtìt
(vi)  ah-gàht mâi dee
(vii)  kon mâi kôy nâirn
(viii)  rót dtìt jung ler-ee
(ix)  dtèuk sǒong sǒong mâi kôy mee
(x)  ngern deu-un mâi kôy dee

**3** How would you translate *like* in the sentences below? Choose from (i) **kǒr** ... (ii) **yàhk ja** (iii) **chôrp** and (iv) **měu-un**.

(*a*)  I don't like Thai food.
(*b*)  I'd like to visit Phuket.
(*c*)  I'd like a plate of fried rice, please.
(*d*)  I like crab fried rice.
(*e*)  It's not like English food.
(*f*)  I'd like to send it by air.

—— **àhn láir kĕe-un** อ่านและเขียน ——

## 1 Consonants

| ฆ | ธ | ภ | ญ | ณ |
|---|---|---|---|---|
| k | t | p | y* | n |

\* pronounced 'n' at the end of a word

This third group of *low class* consonants have the same sounds as other low class consonants that you have already learned in Units 1 and 4. The new consonants do not occur as frequently as those you met earlier, but they cannot be ignored as they appear in a number of common words. These include:

| ฆ่า | kâh | *to kill* |
|---|---|---|
| ภาษา | pah-săh | *language* |
| หญิง | yĭng | *lady* |
| ใหญ่ | yài | *big* |
| ญี่ปุ่น | yêe-bpÒOn | *Japan* |
| คุณ | kOOn | *you, Khun* |

## 2 Vowels

เ-า เ-ีย เ-ือ -ัว เ-ิ -ะ

| เ-า | เ-ีย | เ-ือ | -ัว* | เ-ิ** | -ะ |
|------|-------|-------|---------|--------|------|
| -ao | -ee-a | -eu-a | -oo-a | -er | -a |
| (short) | (long) | (long) | (long) | (long) | (short) |

Several new vowels are now being added, most of which are made up of combinations of symbols you have already met. Many learners worry that when reading words where a vowel surrounds a consonant, such as เ-า, they will try to read it as two separate vowels (เ- and -า) instead of recognising it as a single vowel. In fact most find the problem evaporates as soon as they start to practise reading. Even so, it is worth remembering that whenever you encounter the symbol เ- you need to scan the next couple of letters briefly to see whether it is a vowel in its own right or just a part of a 'wrap-around' vowel.

\* When -ัว is followed by another consonant symbol it omits the top part ( -ั ) of the vowel symbol.

| หัว | ตัว | วัว |
|------|------|------|
| hǒo-a | dtoo-a | woo-a |

*but*

| ด้วย | สวน | รวย |
|------|------|------|
| dôo-ay | sǒo-un | roo-ay |

\*\* When เ-ิ is *not* followed by a consonant it drops the top part of the vowel symbol ( -ิ ) *but adds* the zero-consonant symbol (อ) at the end of the word.

| เดิน | เปิด | เกิด |
|------|------|------|
| dern | bpèrt | gèrt |

*but*

| เธอ | เจอ |
|-----|-----|
| ter | jer |

#  —— **bàirp fèuk àhn** แบบฝึกอ่าน ——

1 Once you have learned the vowels and consonants from this únit, you should be able to read these words from the Dialogue.

| เหมือน | เงิน | เดือน | เบื่อ |
|--------|------|-------|-------|
| เสีย | ชั่วโมง | นะ | สะอาด |
| คุณ | คะ | เมื่อ | สวย |
| ภาค | เกิด | ภูเก็ต | |

2 These phrases taken from earlier units, all include some of the new letters from this unit.

| คุณชื่ออะไร | สีแดงสวยมาก | เรียกว่าน้อยหน่า |
|-------------|-------------|------------------|
| โลละเท่าไร* | เลี้ยวซ้ายที่นี่ | เอาน้ำอะไรคะ** |
| ขอเป๊ปซี่ขวดหนึ่ง | เอาขวดใหญ่ | อยากจะลงทะเบียนด้วย |
| พูดภาษาไทยเป็นไหม | ลูกชายอายุสามขวบ | จะแลกเปลี่ยนสองร้อย |

\* เท่าไร pronounced **tâo-rài** with a low tone on the second syllable

\*\* น้ำ pronounced **náhm** with a long vowel, unless it is part of a compound word such as น้ำส้ม **núm sôm**

**3** Peter is asking Somchai about his origins ...

| Peter | คุณสมชายเป็นคนภาคเหนือใช่ไหม |
|---|---|
| Somchai | ใช่ ผมเกิดที่เชียงใหม่ |
| | พ่อแม่ย้ายมาอยู่ที่นี่เมื่อสามสิบปีก่อน |
| | เมื่อผมยังเด็ก |
| Peter | ชอบอยู่ที่นี่ไหม |
| Somchai | ไม่ค่อยชอบ |
| | ที่นี่รถติดจังเลย |
| | อยู่เชียงใหม่อากาศสะอาด |
| | รถไม่ติดเหมือนที่นี่ |

(*a*) Where does Somchai come from?
(*b*) How long has he lived in Bangkok?
(*c*) How does his place of birth compare with Bangkok?

**4** Write answers to these questions:

๑. คุณทำงานอะไร

๒. คุณทำงานที่ไหน

๓. งานของคุณเป็นอย่างไร

๔. เงินเดือนดีไหม

๕. ไปทำงานคุณเสียเวลากี่ชั่วโมง (กี่นาที)

## ———— bòt àhn  บทอ่าน ————

Here is a little more information about Chanida's family. What was her father's occupation? How old was she when she left Phuket? What was her older brother's ambition when he was at school?

คุณชนิดาเป็นคนภาคใต้ เกิดที่จังหวัดภูเก็ต พ่อเป็นตำรวจ

แม่เป็นแม่บ้าน มีลูกห้าคน พ่อแม่คุณชนิดากับพี่น้องย้ายมาอยู่ที่นี่
เมื่อคุณชนิดาอายุห้าขวบ พี่ชายคุณชนิดาชื่อวิท ที่โรงเรียนวิทเรียนเก่ง
เขาบอกว่าอยากจะเป็นหมอ

---

ตำรวจ  *policeman* (dtum-ròo-ut\*)

โรงเรียน  school

---

\*Note that the second syllable is pronounced with a *low* tone, not a falling tone, as might be expected from the rules you have learned.

# 10

## tahn pèt bpen mái?

*Can you eat spicy food?*

ทานเผ็ดเป็นไหม

### In this lesson you will learn

- the names of more Thai foods
- *anything, anywhere, anyone*
- the verb **hâi**
- how to express opinions: *too ...*
- how to read words that begin with two consonants

## bòt sŏn-ta-nah   บทสนทนา

Chanida has taken Peter and Sue to a restaurant.

| Waiter | sùng rĕu yung krúp? | สั่งหรือยังครับ |
|---|---|---|
| Chanida | yung kâ. | ยังค่ะ |
| | kŏr doo may-noo nòy. | ขอดูเมนูหน่อย |
| | kOOn Peter chôrp tahn a-rai? | คุณ Peter ชอบทานอะไร |
| Peter | a-rai gôr dâi krúp. | อะไรก็ได้ครับ |

|  | hâi kOOn Cha-ní-dah sùng dee gwàh. | ให้คุณชนิดาสั่งดีกว่า |
|---|---|---|
| **Chanida** | kOOn Sue tahn pèt bpen mái? | คุณSue ทานเผ็ดเป็นไหม |
| **Sue** | bpen kâ tâh mâi pèt mâhk. | เป็นค่ะ ถ้าไม่เผ็ดมาก |
| **Chanida** | gairng gài pèt mâhk mái ká? | แกงไก่เผ็ดมากไหมคะ |
| **Waiter** | mâi pèt mâhk krúp. | ไม่เผ็ดมากครับ |
| **Chanida** | tâh yàhng nún kǒr gairng gài | ถ้าอย่างนั้น ขอแกงไก่ |
|  | néu-a pùt núm mun hǒy | เนื้อผัดน้ำมันหอย |
|  | láir-o gôr dtôm yum gÔOng. | แล้วก็ต้มยำกุ้ง |
|  | dtôm yum mâi ao pèt mâhk ná. | ต้มยำไม่เอาเผ็ดมากนะ |
|  | ao kâo dôo-ay ná. | เอาข้าวด้วยนะ |
| **Waiter** | krúp. láir-o rúp náhm a-rai krúp? | แล้วรับน้ำอะไรครับ |
| **Chanida** | kǒr núm sôm kún sǒrng gâir-o kâ. | ขอน้ำส้มคั้นสองแก้วค่ะ |
|  | láir-o kOOn Peter rúp bee-a | แล้วคุณPeter รับเบียร์ |
|  | châi mái? | ใช่ไหม |

| **sùng** | *to order* | สั่ง |
|---|---|---|
| **tahn** | *to eat* | ทาน |
| **a-rai gôr dâi** | *anything* | อะไรก็ได้ |
| **hâi** | *to get someone to do something* | ให้ |
| **pèt** | *spicy* | เผ็ด |
| **tâh** | *if* | ถ้า |
| **gairng** | *curry* | แกง |
| **gairng gài** | *chicken curry* | แกงไก่ |
| **tâh yàhng nún** | *in that case* | ถ้าอย่างนั้น |
| **néu-a** | *beef* | เนื้อ |
| **pùt** | *to stir fry* | ผัด |

| **núm mun hǒy** | *oyster sauce* | น้ำมันหอย |
| **néu-a pùt núm mun hoy** | *beef fried in oyster sauce* | เนื้อผัดน้ำมันหอย |
| **dtôm yum gÔOng** | *shrimp 'tom yam'* | ต้มยำกุ้ง |
| **rúp** | *to receive, take* | รับ |
| **núm sôm** | *orange juice* | น้ำส้ม |
| **núm sôm kún** | *fresh orange juice* | น้ำส้มคั้น |

After the main course the waiter returns.

| | | |
|---|---|---|
| **Waiter** | rúp kǒrng wǎhn mái krúp? | รับของหวานไหมครับ |
| **Chanida** | mee a-rai bâhng ká? | มีอะไรบ้างคะ |
| **Waiter** | mee pǒn-la-mái mee ka-nǒm | มีผลไม้ มีขนม |
| | láir-o gôr mee ai dtim. | แล้วก็มีไอสครีม |
| **Chanida** | ka-nǒm têe-nêe a-ròy ná. | ขนมที่นี่อร่อยนะ |
| | kOOn Sue tahn ka-nǒm mái? | คุณ Sue ทานขนมไหม |
| **Sue** | mâi dâi kâ. ìm láir-o. | ไม่ได้ค่ะ อิ่มแล้ว |
| **Chanida** | láir-o kOOn Peter lâ? | แล้วคุณ Peter ล่ะ |
| **Peter** | tahn ka-nǒm tai mâi bpen krúp. | ทานขนมไทยไม่เป็นครับ |
| | kít wâh mâi kôy a-ròy. | คิดว่าไม่ค่อยอร่อย |
| | wǎhn gern bpai. | หวานเกินไป |

| **kǒrng wǎhn** | *sweet, dessert* | ของหวาน |
| **... bâhng** | *(see kum ut-ti-bai (5))* | ... บ้าง |
| **pǒn-la-mái** | *fruit* | ผลไม้ |
| **ka-nǒm** | *cake, dessert* | ขนม |
| **ai dtim** | *ice-cream* | ไอสครีม |
| **ìm** | *to be full* | อิ่ม |
| **... gern bpai** | *too ...* | ... เกินไป |

At the end of the meal, Khun Somchai offers Peter a cigarette.

| Somchai | sòop bOO-rèe mái krúp? | สูบบุหรี่ไหมครับ |
| Peter | mâi sòop krúp. | ไม่สูบครับ |
| | lêrk láir-o. | เลิกแล้ว |
| Somchai | nórng, nórng! | น้องๆ |
| | kǒr têe-kèe-a bOO-rèe nòy. | ขอที่เขี่ยบุหรี่หน่อย |
| | chék bin dôo-ay. | เช็คบิลด้วย |

| bOO-rèe | cigarette | บุหรี่ |
| sòop bOO-rèe | to smoke | สูบบุหรี่ |
| lêrk | to cease, give up | เลิก |
| nórng, nórng | waiter! | น้องๆ |
| têe-kèe-a bOO-rèe | ashtray | ที่เขี่ยบุหรี่ |
| chék bin | can I have the bill? | เช็คบิล |

## *Comprehension*

1 Can Sue eat hot food?
2 What dishes does Khun Chanida order?
3 What do they have to drink with their meal?
4 Why doesn't Sue want any dessert?
5 Why doesn't Peter like Thai desserts?
6 What does Somchai ask the waiter for?

# — pah-săh láir sŭng-kom ภาษาและสังคม —

If you are eating alone in a restaurant, you are most likely to order a rice or noodle dish (see Unit 4) which are served quickly. But if you go out for an evening meal with a number of friends, you are more likely to order rice and a variety of side dishes. These may be brought to the table once they are cooked and the meal can begin before all the dishes have arrived. If you are invited to select one of the dishes, you should be aware that it is not for your exclusive consumption but is supposed to blend in with all the other dishes. If you are not very confident about what to choose, you can always relinquish the responsibility by saying, **hâi kOOn** x **sùng dee gwàh** (*It's better to let Khun* x *order*). If you do opt out, watch what Thais order, so that on future occasions you will be able to make appropriate combinations yourself. Thais use a spoon and fork (although chopsticks are used in noodle shops) to eat. After rice has been served onto the plate, a spoonful or two is normally taken from one of the side dishes, and mixed with the rice before eating. A meal is thus a constant 'dipping-in' process. In some restaurants a serving spoon will be provided with each side dish, but in others, you simply use the spoon and fork that you eat with.

Expect to be asked questions about whether you can eat Thai food **(tahn ah-hăhn tai bpen mái?)**, whether you can eat spicy food **(tahn ah-hăhn pèt bpen mái?)**, whether Thai food is tasty **(ah-hăhn tai a-ròy mái?)**, whether Thai food is spicy **(ah-hăhn tai pèt mái?)** and so on. At the end of a meal, the host or senior person present will normally pick up the bill.

Although Thai cigarette packs have introduced health warnings in the last few years, many Thai men smoke. Smoking is still seen as manly in men and sophisticated in *some* women. When offering a cigarette, a Thai may ask **sòop bOO -rèe mái?** or, more surprisingly to the westerner, **sòop bOO -rèe bpen mái?** (literally, **Can** *you smoke?*). The latter question does not require a pedantic explanation along the lines of 'Yes-I-can-*but-actually-I-don't-any*' *more-because-it's-bad-for-the-health;* a simple **mâi sòop krúp (kâ)** or, if accepting, **kòrp-kOOn krúp (kâ)** is quite sufficient. While smoking is banned in certain places, such as hospital waiting rooms and cinemas, the non-smoking work environment is a long way from realisation in Thailand.

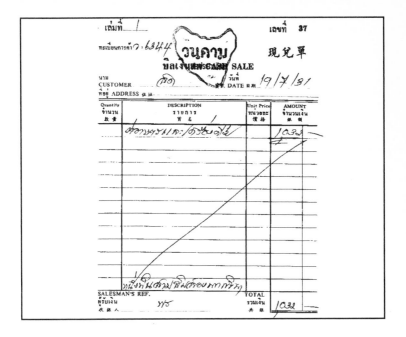

# sǔm-noo-un สำนวน

How to:

- ask your friend to order for you
  hâi kOOn X sùng dee gwàh

  ให้คุณ x สั่งดีกว่า

- ask if a dish is very spicy
  ... pèt mâhk mái?

  ... เผ็ดมากไหม

- tell the waiter you don't want it too hot
  mâi ao pèt mâhk ná

  ไม่เอาเผ็ดมากนะ

- say you are full
  ìm láir-o

  อิ่มแล้ว

- say you can't eat something

  tahn (gin) ... mâi bpen       ทาน (กิน) ... ไม่เป็น

- say something is too sweet / spicy

  wǎhn / pèt gern bpai       หวาน/เผ็ดเกินไป

- say you don't smoke

  mai sòop       ไม่สูบ

## kum ùt-tí-bai คำอธิบาย

### 1 ...gôr dâi ก็ได้

... **gôr dâi** occurs commonly with question words in the following indefinite expressions, which in conversational English, often tag *you like* or *will do* on to the end:

| | |
|---|---|
| a-rai gôr dâi | *anything* |
| krai gôr dâi | *anyone* |
| têe-nǎi gôr dâi | *anywhere* |
| mêu-rai gôr dâi | *any time* |
| póp gun têe-nai? | *Where shall we meet?* |
| – têe-nǎi gôr dâi | *– Anywhere you like.* |
| rao ja bpai mêu-rai? | *When shall we go?* |
| – mêu-rai gôr dâi | *– Any time will do.* |

### 2 hâi ให้

**hâi** is an important verb in Thai with a number of distinct usages. It can mean *to get someone to do something, to give* and *for*. In the expression **hâi kOOn X sùng dee gwàh** it has the first meaning of getting someone to do something. In the dialogue, the pronoun *I* is omitted because it is understood from the context. Here are some more examples:

| | |
|---|---|
| káo hâi pǒm séu bOO-rèe | *He got me to buy some cigarettes.* |
| pǒm hâi káo glùp bâhn | *I got him to go home.* |
| káo hâi rao bpai tahng reu-a | *They got us to go by boat.* |

## 3 tahn ทาน

**tahn** is a polite, slightly formal word for *to eat*, rather like **sâhp** (Unit 7) was the formal word for *to know*. You would use these words in formal situations and when speaking to people of equal or more senior status. The more informal word for *to eat* is **gin** (กิน).

## 4 rúp รับ

The waiter uses the more polite and formal verb **rúp** *(to receive)* when asking the diners what they would like, whereas the waitress in the coffee shop in Unit 4 used the less formal **ao**.

## 5 a-rai bâhng อะไรบ้าง

When the word **bâhng** (บ้าง) *(some, somewhat)* appears after a question word, it assumes that the answer will be in the form of some kind of list. Notice that this **bâhng**, which occurs at the end of a question, is spelt differently from **bahng** (บาง) in Unit 9, where it occurred in front of a noun.

| | |
|---|---|
| mee pǒn-la-mái a-rai bâhng? | *What fruits do you have?* |
| – mee sùp-bpa-rót, ma-la-gor láir-o gôr dtairng moh | *– There's pineapple, papaya and water melon.* |
| bpai têe-o têe-nai bâhng? | *Where did you visit?* |
| – bpai chee-ung-mài, pút-ta-yah láir-o gôr poo-gèt | *– I went to Chiangmai, Pattaya and Phuket.* |
| róo-jùk krai bâhng? | *Who do you know?* |
| – róo-jùk kOOn Som-chai, kOOn Mah-lee láir-o gôr kOOn Sa-ngàh | *– I know Khun Somchai, Khun Malee and Khun Sa-nga.* |

# 6 gern bpai เกินไป

**gern bpai** *(too ...)* occurs after an adjective. In spoken Thai, it is common to omit the word **gern**.

| | |
|---|---|
| wǎhn (gern) bpai | *too sweet* |
| pèt (gern) bpai | *too hot, spicy* |
| pairng (gern) bpai | *too expensive* |
| lék (gern) bpai | *too small* |

## 7 Thai food

Here is a list of some basic foods and dishes. In many restaurants catering for a foreign clientele, dishes will be listed in Thai script and romanised Thai, perhaps with a description in English. Systems of romanising Thai words however, will vary considerably from one restaurant to another; but if you have followed the script lessons carefully up to now, you won't need to look at romanised Thai anyway!

### *Curries and soups*

| | | |
|---|---|---|
| แกง | gairng | *'wet' curry* (i.e. with a lot of liquid) |
| แพนง | pa-nairng | *'dry' curry* |
| แกงไก่ | gairng gài | *chicken curry* |
| แกงเนื้อ | gairng néu-a | *beef curry* |
| แกงมัสมั่น | gairng mút-sa-mun | *'Muslim' curry* |
| แกงจืด | gairng jèut | *bland, clear soup* |
| ต้มยำ | dtôm yum | *'tom yam'* (a spicy soup made with lemon grass) |

| ต้มยำกุ้ง | dtôm yum gÔOng | shrimp 'tom yam' |
| ต้มยำปลา | dtôm yum bplah | fish 'tom yam' |

## Meat and fish

| ไก่ | gài | chicken |
| ไก่ผัดหน่อไม้ | gài pùt nòr-mái | chicken fried with bamboo shoots |
| ไก่ผัดขิง | gài pùt kǐng | chicken fried with ginger |
| ไก่ผัดพริก | gài pùt prík | chicken fried with chilli |
| ไก่ผัดใบกะเพรา | gài pùt bai ga-prao | chicken fried with basil leaves |
| ไก่ทอดกระเทียม พริกไทย | gai tôrt gra-tee-um prík tai | chicken fried with garlic and pepper |
| ไก่ผัดเปรี้ยวหวาน | gài pùt bprêe-o wǎhn | sweet and sour chicken |
| ไก่ย่าง | gài yâhng | barbecued chicken |
| เนื้อ | néu-a | beef |
| เนื้อผัดขิง | néu-a pùt kǐng | beef fried with ginger |
| เนื้อผัดพริก | néu-a pùt prík | beef fried with chilli |
| เนื้อผัดน้ำมันหอย | néu-a pùt núm mun hǒy | beef fried in oyster sauce |
| หมู | mǒo | pork |
| หมูผัดขิง | mǒo pùt kǐng | pork fried with ginger |
| หมูผัดพริก | mǒo pùt prík | pork fried with chilli |
| หมูผัดหน่อไม้ | mǒo pùt nòr-mái | pork fried with bamboo shoots |

| หมูผัดใบกะเพรา | mǒo pùt bai ga-prao | pork fried with basil leaves |
| หมูผัดเปรี้ยวหวาน | mǒo pùt bprêe-o wǎhn | sweet and sour pork |
| เป็ด | bpèt | duck |
| เป็ดย่าง | bpèt yâhng | roast duck |

## Fish dishes

| ปู | bpoo | crab |
| ปลา | bplah | fish |
| กุ้ง | gÔOng | shrimp |
| กุ้งใหญ่ | gÔOng yài | lobster |
| ปลาเปรี้ยวหวาน | bplah bprêe-o wǎhn | sweet and sour fish |
| กุ้งผัดพริก | gÔOng pùt prík | shrimp fried with chilli |
| กุ้งผัดใบกะเพรา | gÔOng pùt bai ga-prao | shrimp fried with basil leaves |

## Egg dishes

| ไข่ | kài | egg |
| ไข่ดาว | kài dao | fried egg |
| ไข่เจียว | kài jee-o | omelette |
| ไข่ยัดไส้ | kài yút sâi | stuffed omelette |

# bàirp fèuk hùt   แบบฝึกหัด

**1** How would you answer if a Thai asked you the following questions?

   (a)  tahn ah-hǎhn tai bpen mái?
   (b)  ah-hǎhn tai pèt mái?
   (c)  tahn pèt bpen mái?
   (d)  ah-hǎhn tai a-ròy mái?
   (e)  tahn ka-nǒm tai bpen mái?
   (f)  sòop bOO-rèe mái?

**2** rúp a-rai krúp?

You have taken some non-Thai speaking friends to a restaurant and they expect you to do the talking. How would you order the following?

beef curry
sweet and sour fish
chicken fried with ginger
shrimp 'tom yam'

**3** How would you:

   (a)  tell the waiter you don't want the 'tom yam' to be too hot?
   (b)  ask the waiter if the beef curry is spicy?
   (c)  say that the chicken fried with ginger is very tasty?
   (d)  ask the waiter what fruit the restaurant serves?
   (e)  tell the waiter Thai desserts are too sweet and ask if they serve ice-cream?

—— **àhn láir kĕe-un** อ่านและเขียน ——

## 1 Words beginning with consonant clusters

All of the words that you have read up to now have begun with either a single consonant or a vowel sound. In this unit we are going to learn how to read words that begin with a consonant cluster (two consonant sounds) – words like **krúp, glùp, gwàh** and so on. The following consonant clusters exist in Thai; knowing which consonant clusters can exist at the beginning of a word will help you to avoid misreading certain two-syllable words.

| กร- | คร-, ขร- | ตร- | ปร- | พร- |
|-----|----------|-----|-----|-----|
| gr- | kr-      | dtr-| bpr-| pr- |
| กล- | คล-, ขล- |     | ปล- | พล- |
| gl- | kl-      |     | bpl-| pl- |
| กว- | คว-, ขว- |     |     |     |
| gw- | kw-      |     |     |     |

When it comes to reading a word like ครับ, the tone should clearly be *high*, since (i) it is a *dead syllable*, (ii) both consonants in the cluster are *low class*, and (iii) the vowel is *short*.

However, in many words the two consonants at the beginning of a word belong to different classes. In such cases, it is the class of the *first* consonant which determines the tone.

| ขวา | ใกล้ | ปลูก |
|-----|------|------|
| kwǎh | glâi | bplòok |

## 2 Words with no vowel symbols

In Unit 4 you met words like **kon** and **hòk** which consisted of two consonants but no written vowel symbol. Two syllable words, consisting of three consonant symbols and no vowel symbols are much less common. In such cases the first vowel is -**a** and the second -**o**.

| ถนน | สงบ | ขนม |
|------|------|------|
| ta-nǒn | sa-ngòp | ka-nǒm |

More common are words in which there is a vowel symbol in the second syllable, but where a short -**a** vowel has to be supplied in the first.

| ตลาด | สนาม | สบาย | ชนิดา |
|------|------|------|------|
| dta-làht | sa-nǎhm | sa-bai | cha-ní-dah |

In having two consonants at the beginning, the words above look very similar to those that begin with a consonant cluster. But if you check the consonant cluster chart above, you will see that the sounds *dtl-, sn-, sb-* and *chn* do not exist at the beginning of Thai words. So the short -**a** vowel has to be added after the initial consonant. The first syllable in words like this is pronounced with a mid tone.

The tone of the second syllable is determined by the *second* consonant in the cluster *unless* it is one of those consonants you learned in Unit 1 (i.e. ง น ม ร ย ล ว); if the second consonant is a Unit 1 consonant then the class of the *first* consonant determines the tone.

| ขบวน | สภาพ | สนาม | สง่า |
|------|------|------|------|
| ka-boo-un | sa-pâhp | sa-nǎhm | sa-ngàh |

*Note:* Words beginning บริ- are pronounced with an -**or** vowel between the first and second consonants, *not* an -**a** vowel.

| บริการ | บริเวณ | บริษัท |
|------|------|------|
| bor-ri-gahn | bor-ri-wayn | bor-ri-sùt |

# 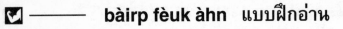 bàirp fèuk àhn แบบฝึกอ่าน

1 In all of these words two consonant symbols appear before there is any vowel symbol. Some are consonant clusters, others require you to supply a short vowel.

| | | | | |
|---|---|---|---|---|
| กว่า | ขวา | กรุง | ประตู | ปลา |
| เปล่า | ตรง | ไกล | ใกล้ | กลับ |
| ใคร | คล้าย | ประเทศ | พระ | ถนน |
| ขนาด | สนุก | สถาน | สบาย | บริษัท |

2 What's it (stir) fried with? On a Thai menu you will find a large number of items consisting of the name of the meat (e.g. **gài, néu-a, moo**) followed by the word **pùt** *(stir fried)* and then the vegetable with which it is fried. Match up the Thai script with the English description.

(i) ... ผัดขิง  (a) ... fried with basil leaves

(ii) ... ผัดพริก  (b) ... fried with ginger

(iii) ... ผัดหน่อไม้  (c) ... fried with chilli

(iv) ... ผัดใบกะเพรา  (d) ... fried with bamboo shoots

3 No pork, please. If you were eating with a friend who didn't like pork, which of these dishes should be avoided?

๑. เนื้อผัดน้ำมันหอย

๒. หมูเปรี้ยวหวาน

๓. ไก่ผัดหน่อไม้

๔. หมูผัดขิง

๕. กุ้งผัดพริก

4 That's not what I ordered!

This was what the waiter noted down for your order (see **bàirp fèuk hùt 2**). How many dishes did he get right? And what unexpected delicacies arrived at your table?

๑. แกงเนื้อ
๒. หมูเปรี้ยวหวาน
๓. ไก่ผัดขิง
๔. ต้มยำปู

—————— **bòt àhn** บทอ่าน ——————

Each year thousands of people leave their villages in rural Thailand and flock to Bangkok in search of work. While some are seasonal migrants, others, through either poverty or ambition, will never return. In this passage, a young girl, Tui, talks about leaving home and going to work in a noodle shop in Bangkok. (Note that she refers to herself as 'Tui' rather than using **chún**. Using one's name or nickname instead of *I* is very common in the speech of girls; a lot of foreign men pick up the habit and sound rather strange to Thais!)

เป็นคนอีสาน อยู่หมู่บ้านเล็กๆ ที่จังหวัดหนองคาย
ที่บ้านไม่ค่อยมีงานทำ นอกจากทำนา ตุ่ยไม่ชอบทำนา
มันยากลำบาก ก็คิดว่ามาทำงานที่นี่ดีกว่า
เดี๋ยวนี้ทำงานที่ร้านก๋วยเตี๋ยว ล้างชามล้างจานทั้งวัน
บางวันคิดว่าน่าเบื่อ อยากกลับบ้านต่างจังหวัด
แต่เงินไม่ค่อยมี

| คนอีสาน | a North-Easterner |
|---|---|
| หมู่บ้าน | village |
| เล็ก ๆ | lék lék |
| | (The symbol ๆ means 'repeat' the previous word.) |
| หนองคาย | Nongkhai |
| งาน | work (noun) |
| นอกจาก | apart from |
| ทำนา | rice farming |
| ชอบ | to like |
| มัน | it |
| ยาก | difficult |
| ลำบาก | difficult |
| เดี๋ยวนี้ | now |
| ร้านก๋วยเตี๋ยว | noodle shop |
| ล้าง | to wash |
| ทั้งวัน | all day |
| เงิน | money |

## *Comprehension*

(*a*)   What work opportunities are there for Tui in her village?

(*b*)   Why doesn't she want to do this?

(*c*)   What does she do all day long in the noodle shop?

(*d*)   Is she happy in her work?

(*e*)   Why can't she go home?

# 11

## kOOn pôot tai gèng

*You speak Thai well*

## คุณพูดไทยเก่ง

## In this lesson you will learn

- how to talk about your knowledge of Thai
- *why?* questions
- to talk about things that happened in the past: **ker-ee**
- to talk about things that are happening now: **gum-lung**
- abstract nouns
- the final group of consonants

## bòt sŏn-ta-nah    บทสนทนา

A taxi driver strikes up a conversation with Peter ...

| | | |
|---|---|---|
| **Taxi** | bpen kon a-may-ri-gun châi mái? | เป็นคนอเมริกันใช่ไหม |
| **Peter** | mâi châi bpen kon ung-grìt. | ไม่ใช่ เป็นคนอังกฤษ |
| **Taxi** | oh kon ung-grìt lěr? | โอ คนอังกฤษหรือ |
| | yòo meu-ung tai nahn mái? | อยู่เมืองไทยนานไหม |
| **Peter** | mâi nahn krúp. | ไม่นานครับ |

| Taxi | tum-mai kOOn pôot tai gèng? | ทำไมคุณพูดไทยเก่ง |
|------|------------------------------|-------------------|
| Peter | mâi gèng ròrk krúp. | ไม่เก่งหรอกครับ |
| | pôot dâi nít-nòy tâo-nún. | พูดได้นิดหน่อยเท่านั้น |
| Taxi | gèng sí krúp. | เก่งซิครับ |
| | mee mee-a kon tai châi mái krúp? | มีเมียคนไทยใช่ไหมครับ |
| Peter | mâi châi krúp. ker-ee ree-un | ไม่ใช่ครับ เคยเรียน |
| | têe ung-grìt mah gòrn. | ที่อังกฤษมาก่อน |
| Taxi | ree-un pah-sǎh tai têe ung-grìt | เรียนภาษาไทยที่อังกฤษ |
| | dâi lěr? | ได้หรือ |
| Peter | dâi krúp. | ได้ครับ |
| Taxi | mee kon tai sǒrn mái? | มีคนไทยสอนไหม |
| Peter | mee krúp. mee túng fa-rùng láir | มีครับ มีทั้งฝรั่งและ |
| | kon tai sǒrn. | คนไทยสอน |
| Taxi | láir-o kOOn àhn láir kěe-un | แล้วคุณอ่านและเขียน |
| | pah-sǎh tai dâi mái? | ภาษาไทยได้ไหม |
| Peter | gum-lung ree-un krúp. | กำลังเรียนครับ |

| tum-mai | *why?* | ทำไม |
|---------|--------|------|
| sí | *particle* | ซิ |
| mee-a | *wife* (informal) | เมีย |
| ker-ee | *used to; to have ever done* | |
| | *something* | เคย |
| ker-ee ... mah gòrn | *to have ever done something* | เคย ... มาก่อน |
| ree-un | *to study, learn* | เรียน |
| sǒrn | *to teach* | สอน |
| túng ... láir ... | *both ... and ...* | ทั้ง ... และ ... |

| | | |
|---|---|---|
| **àhn** | *to read* | อ่าน |
| **kěe-un** | *to write* | เขียน |
| **gum-lung ...** | *to be in the process of ...* | กำลัง... |

Chanida is meanwhile asking Sue how she finds learning Thai.

| | | |
|---|---|---|
| **Chanida** | pah-sǎh tai yâhk mái, | ภาษาไทยยากไหม |
| | kOOn Sue? | คุณ Sue |
| **Sue** | chún wâh pôot yâhk prór wâh | ฉันว่าพูดยาก เพราะว่า |
| | pah-sǎh tai mee sěe-ung sǒong | ภาษาไทยมีเสียงสูง |
| | sěe-ung dtùm. gloo-a wâh ja | เสียงต่ำ กลัวว่าจะ |
| | pôot pìt sa-měr. | พูดผิดเสมอ |
| **Chanida** | mâi dtôrng gloo-a ròrk. | ไม่ต้องกลัวหรอก |
| | pôot chút jing jing. | พูดชัดจริงๆ |
| | kOOn Sue ker-ee ree-un têe-nǎi? | คุณSueเคยเรียนที่ไหน |
| **Sue** | têe lorn-dorn kâ, | ที่ลอนดอนค่ะ |
| | têe ma-hǎh-wít-ta-yah-lai. | ที่มหาวิทยาลัย |
| **Chanida** | lěr? mee kroo kon tai mái? | หรือ? มีครูคนไทยไหม |
| **Sue** | mee kâ. láir-o mee kroo fa-rùng | มีค่ะ แล้วมีครูฝรั่ง |
| | dôo-ay. | ด้วย |
| **Chanida** | láir-o kOOn Sue ree-un àhn | แล้วคุณ Sue เรียนอ่าน |
| | láir kěe-un dôo-ay châi mái? | และเขียนด้วยใช่ไหม |
| **Sue** | châi kâ. fa-rùng bahng kon kít wâh | ใช่ค่ะ ฝรั่งบางคนคิดว่า |
| | àhn pah-sǎh tai kong yâhk. | อ่านภาษาไทยคงยาก |
| | chún wâh mâi kôy yâhk tâo-rài. | ฉันว่าไม่ค่อยยากเท่าไร |
| | kwahm jing kít wâh àhn láir | ความจริงคิดว่าอ่านและ |
| | kěe-un ngâi gwàh pôot. | เขียนง่ายกว่าพูด |

| yâhk | difficult | ยาก |
| prór wâh | because | เพราะว่า |
| sěe-ung | sound; tone | เสียง |
| sǒong | high | สูง |
| dtùm | low | ต่ำ |
| gloo-a | to be afraid | กลัว |
| pìt | wrong | ผิด |
| sa-měr | always | เสมอ |
| mâi dtôrng | there's no need (to) | ไม่ต้อง |
| ma-hǎh-wít-ta-yah-lai | university | มหาวิทยาลัย |
| kroo | teacher | ครู |
| kong | bound to be, sure to be | คง |
| mâi kôy ... tâo-rài | not very ... | ไม่ค่อย ... เท่าไร |
| kwahm jing | (in) truth; truly; actually | ความจริง |
| ngâi | easy | ง่าย |

## Comprehension

1  What wrong assumptions does the taxi driver make about Peter?
2  Where did Peter learn Thai?
3  Who taught him?
4  Can Peter read Thai?
5  Why does Sue find it hard to speak Thai?
6  What is she afraid of?
7  How does Chanida reassure her?
8  How easy does Sue find the Thai script?

# —pah-sǎh láir sǔng-kom   ภาษาและสังคม—

One of the most enjoyable aspects of speaking Thai in Thailand is that there always seem to be lots of Thais eager to tell you how well you speak their language. Even the most faltering attempts are likely to prompt a complimentary **pôot tai gèng** (*You speak Thai well*). Such encouragement is a wonderful incentive to practise more, but don't take it too literally. Mutual compliments are an important part of Thai social relations and Thais are simply trying to be friendly and express their appreciation that the foreigner has made an effort to learn something of their language, rather than objectively evaluating his or her linguistic competence. The appropriate response is a suitably modest one of denial such as **mâi gèng ròrk** or **bplào** (see Unit 8) or **pôot dâi nít-nòy tâo-nún**. Generally speaking, it doesn't hurt to compliment Thais on their command of English; unless, of course, they spent their formative years in an English boarding school or have just returned from the United States with an MBA, in which case you risk sounding a little condescending!

# ——— sǔm-noo-un   สำนวน ———

How to say:

- I only speak a little (Thai)

  pôot (pah-sǎh tai) dâi         พูด(ภาษาไทย)ได้

  nít-nòy tâo-nún                 นิดหน่อยเท่านั้น

- I studied it before

  ker-ee ree-un mah gòrn         เคยเรียนมาก่อน

- I am studying it

  gum-lung ree-un                 กำลังเรียน

- It's difficult to speak because it has tones

  pôot yâhk prór wâh mee sěe-ung sǒong   พูดยากเพราะว่ามีเสียงสูง

sěe-ung dtùm           เสียงต่ำ

● I'm always afraid I'll make a mistake

gloo-a ja pôot pìt sa-měr      กลัวจะพูดผิดเสมอ

## 🔘 ————— kum ùt-tí-bai   คำอธิบาย ————

### 1 tum-mai? ทำไม

The question word **tum-mai** *(why?)* can occur either at the beginning or at the end of the question.

tum-mai pôot tai gèng?     *Why do you speak Thai so well?*
bpai tum-mai?             *Why are you going?*

You can answer 'why?' questions using **prór wâh** (เพราะว่า) *because.*

prór wâh mâir bpen kon tai   *Because my mother is Thai.*
prór wâh yàhk bpai        *Because I'd like to go.*

### 2 sí ซิ

In Thai there are many 'particles' – untranslatable words which are used to convey meaning in much the way we use stress and intonation in English. In the conversation the taxi driver uses **sí** to emphasise his statement:

**Taxi**   tum-mai kOOn pôot tai gèng?  *Why do you speak Thai so well?*
**Peter**  mâi gèng ròrk krúp.        *I don't.*
**Taxi**   gèng sí krúp.             *Yes you do.*

### 3 mee-a เมีย

**mee-a** is an informal, even slightly vulgar word for *wife*. While a taxi driver may use it quite naturally, it is much more appropriate and safer for the foreigner to use the formal word, **pun-ra-yah** (ภรรยา). **pǒo-a** (ผัว) is the informal word for *husband* and **sǎh-mee** (สามี) the more polite term.

# 4  ker-ee เคย

The word **ker-ee** occurs in front of a main verb and indicates that the action of the verb has occurred at least once in the past. The negative, **mâi ker-ee** (ไม่เคย) means *never*.

| | |
|---|---|
| pǒm ker-ee ree-un | *I have studied it. / I used to study it.* |
| káo mâi ker-ee bpai | *She has never been.* |
| ker-ee gin ah-hǎhn tai mái? | *Have you ever eaten Thai food?* |

# 5  gum-lung กำลัง

When **gum-lung** occurs before a verb it usually indicates that the action of the verb is taking place at present. It is best translated by the *-ing* form of the verb in English.

| | |
|---|---|
| pǒm gum-lung ree-un pah-sǎh tai | *I am studying Thai.* |
| rao gum-lung gin kâo | *We are eating.* |
| káo gum-lung doo tee-wee | *He is watching T.V.* |

# 6  kong คง

**kong** or **kong ja** occurs before a main verb and means *bound to* or *sure to*.

| | |
|---|---|
| àhn pah-sǎh tai kong yâhk | *Reading Thai is sure to be difficult.* |
| káo kong mâi mah | *It's certain he's not coming.* |
| káo kong mâi mee | *They are bound not to have any.* |

# 7  kwahm ความ

The word **kwahm** is used to transform a verb or adjective into an abstract noun. In the dialogue it occurs with **jing** *(true)* to mean *truth* and can be translated as *the truth is* or *actually*. Here are some more examples:

| dee | *good* | kwahm dee | *goodness* |
| kít | *to think* | kwahm kít | *idea* |
| rúk | *to love* | kwahm rúk | *love* |
| sÒOk | *to be happy* | kwahm sÒOk | *happiness* |

## ☑ ——— bàirp fèuk hùt    แบบฝึกหัด ———

**1** How would you respond to the following questions and comments?

   *(a)* kOOn pôot tai gèng.
   *(b)* ker-ee ree-un pah-săh tai mái?
   *(c)* kOOn ree-un pah-săh tai nahn mái?
   *(d)* kOOn ree-un pah-săh tai têe-nai?
   *(e)* kOOn àhn pah-săh tai dâi mái?
   *(f)* kOOn kěe-un pah-săh tai bpen mái?
   *(g)* pah-săh tai yâhk mái?

**2** Here is a company's summary of its staff's spoken language proficiency in the languages of the Far East.

|  | **jeen** | **yêe-bpÒO n** | **gao-lěe** | **wêe-ut-nahm** |
| --- | --- | --- | --- | --- |
| **klôrng** | Stephen | Kevin | Sharon | Nicola |
| **gèng** | Paula | Stephen | Sarah | Kathy |
| **nít-nòy** | Nicola | Sarah | Kevin | Paula |

| **klôrng** | *fluent* |
| **gao-lěe** | *Korea* |
| **wêe-ut-nahm** | *Vietnam* |

Make up sentences describing the company's strength in each language. The first sentence is done for you.

Stephen pôot pah-sǎh jeen dâi klôrng
Paula pôot pah-sǎh jeen ...
Nicola ...

—— **àhn láir kěe-un**    อ่านและเขียน ——

## 1 Consonants

The consonants in this unit are not very common and at this stage you need not worry about memorising them. The class of each consonant is indicated beneath the symbol.

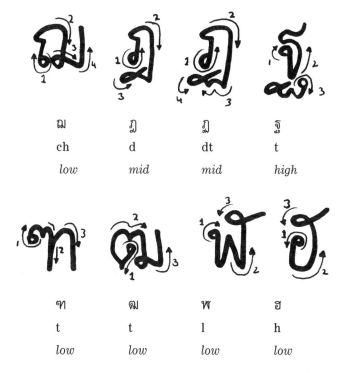

| ฌ | ฎ | ฏ | ฐ |
|------|------|------|------|
| ch | d | dt | t |
| *low* | *mid* | *mid* | *high* |

| ฑ | ฒ | ฬ | ฮ |
|------|------|------|------|
| t | t | l | h |
| *low* | *low* | *low* | *low* |

## 2 Vowel shortener: –ะ

In Unit 9 you met the vowel symbol –ะ.
The same symbol also has a completely different function, in shortening the following long vowels: เ–, แ–, โ–, เ–อ, and เ–า.

เ–ะ   แ–ะ   โ–ะ   เ–อะ   เ–าะ

| เ–ะ | แ–ะ | โ–ะ | เ–อะ | เ–าะ |
|-----|-----|-----|------|------|
| -e  | -air | -o  | -er  | -o   |

Here are some of the more common words that you will meet in which –ะ acts as a vowel shortener.

| เยะ | yé | *a lot* |
| และ | láir | *and* |
| โต๊ะ | dtó | *table* |
| เยอะ | yér | *a lot* |
| เพราะ | prór | *because* |
| เกาะ | gòr | *island* |

# ✓ ——— bàirp fèuk àhn    แบบฝึกอ่าน ———

1  The phrases in this section offer some more examples of some of
   the key structures introduced in this unit.

| | | |
|---|---|---|
| ไม่ค่อยเก่งเท่าไร | ไม่ค่อยอร่อยเท่าไร | ไม่ค่อยแพงเท่าไร |
| ทำไมพูดไทยชัด | ทำไมไม่ชอบ | ทำไมไม่กิน |
| เพราะว่าแม่เป็นคนไทย | เพราะว่าไม่สวย | เพราะว่าไม่อร่อย |
| เคยไปไหม | เคยดูไหม | เคยกินไหม |

2  Khun Sa-nga's company is involved in trade with Cambodia and
   he has been asked to recruit a Thai who knows Cambodian. Here
   he is, interviewing an applicant from Buriram Province in North
   East Thailand which has a large Cambodian-speaking population.

| | |
|---|---|
| **Sa-nga** | คุณชื่ออะไรครับ |
| **Applicant** | ชื่อ สุกัญญา ค่ะ |
| | นามสกุล แสงจันทร์ |
| **Sa-nga** | อายุเท่าไรครับ |
| **Applicant** | ๒๒ ค่ะ |
| **Sa-nga** | ทำไมคุณพูดภาษาเขมรได้ |
| **Applicant** | ดิฉันมาจากจังหวัดบุรีรัมย์*ค่ะ |
| | ที่บ้านเราพูดภาษาเขมรเสมอ |
| **Sa-nga** | พูดได้คล่องใช่ไหม |
| **Applicant** | ค่ะ |
| **Sa-nga** | แล้วคุณอ่านและเขียนภาษาเขมรเป็นไหม |
| **Applicant** | ไม่เป็นค่ะ |

*บุรีรัมย์ Buriram (The symbol over the final letter indicates that
 it is not pronounced.)

(a)  What is the applicant's name?
(b)  How old is she?
(c)  How well does she speak Cambodian?
(d)  How well does she read and write it?

3  Look at the application form on the next page, submitted by another candidate for the same job. You will not understand everything on the form, but a full translation is provided in the Key. Before you refer to this, try to extract the following information:

(a)  Applicant' s name
(b)  Date of birth
(c)  Address
(d)  Current salary
(e)  Educational background
(f)  Work experience
(g)  Competence in Cambodian

# bòt àhn   บทอ่าน

Magazines in Thailand sometimes feature interviews with western residents and questions about language inevitably occur. Here is an interview with a British businessman.

| | |
|---|---|
| **Interviewer** | คุณอยู่เมืองไทยนานไหมครับ |
| **Businessman** | ไม่นานครับ |
| | ประมาณ ๖ เดือนเท่านั้น |
| **Interviewer** | คุณพูดไทยเก่งมากครับ |

ใบสมัครงานชั่วคราว

ชื่อ **นายวิชัย** นามสกุล **สายทอง**

เกิดวันที่ **๘** เดือน **ธันวาคม** พ.ศ. **๒๕๙๖**

อยู่บ้านเลขที่ **๒๑/๒** ซอย **อารี** ถนน **พหลโยธิน**

ตำบล ............. อำเภอ **พญาไท** จังหวัด **กรุงเทพฯ**

สัญชาติ **ไทย**

ตำแหน่งปัจจุบัน **ข้าราชการ** เงินเดือน **๑๕,๕๐๐**

ประวัติการศึกษา

**๒๕๑๘ จนปริญญาตรีจากมหาวิทยาลัย**

ประสบการณ์การทำงาน **รามกำแหง**

**๒๕๑๘ - ๒๕๒๕ ทำงานกับ UNHCR ที่อรัญประเทศ**

**๒๕๒๕ - ปัจจุบัน ทำงานที่กระทรวงการต่าง** **จ. ปราจีนบุรี**

ความรู้ภาษาเขมร **ประเทศ**

| | พูด | อ่าน | เขียน |
|---|---|---|---|
| คล่อง | ✓ | | |
| เก่ง | | ✓ | |
| นิดหน่อย | | | ✓ |

|              | เหมือนเป็นเจ้าของภาษา |
|--------------|---------------------------|
|              | เคยเรียนที่ไหน |
| **Businessman** | เรียนเองครับ |
|              | ไม่มีเวลาไปเรียนที่โรงเรียน |
|              | ใช้ตำราและเทป |
| **Interviewer** | เรียนเองยากไหมครับ |
| **Businessman** | ก็ไม่ค่อยยากเท่าไร |
|              | ถ้าไม่มีเทป คิดว่าคงยากกว่า |
|              | เพราะว่าภาษาไทยมีเสียงสูงเสียงต่ำ |
| **Interviewer** | แล้วคุณอ่านและเขียนภาษาไทยได้ไหม |
| **Businessman** | อ่านได้นิดหน่อยครับ ถ้าเป็นคำง่ายๆ |
|              | แต่เขียนไม่ค่อยได้ |

| เหมือน | *like* |
|--------|--------|
| เจ้าของภาษา | *native speaker* (lit. owner of the language) |
| เอง | *self* |
| เรียนเอง | *(I) studied on my own* |
| เวลา | *time* |
| โรงเรียน | *school* |
| ใช้ | *to use* |
| ตำรา | *textbook* |
| เทป | *tape* |
| ถ้า | *if* |

## *Comprehension*

(a)  How long has he been in Thailand?
(b)  How did he learn Thai?
(c)  What aids did he have in learning Thai?
(d)  Can he read and write Thai?

# 12

## — mâi kâo jai *I don't understand* —
## ไม่เข้าใจ

### *In this unit you will learn*

- strategies for coping when you don't understand
- *how?* questions
- more ways of saying *I don't understand!*
- *don't ...*
- some spelling irregularities and miscellaneous diacritics

## — bòt sǒn-ta-nah   บทสนทนา —

Sue has accompanied some Thai friends to a restaurant.

| Chanida | bplah kem mâhk mái ká | ปลาเค็มมากไหมคะ |
| | kOOn Sue? | คุณ  Sue |
| Sue | a-rai ná ká? | อะไรนะคะ |
| | pôot èek tee dâi mái? | พูดอีกทีได้ไหม |
| Chanida | bplah kem mâhk mái? | ปลาเค็มมากไหม |
| Sue | mâi kâo jai. | ไม่เข้าใจ |

|          | pôot cháh cháh nòy dâi mái?        | พูดช้าๆ หน่อยได้ไหม |
| -------- | ---------------------------------- | -------------------- |
| **Chanida** | bplah – kem – mái?              | ปลา-เค็ม-ไหม |
| **Sue**  | mâi róo-jùk kum wâh 'kem'.          | ไม่รู้จักคำว่า 'เค็ม' |
|          | pah-sǎh ung-grìt bplair            | ภาษาอังกฤษแปลว่าอะไร |
|          | wâh a-rai?                         |  |
| **Chanida** | bplair wâh 'salty'              | แปลว่า 'salty' |
| **Sue**  | kâo jai láir-o.                    | เข้าใจแล้ว |
|          | kem kâ.                            | เค็มค่ะ |
|          | 'kem' sa-gòt yung-ngai?            | 'เค็ม' สะกดอย่างไร |

| bplah              | *fish*           | ปลา |
| ------------------ | ---------------- | ------------ |
| kem                | *salty*          | เค็ม |
| tee                | *time*           | ที |
| èek tee            | *again*          | อีกที |
| kâo jai            | *to understand*  | เข้าใจ |
| cháh               | *slow*           | ช้า |
| kum                | *word*           | คำ |
| bplair             | *to translate*   | แปล |
| ... bplair wâh a-rai? | *what does ... mean?* | แปลว่าอะไร |
| sa-gòt             | *to spell*       | สะกด |
| yung-ngai?         | *how?*           | อย่างไร |

Peter is also in a restaurant. His Thai companions are busy chattering away in Thai until Somchai suddenly turns to him ...

| **Somchai** | kOOn Peter fung róo rêu-ung mái? | คุณ Peter ฟังรู้เรื่องไหม |
| ----------- | --------------------------------- | -------------------------- |
| **Peter**   | a-rai ná krúp?                    | อะไรนะครับ |

| Malee | fa-rùng ngong. | ฝรั่งงง |
| Somchai | fung róo rêu-ung mái? | ฟังรู้เรื่องไหม |
| Peter | mâi róo rêu-ung. | ไม่รู้เรื่อง |
| | tâh pôot ray-o mâhk | ถ้าพูดเร็วมาก |
| | mâi róo rêu-ung ler-ee. | ไม่รู้เรื่องเลย |
| Malee | mâi bpen rai ròrk. | ไม่เป็นไรหรอก |
| | rao nin-tah kOOn tâo-nún. | เรานินทาคุณเท่านั้น |
| Peter | nin-tah mǎi-kwahm | 'นินทา' หมายความว่าอะไร |
| | wâh a-rai? | |
| Somchai | bplair wâh 'gossip'. | แปลว่า 'gossip' |
| | dtàir yàh bpai chêu-a kOOn | |
| | Malee ná. | แต่อย่าไปเชื่อคุณมาลีนะ |
| | kOOn Malee chôrp pôot | |
| | lên sa-měr. | คุณมาลีชอบพูดเล่นเสมอ |

| fung róo rêu-ung | to understand | ฟังรู้เรื่อง |
|---|---|---|
| ngong | to be dazed, confused | งง |
| mâi róo rêu-ung | I don't understand | ไม่รู้เรื่อง |
| ray-o | quick | เร็ว |
| nin-tah | to gossip | นินทา |
| ... mǎi-kwahm wâh a-rai? | what does ... mean? | ... หมายความว่าอะไร |
| yàh | don't | อย่า |
| chêu-a | to believe | เชื่อ |
| pôot lên | to joke | พูดเล่น |

## Comprehension

1 What was the Thai word that Sue did not know?
2 How did she try to ensure that she would remember it?
3 How did she answer Chanida's original question?
4 Why couldn't Peter understand what his companions were saying?
5 What joke did Malee make?
6 Why didn't Peter get the joke?

# — pah-sǎh láir sǔng-kom ภาษาและสังคม —

Although you will find Thais extremely complimentary about your attempts to learn Thai, you will almost certainly feel that your linguistic inadequacies are exposed with alarming frequency in the initial stages. One obvious problem is vocabulary. Thai words sound quite unlike any European language and so there is little scope for latching onto a familiar word and then guessing what people are talking about. Even when you stay within your linguistic limitations, you may find a Thai looking absolutely bewildered by your best attempts, only to repeat, with a sudden expression of enlightenment, *exactly* what you just said. (Well, *almost* exactly!) Maybe you got a tone wrong, a vowel not quite right, or maybe your Thai friend was simply accustomed to foreigners speaking Thai with a German accent.

The important thing is not to be discouraged by these little setbacks. Relax. Recognise that some days you are on better form than others. Don't worry if everything is going over your head. Be prepared to laugh at yourself. But most important of all, have a positive strategy for dealing with communication breakdowns and try to analyse where your individual weaknesses lie. Learn different ways of asking someone to repeat something – for even the most patient of Thais may tire of the farang whose every other utterance is **a-rai ná?** A knowledge of Thai script is invaluable here, because you can always ask how something is written in Thai (**pah-sǎh tai kěe-un yung-ngai?**); and if you weren't sure what tone the word was when you heard it, you can check from the spelling.

# sǔm-noo-un สำนวน

How to say:

- Pardon?

  a-rai ná? อะไรนะ

- Could you say that again?

  ... pôot èek tee dâi mái? พูดอีกทีได้ไหม

- I don't understand

  mâi kâo jai ไม่เข้าใจ

  mâi róo rêu-ung ไม่รู้เรื่อง

- Could you speak slowly please?

  pôot cháh cháh nòy dâi mái? พูดช้าๆ หน่อยได้ไหม

- I don't know the word ...

  mâi róo-jùk kum wâh ... ไม่รู้จักคำว่า ...

- What's that in English?

  pah-sǎh ung-grìt bplair wâh a-rai? ภาษาอังกฤษแปลว่าอะไร

- How do you spell it?

  sa-gòt yung-ngai? สะกดอย่างไร

- What does ... mean?

  ... mǎi-kwahm wâh a-rai? ... หมายความว่าอะไร

  ... bplair wâh a-rai? ... แปลว่าอะไร

———————— **kum ùt-tí-bai** คำอธิบาย ————————

## 1 'What does that mean?'

There are two ways of asking what something means. Strictly speaking, **bplair wâh a-rai?** (แปลว่าอะไร) is a request for a translation, while **mai-kwahm wâh a-rai?** (หมายความว่าอะไร) is used to ask for clarification or an explanation.

## 2 yung-ngai? อย่างไร

The question word **yung-ngai?** (อย่างไร) *how?* always occurs at the end of a sentence.

| | |
|---|---|
| bpen yung-ngai? | *How are things?* |
| sa-gòt yung-ngai? | *How do you spell it?* |
| bpai yung-ngai? | *How are we going?* |

If you look at the Thai spelling you will notice that the correct pronunciation would appear to be **yàhng-rai** rather than **yung-ngai**. In normal speech, however, the first vowel is shortened, the low tone changes to a neutral mid tone and the final **ng** in the first syllable and initial **r** in the second syllable are assimilated into a **ng** sound. In fact, when greeting each other informally, Thais will often go a step further and say simply, **bpen ngai?**

## 3 róo rêu-ung รู้เรื่อง

**róo rêu-ung** like **kâo jai** (เข้าใจ) means *to understand*. It often occurs with the verbs **fung** (ฟัง) *to listen* and **àhn** (อ่าน) *to read* to specify aural or visual comprehension. Notice the position of the word **mâi** in negative statements.

| | |
|---|---|
| fung róo rêu-ung mái? | *Do you understand?* (by listening) |
| fung **mâi** róo rêu-ung | *I don't understand.* |
| àhn róo rêu-ung mái? | *Do you understand?* (by reading) |
| àhn **mâi** róo rêu-ung | *I don't understand.* |

Sometimes Thais will shorten the question to simply **fung róo mái?**

To answer *yes* to **fung róo (rêu-ung) mái?** you can say **róo** or **róo rêu-ung** (but not **fung**); a *no* answer is **mâi róo** or **mâi róo rêu-ung**.

## 4 yàh อย่า

yàh (*don't*) is used at the beginning of negative commands. Very often in speech it is used with the particle **ná** *(right?, O.K?)*.

| | |
|---|---|
| yàh leum ná | *Don't forget, O.K?* |
| yàh kùp ray-o ná | *Don't drive (too) quickly, right?* |

In the conversation, notice that Somchai says **yàh** bpai **chêu-a kOOn Malee ná**. This usage of **bpai** has an exact equivalent in the English, *Don't* **go** *believing Khun Malee*.

## 5 pôot lên พูดเล่น

When the word **lên** (เล่น) *to play* follows another verb, it indicates that the action of the first verb is being carried out for fun.

| pôot | *to speak* | pôot lên | *to joke* |
|---|---|---|---|
| dern | *to walk* | dern lên | *to go for a walk* |
| àhn | *to read* | àhn lên | *to read for pleasure* |
| gin | *to eat* | gin lên | *to eat 'for fun'* (e.g. between-meal snacks) |

## ☑ —— bàirp fèuk hùt แบบฝึกหัด ——

1   A Korean businessman who speaks no English and less Thai than Peter is having difficulty following a conversation among his Thai  hosts. He keeps asking Peter what various words mean. How  should Peter respond?

(a) 'pun-ra-yah' bplair wâh a-rai?  'ภรรยา' แปลว่าอะไร

(b) 'tahn' bplair wâh a-rai?  'ทาน' แปลว่าอะไร

(c) 'sâhp' bplair wâh a-rai?  'ทราบ' แปลว่าอะไร

(d) 'rúp a-rai?' bplair wâh a-rai?  'รับอะไร' แปลว่าอะไร

2  Here's Peter, locked in conversation with Malee and stubbornly refusing to be defeated by his limited vocabulary. What do you think he said?

| Malee | ker-ee bpai doo nǔng tai mái? | เคยไปดูหนังไทยไหม |
|-------|-------------------------------|------------------|
| Peter | ................................ | ................................ |
| Malee | ker-ee bpai doo nǔng tai mái? | เคย ไป ดู หนัง ไทย ไหม |
| Peter | ................................ | ................................ |
| Malee | ker-ee – bpai – doo – nǔng – tai – mái? | เคย-ไป-ดู-หนัง-ไทย-ไหม |
| Peter | ................................ | ................................ |
| Malee | nǔng bplair wâh 'movie.' kâo jai mái? | 'หนัง' แปลว่า 'movie.' เข้าใจไหม |
| Peter | ................................ | ................................ |
| Malee | ker-ee bpai doo mái? | เคยไปดูไหม |
| Peter | mâi ker-ee. | ไม่เคย |

---

📻 —— **àhn láir kěe-un**  อ่านและเขียน ——

You have now covered the principal features of the Thai writing system. This unit gives examples of the most common spelling irregularities and lists miscellaneous diacritics which you are likely to encounter in reading an ordinary passage of Thai.

# 1 The letter ร

The letter ร is normally pronounced as *n* at the end of a word:

| อาหาร | ah-hǎhn | *food* |
| ควร | koo-un | *should* |
| ผู้จัดการ | pôo-jùt-gahn | *manager* |

In a number of words, however, it is pronounced *orn:*

| นคร | na-korn | *Nakhorn* (in place names) |
| ละคร | la-korn | *theatre* |
| พร | porn | *gift, blessing* |

In certain words it is not pronounced at all:

| จริง | jing | *true* |
| สระ | sà | *swimming pool* |

When ทร occurs at the beginning of a word, the cluster is pronounced *s:*

| ทราบ | sâhp | *to know* |

When –รร occurs at the end of a word or syllable it is pronounced *-un* and *-u* if it is followed by a consonant:

| รถบรรทุก | rót bun-tóOk | *lorry* |
| พรรค | púk | *party* (political) |

# 2 'r' in ung-grìt อังกฤษ

You will have noticed that the Thai spelling of **ung-grìt** *(English)* uses neither the letter ร nor the vowel ◌ิ. Instead it is written with the symbol ฤ which in this word represents a *ri* sound. It is most unlikely that you will encounter this symbol in any word other than **ung-grìt.**

# 3  Letters that are not pronounced at the end of a word

When the symbol ́ occurs above a consonant, that consonant is not pronounced. It occurs in words of foreign origin, where the foreign spelling has been retained.

| เบอร์ | ber | *number* |
| จอห์น | jorn | *John* |
| เสาร์ | săo | *Saturday* |
| อาทิตย์ | ah-tít | *Sunday, week* |

Sometimes it is not only the consonant below the symbol which is not pronounced but also the one immediately preceding it:

| จันทร์ | jun | *Monday, moon* |
| ศาสตร์ | sàht | *science* |

In some cases, even though there is no 'consonant killer' ( ́), the final consonant is still not pronounced:

| บัตร | bùt | *card* |
| สมัคร | sa-mùk | *to join* |

And in other cases, a final short vowel is not pronounced:

| ชาติ | châht | *nation* |
| เหตุ | hàyt | *reason* |

# 4  Linker syllables

There are a number of words which appear to have two syllables but which are pronounced as three syllables, with a short **a** vowel in the middle. In such words the final consonant of the first syllable also functions as the initial consonant in the second syllable:

| ชนบท | chon-na-bòt | *countryside* |
| ผลไม้ | pǒn-la-mái | *fruit* |

## 5 Mis-match between pronunciation and spelling

There are a few common words that in normal conversation are pronounced with a high tone when the written form suggests the tone should be rising:

| ไหม | mái | *(question word)* |
| ฉัน | chún | *I* |
| เขา | káo | *he, she, they* |

## 6 Symbols ฯ and ๆ

The symbol ฯ you will first meet in the word **grOOng-tâyp**–the Thai name for Bangkok. It really means *etc.* and is used to abbreviate the extremely long full name of the capital. The second symbol indicates that the preceding word should be repeated:

| กรุงเทพฯ | grOOng-tâyp | *Bangkok* |
| ช้าๆ | cháh cháh | *slow* |

✔ —— **bàirp fèuk àhn** แบบฝึกอ่าน ——

**1** Here are some of the key phrases from the Dialogue.

| อะไรนะ | พูดอีกทีได้ไหม | พูดช้าๆ หน่อยได้ไหม |
| แปลว่าอะไร | ไม่เข้าใจ | สะกดอย่างไร |
| เขียนอย่างไร | ฟังรู้เรื่อง | ไม่รู้เรื่อง |

2  Silent letters. Here are some words from earlier units with the 'killer' symbol over one of the letters. Some of these words are recognisably borrowed from English. Others are borrowed from Sanskrit, the classical language of India.

ซอยเกษมสันต์  เบียร์สิงห์  เก็บสตางค์

ไปรษณีย์  โปสการ์ด  แสตมป์

3  A number of provinces include the word **na-korn** in their name. **na-korn** in fact comes from Sanskrit and means *city*. Match the Thai script spelling with the normal romanisation of these place names. Look at the provinces on the map on page 180.

|  |  |  |  |
|---|---|---|---|
| (i) | นครปฐม | (a) | Nakhorn Ratchasima |
| (ii) | นครนายก | (b) | Nakhorn Phanom |
| (iii) | นครสวรรค์ | (c) | Sakol Nakhorn |
| (iv) | นครราชสีมา | (d) | Nakhorn Srithammarat |
| (v) | นครพนม | (e) | Nakhorn Sawan |
| (vi) | สกลนคร | (f) | Nakhorn Nayok |
| (vii) | นครศรีธรรมราช | (g) | Nakhorn Pathom |

4  Write answers to these questions.

๑.  คุณเรียนภาษาไทยนานไหม

๒.  คุณเรียนภาษาไทยที่ไหน

๓.  คุณเรียนภาษาไทยเองไหม

๔.  คุณมีครูสอนภาษาไทยไหม

๕.  อ่านภาษาไทยยากไหม

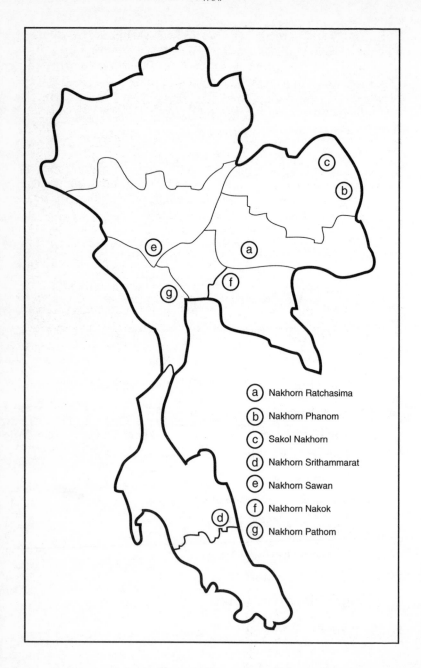

(a) Nakhorn Ratchasima

(b) Nakhorn Phanom

(c) Sakol Nakhorn

(d) Nakhorn Srithammarat

(e) Nakhorn Sawan

(f) Nakhorn Nakok

(g) Nakhorn Pathom

Thai farmers transplanting rice seedlings.

# ——— **bòt àhn** บทอ่าน ———

A Thai woman talks about her language problems when she first came to live in England.

เราแต่งงานที่กรุงเทพฯ

สามีเป็นคนอังกฤษ

ทำงานอยู่ที่บริษัทใหญ่แห่งหนึ่ง

เรากลับมาอยู่ที่นี่สามปีก่อน

ความจริงฉันไม่อยากมาอยู่อังกฤษเลย

เพราะว่าพูดภาษาอังกฤษไม่ค่อยเป็น

เคยเรียนที่โรงเรียน แต่เรียนไม่เก่ง

คนอังกฤษพูด ฉันฟังไม่รู้เรื่องเลย

สามีก็ให้ฉันไปเรียนภาษาที่โรงเรียนแถวๆ บ้าน

ที่โรงเรียนมีนักเรียนทุกชาติ ญี่ปุ่นก็มี จีนก็มี

เยอรมันก็มี อาฟริกาก็มี แล้วก็มีอาหรับด้วย

ฉันต้องไปเรียนทุกวัน วันละ ๒-๓ ชั่วโมง

หลังจากเรียนประมาณ ๖ เดือนแล้ว ก็คิดว่า

ภาษาอังกฤษดีขึ้นมากเลย

| สามี | husband |
| --- | --- |
| แห่ง | (classifier for companies) |
| โรงเรียน | school |
| นักเรียน | pupil |
| ชาติ | nation |
| ญี่ปุ่น | Japanese |

| | |
|---|---|
| จีน | *Chinese* |
| เยอรมัน | *German* |
| อาฟริกา | *Africa(n)* |
| อาหรับ | *Arab* |
| หลังจาก | *after* |
| เดือน | *month* |
| ดีขึ้น | *to improve* |

## *Comprehension*

(a)  Why is the woman living in England?
(b)  How long has she been living here?
(c)  How did she feel about coming to live in England?
(d)  What steps did she take to improve her English?
(e)  What was the effect after six months?

## ——— How are you progressing? ———

You have now covered the major features of the Thai writing system and you should find that if you cover up the romanised part of the dialogues and study the Thai script sections, you can read every word. At this point, it is worth going back over the earlier units and working through the Thai script dialogues. It will almost certainly be slow work at first; but if you keep re-reading the same dialogues, you will find that your reading speed steadily improves and that your eye begins to skim quickly over letters without having to pause to think carefully about each one. The reading speed you develop on familiar passages will gradually transfer itself to new, unseen materials.

# 13

## rót òrk gèe mohng?

### *What time does the bus leave?*
### รถออกกี่โมง

## *In this unit you will*

- learn how to make travel arrangements
- learn how to tell the time
- practise reading some more province names
- attempt to extract information from some authentic travel guides

## bòt sǒn-ta-nah    บทสนทนา

Peter is at the Northern Bus Terminal in Bangkok, trying to book tickets for a trip to the Northeast.

| Peter | kǒr-tôht krúp | ขอโทษครับ |
|---|---|---|
| | bpai na-korn pa-nom jorng dtǒo-a | ไปนครพนมจองตั๋ว |
| | têe-nǎi? | ที่ไหน |
| Clerk | têe-nêe kâ. | ที่นี่ค่ะ |
| | ja bpai mêu-rai? | จะไปเมื่อไร? |

| Peter | kít ja bpai prôOng née. | คิดจะไปพรุ่งนี้ |
| Clerk | prôOng née cháo dtem láir-o. | พรุ่งนี้เช้าเต็มแล้ว |
| | keun prôOng née dâi mái kâ? | คืนพรุ่งนี้ได้ไหมคะ |
| Peter | dâi krúp. rót may òrk gèe mohng? | ได้ครับ รถเมล์ออกกี่โมง |
| Clerk | òrk sǒrng tÔOm krêung kâ. | ออกสองทุ่มครึ่งค่ะ |
| Peter | chái way-lah dern tahng | ใช้เวลาเดินทาง |
| | gèe chôo-a-mohng krúp? | กี่ชั่วโมงครับ |
| Clerk | sìp-sǒrng chôo-a-mohng kâ. | สิบสองชั่วโมงค่ะ |
| | těung na-korn pa-nom bpra-mahn | ถึงนครพนมประมาณ |
| | sǎhm mohng cháo. | สามโมงเช้า |
| Peter | dtǒo-a bai la tâo-rài krúp? | ตั๋วใบละเท่าไรครับ |
| Clerk | bai la sǒrng róy-hâh-sip bàht kâ. | ใบละสองร้อยห้าสิบบาทค่ะ |
| Peter | dee krúp. ao sǒrng bai. | ดีครับ เอาสองใบ |
| | láir-o kêun rót-may têe-nǎi? | แล้วขึ้นรถเมล์ที่ไหน |

| | | |
|---|---|---|
| **na-korn pa-nom** | *Nakhorn Phanom* | นครพนม |
| **jorng** | *to book* | จอง |
| **dtǒo-a** | *ticket* | ตั๋ว |
| **prôOng née** | *tomorrow* | พรุ่งนี้ |
| **cháo** | *morning* | เช้า |
| **dtem (láir-o)** | *full* | เต็ม (แล้ว) |
| **keun** | *night* | คืน |
| **rót may** | *bus* | รถเมล์ |
| **gèe mohng?** | *what time?* | กี่โมง |
| **sǒrng tÔOm** | *8.00 p.m.* | สองทุ่ม |

| | | |
|---|---|---|
| **krêung** | *half* | ครึ่ง |
| **sǒrng tôOm krêung** | *8.30 p.m.* | สองทุ่มครึ่ง |
| **chái** | *to use* | ใช้ |
| **chái way-lah** | *to take time* | ใช้เวลา |
| **dern tahng** | *to travel* | เดินทาง |
| **sǎhm mohng cháo** | *9.00 a.m.* | สามโมงเช้า |
| **bai** | (classifier for ticket) | ใบ |
| **kêun** | *to get on* | ขึ้น |

The following evening, the overnight coach to Nakhorn Phanom passes through a large town and stops at a restaurant/coach park. This is the announcement the courier makes:

tûn pôo doy-ee sǎhn ká     ท่านผู้โดยสารคะ

rao mah těung na-korn râht-cha-sěe-mah     เรามาถึงนครราชสีมา

rêe-up róy láir-o kâ.     เรียบร้อยแล้วค่ะ

láir-o rao ja yÒOt púk gin kâo dtôm     แล้วเราจะหยุดพักกินข้าวต้ม

sùk krêung chôo-a mohng.     สักครึ่งชั่วโมง

way-lah née têe-ung krêung ná ká     เวลานี้ เที่ยงครึ่งนะคะ

rót máy ja òrk mài     รถเมล์จะออกใหม่

way-lah dtee nèung dtrong ná ká     เวลาตีหนึ่งตรงนะคะ

tûn pôo doy-ee sǎhn chôo-ay glùp mah     ท่านผู้โดยสารช่วยกลับมา

têe rót gòrn way-lah nún ná ká.     ที่รถก่อนเวลานั้นนะคะ

way-lah long rót láir-o chôo-ay ao     เวลาลงรถแล้วช่วยเอา

dtǒo-a rót may bpai dôo-ay.     ตั๋วรถเมล์ไปด้วย

yàh leum ná ká prór wâh dtôrng     อย่าลืมนะคะเพราะว่าต้อง

ao bpai sa-dairng nai ráhn ah-hǎhn.     เอาไปแสดงในร้านอาหาร

mâi mee dtǒo-a dtìt dtoo-a gôr dtôrng     ไม่มีตั๋วติดตัว ก็ต้อง

sěe-a kâh ah-hǎhn eng ná ká.     เสียค่าอาหารเองนะคะ

| tûn | you (polite) | ท่าน |
| --- | --- | --- |
| pǒo-doy-ee sǎhn | passenger | ผู้โดยสาร |
| mah tǔeng | to reach | มาถึง |
| na-korn râht-cha-sěe-mah | Nakhorn Ratchasima | นครราชสีมา |
| rêe-up róy | safely | เรียบร้อย |
| yòot | to stop | หยุด |
| púk | to rest | พัก |
| kâo dtôm | rice porridge | ข้าวต้ม |
| krêung chôo-a mohng | half an hour | ครึ่งชั่วโมง |
| têe-ung krêung | 12.30 a.m. | เที่ยงครึ่ง |
| dtee nèung | 1.00 a.m. | ตีหนึ่ง |
| dtrong | straight, exact | ตรง |
| long | to get off (a bus) | ลง |
| ao ... bpai | to take | เอา ... ไป |
| dôo-ay | too; with | ด้วย |
| leum | to forget | ลืม |
| sa-dairng | to show | แสดง |
| dtoo-a | body | ตัว |
| dtìt dtoo-a | on you; with you | ติดตัว |
| kâh | cost | ค่า |
| eng | self | เอง |

## Comprehension

1 When does Peter want to go to Nakhorn Phanom?
2 What time does his bus leave?
3 How long is the journey?
4 How much does his ticket cost?
5 What time does the bus reach Nakhorn Ratchasima?
6 How long will it stop there?
7 What does the courier remind the passengers to take with them?

# — pah-sǎh láir sǔng-kom ภาษาและสังคม —

Travel outside Bangkok is cheap and convenient. Perhaps the best way to travel up-country is by air-conditioned tour bus; if you can arrange for a day-time rather than overnight departure, this will give you a good opportunity to get an impression of the rural landscape in relative comfort. Tour buses are operated both by the state-owned Mass Transport Organisation (MTO) and private companies. They operate a frequent and efficient service to every province in the country. Refreshments are served en-route and, on longer journeys a simple meal is provided at a highway café on presentation of your ticket. When travelling up-country it is normally necessary to book in advance.

MTO buses, or **rót bor kor sǒr** as they are known by the Thai acronym, can be booked at the Northern, Eastern or Southern bus terminals.

——————— **sǔm-noo-un** สำนวน ———————

How to:

● ask where to book tickets

jorng dtǒo-a têe-nai? จองตั๋วที่ไหน

● ask what time the bus leaves / arrives

rót may òrk gèe mohng? รถเมล์ออกกี่โมง

rót may těung gèe mohng? รถเมล์ถึงกี่โมง

● ask how long the journey takes

chái way-lah dern tahng gèe ใช้เวลาเดินทางกี่

chôo-a mohng? ชั่วโมง

● ask where to get on / off the bus

kêun / long rót may têe-nǎi? ขึ้น(ลง)รถเมล์ที่ไหน

🖊 ——————— **kum ùt-tí-bai** คำอธิบาย ———————

## 1 'tomorrow morning / evening'

Notice that **prÔOng née** (พรุ่งนี้) *tomorrow* occurs before **cháo** (เช้า) *morning* but after **kêun** (คืน) *night*.

| prÔOng née cháo | *tomorrow morning* | พรุ่งนี้เช้า |
| prÔOng née bài | *tomorrow afternoon* | พรุ่งนี้บ่าย |
| prÔOng née yen | *tomorrow (early) evening* | พรุ่งนี้เย็น· |

*but*

keun prÔÔng née     *tomorrow night*      คืนพรุ่งนี้

## 2 Time questions

Note the difference in the following time questions:

| | | |
|---|---|---|
| rót òrk gèe mohng? | *What time does* **the bus leave?** | รถออกกี่โมง |
| gèe chôo-a mohng? | *How many hours? How long?* | กี่ชั่วโมง |
| gèe mohng láir-o? | *What time is it?* | กี่โมงแล้ว |

## 3 sǒrng tÔÔm; sǎhm mohng cháo

Thai uses different words for *o'clock* according to what time of day it is. Between 7 p.m. and midnight, the word **tÔÔm** (ทุ่ม) is used. **tÔÔm nèung** is 7 *p.m.*, **sǒrng tÔÔm** 8 *p.m.*, **sǎhm tÔÔm** 9 *p.m.* and so on. From 6 a.m. to midday, **mohng cháo** (โมงเช้า) is used. Thais count these hours in two ways, as follows:

| | | | |
|---|---|---|---|
| 6 a.m. | hòk mohng cháo | | |
| 7 a.m. | mohng cháo | or | jèt mohng cháo |
| 8 a.m. | sǒrng mohng cháo | or | bpàirt mohng cháo |
| 9 a.m. | sǎhm mohng cháo | or | gâo mohng cháo |
| 10 a.m. | sèe mohng cháo | or | sìp mohng cháo |
| 11 a.m. | hâh mohng cháo | or | sìp-èt mohng cháo |

To the learner, it seems strange that **hòk mohng cháo** is earlier than **sǎhm mohng cháo**; but it is!

## 4 tûn pôo doy-ee sǎhn ท่านผู้โดยสาร

**tûn** (ท่าน) is the polite word for *you* normally used when addressing people of marked superior social status and **pôo doy-ee sǎhn** (ผู้โดยสาร) means *passengers*. So literally, the courier addresses the people on the bus as *You passengers*. You will hear the same expression used in public announcements at Thai airports, and the same formula used by radio announcers when they address their listeners as **tûn pôo fung** (**pôo fung** *listener*).

## 5 Verb serialisation

A common feature of Thai which you will become more aware of as your knowledge of Thai increases is the tendency to string several verbs together, one after the other. The courier puts three together **yÒOt** *(to stop)* **púk** *(to rest)* **gin** *(to eat)* but it is not uncommon to find as many as five or six verbs together.

## 6 ao ... bpai เอา ...ไป

You have already met both **ao** *(want)* and **bpai** *(go)*. They are used together in the pattern **ao ... bpai** to mean *to take*. **ao ... mah** means *to bring*. The noun 'sandwiched' between the two verbs may be omitted when it is clear from the context what is being referred to:

| | |
|---|---|
| ao dtǒo-a bpai dôo-ay | *Take your ticket with you.* |
| ao rót mah | *Bring the car.* |
| ao bpai doo-ay | *Take it with you.* |

## Telling the time

You have already met the word **tÔOm**, for telling the time between 7 p.m. and midnight, and **mohng cháo** used between 6 a.m. and midday. The remaining time words are **dtee** (ตี) for the hours from 1 a.m. to 5 a.m., **bai** (บ่าย), 1 p.m. - 4 p.m., and **yen,** (เย็น) 5 p.m. – 6 p.m.

This is how the hours of the day are expressed:

*midnight* tê-ung keun เที่ยงคืน *midday* tê-ung (wun) เที่ยง(วัน)

| | | | | |
|---|---|---|---|---|
| *1 a.m.* | **dtee** nèung | | *1 p.m.* | **bài mohng** |
| *2 a.m.* | **dtee** sǒrng | | *2 p.m.* | **bài** sǒrng **mohng** |
| *3 a.m.* | **dtee** sǎhm | | *3 p.m.* | **bài** sǎhm **mohng** |
| *4 a.m.* | **dtee** sèe | | *4 p.m.* | **bài** sèe **mohng** |
| *5 a.m.* | **dtee** hâh | | *5 p.m.* | hâh **mohng yen** |
| *6 a.m.* | hòk **mohng cháo** | | *6 p.m.* | hòk **mohng yen** |
| *7 a.m.* | **mohng cháo** | | *7 p.m.* | **tÔOm** nèung |
| *8 a.m.* | sǒrng **mohng cháo** | | *8 p.m.* | sǒrng **tÔOm** |
| *9 a.m.* | sǎhm **mohng cháo** | | *9 p.m.* | sǎhm **tÔOm** |

| | | | |
|---|---|---|---|
| *10 a.m.* | sèe **mohng cháo** | *10 p.m.* | sèe **tÒO m** |
| *11 a.m.* | hâh **mohng cháo** | *11 p.m.* | hâh **tÒOm** |

*Note:* **dtee** and **bài** appear before the number
**dtee** and **tÒOm** do not occur with **mohng**

*Half past the hour* is expressed by adding the word **krêung** (ครึ่ง) *half* to the hour time. For the hours from 7 a.m. to 11 a.m., however, the word **cháo** is usually omitted.

| | | | |
|---|---|---|---|
| *2.30 a.m.* | dtee sǒrng **krêung** | *3.30 p.m.* | bai sǎhm mohng **krêung** |
| *8.30 a.m.* | sǒrng mohng **krêung** | *5.30 p.m.* | hâh mohng yen **krêung** |
| *11.30 a.m.* | hâh mohng **krêung** | *11.30 p.m.* | hâh tÔOm **krêung** |

There is no special word for *quarter-past* or *quarter-to* the hour. Minutes past the hour are expressed as: *hour time + number of minutes* + **nah-tee** (นาที) *(minutes)*.

| | |
|---|---|
| *11.15 a.m.* | hâh mohng sìp-hâh **nah-tee** |
| *3.10 p.m.* | bài sǎhm mohng sìp **nah-tee** |
| *8.15 p.m.* | sǒrng tÔOm sìp-hâh nah-tee |

Minutes to the hour are expressed as: **èek** (อีก) *further, more* + *number of minutes* + *hour time*.

| | |
|---|---|
| *9.45 a.m.* | **èek** sìp-hâh nah-tee sèe mohng cháo |
| *4.40 p.m.* | **èek** yêe-sìp nah-tee hâh mohng yen |
| *11.50 p.m.* | **èek** sìp nah-tee têe-ung keun |

In the twenty-four hour clock system the word **nah-li-gah** (นาฬิกา) is used for *hours*, and half-hours are expressed as *thirty minutes past:*

| | |
|---|---|
| *20.00* | yêe-sìp **nah-li-gah** |
| *22.30* | yêe-sip-sǒrng **nah-li gah** sǎhm-sìp nah-tee |

—————— **bàirp fèuk hùt  แบบฝึกหัด** ——————

**1**  gèe mohng láir-o?

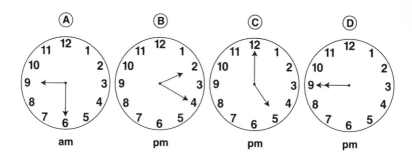

**2**  Match up the following times.

| | |
|---|---|
| (a)  èek sìp-hâh nah-tee têe-ung wun | 05.30 |
| (b)  hâh tÔOm yêe-sìp hâh nah-tee | 16.10 |
| (c)  bài sèe mohng sìp nah-tee | 11.45 |
| (d)  dtee hâh krêung | 23.25 |

**3**  How would you ask:

(a)  where to book a ticket for Chiangmai?
(b)  where to buy (**séu**) a ticket for Songkhla?
(c)  where to get on the bus for Nakhorn Phanom?
(d)  where the Khonkaen bus leaves from?
(e)  what time the Chiangmai bus leaves?
(f)  how long the journey takes?

—— **bàirp fèuk àhn** แบบฝึกอ่าน ——

1 In the last unit you met a number of province names that included the word **Nakhorn**. This lesson introduces thirteen more province names that all have -**buri** as part of their name. (-**buri** means *city* and originally comes from Sanskrit.) Match the Thai spelling with the romanised version and look the map on the next page.

| | | | |
|---|---|---|---|
| (*a*) | Prachinburi | (*i*) | ธนบุรี |
| (*b*) | Chanthaburi | (*ii*) | ราชบุรี |
| (*c*) | Ratburi | (*iii*) | เพชรบุรี |
| (*d*) | Kanchanaburi | (*iv*) | ปราจีนบุรี |
| (*e*) | Nonthaburi | (*v*) | ชลบุรี |
| (*f*) | Saraburi | (*vi*) | จันทบุรี |
| (*g*) | Thonburi | (*vii*) | นนทบุรี |
| (*h*) | Singburi | (*viii*) | สุพรรณบุรี |
| (*i*) | Buriram | (*ix*) | กาญจนบุรี |
| (*j*) | Chonburi | (*x*) | สิงห์บุรี |
| (*k*) | Phetburi | (*xi*) | สระบุรี |
| (*l*) | Suphanburi | (*xii*) | ลพบุรี |
| (*m*) | Lopburi | (*xiii*) | บุรีรัมย์ |

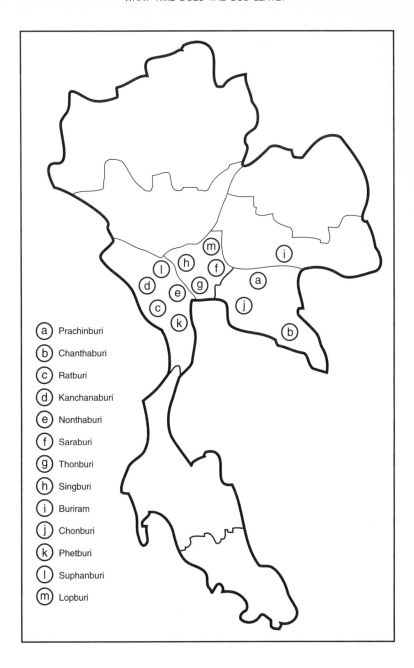

(a) Prachinburi

(b) Chanthaburi

(c) Ratburi

(d) Kanchanaburi

(e) Nonthaburi

(f) Saraburi

(g) Thonburi

(h) Singburi

(i) Buriram

(j) Chonburi

(k) Phetburi

(l) Suphanburi

(m) Lopburi

**2** Here is some information from a tour company's brochure about trips to Nongkhai. Write full sentence answers to the questions below.

หนองคายอยู่ห่างจากกรุงเทพฯ ๖๑๔ กิโลเมตร

บริษัท วี ไอ พี จำกัด มีรถปรับอากาศชั้นหนึ่ง

ออกจากกรุงเทพฯ วันละ ๒ เที่ยว

เวลา ๐๘.๐๐ และ ๒๑.๓๐ นาฬิกา

ใช้เวลาเดินทางประมาณ ๑๐ ชั่วโมง

ค่าโดยสารคนละ ๓๘๐ บาท

| | |
|---|---|
| ห่าง (จาก) | *to be far, distant (from)* |
| บริษัท | *company* |
| จำกัด | *Ltd.* |
| ปรับอากาศ | *air-conditioned* |
| ชั้นหนึ่ง | *first class* |
| วันละ | *per day* |
| เที่ยว | *trip* |
| นาฬิกา | *hrs* |
| ค่าโดยสาร | *fare* |

*Questions:*

๑. หนองคายอยู่ห่างจากกรุงเทพฯ กี่กิโลเมตร

๒. บริษัท วี ไอ พี จำกัด มีรถไปหนองคายวันละกี่เที่ยว

๓. รถไปหนองคายออกกี่โมง

๔. ใช้เวลาเดินทางกี่ชั่วโมง

๕. ค่าโดยสารเท่าไร

## bòt àhn บทอ่าน

The passage in this section is an extract from a tour guide which gives information about various ways of travelling from Bangkok to Nongkhai. You won't be able to understand everything at this stage, but see how many details you can fill in on the chart.

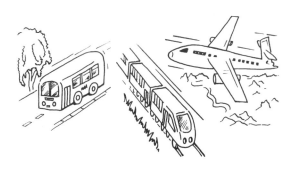

## การเดินทาง

**ทางรถยนต์** หนองคายอยู่ห่างจากกรุงเทพฯ ตามทางหลวงหมายเลข ๑ ถึงสระบุรีเข้าสู่ทางหลวงหมายเลข ๒ ผ่านนครราชสีมา ขอนแก่น อุดรธานี ถึงหนองคายเป็นระยะทางทั้งสิ้น ๖๑๔ กิโลเมตร บริษัทขนส่งจำกัด มีรถ ปรับอากาศชั้นหนึ่งออกจากสถานีขนส่งสายเหนือ ตลาดหมอชิตวันละ ๒ เที่ยว เวลา ๐๘.๐๐ และ ๒๑.๓๐ นาฬิกา ใช้เวลาเดินทางประมาณ ๑๐ ชั่วโมง ค่าโดยสารคนละ ๒๐๙ บาท

**ทางรถไฟ** ขบวนรถด่วนหมายเลข ๓ กรุงเทพฯ – หนองคาย ออกจาก สถานีกรุงเทพฯ ทุกวันเวลา ๒๑ นาฬิกา ถึงหนองคายเวลา ๐๘.๐๐ นาฬิกา ขบวนรถเร็วที่ ๓๓ ออกจากกรุงเทพฯ ทุกวันเวลา ๐๖.๑๐ นาฬิกา ถึงหนองคายเวลา ๑๗.๑๐ นาฬิกา อัตราค่าโดยสารกรุงเทพฯ – หนองคาย

ชั้นหนึ่ง ๒๔๑ บาท ชั้นสอง ๑๒๗.๕๐ บาท ชั้นสาม ๖๘.๕๐ บาท

ระยะทางรถไฟกรุงเทพฯ ถึงหนองคาย ๖๒๔ กิโลเมตร

**ทางเครื่องบิน** จะต้องเดินทางด้วยเครื่องบิน บดท. ไปลงที่จังหวัดอุดรธานี แล้วนั่งรถแท็กซี่หรือรถประจำทางไปหนองคายอีกทีหนึ่ง บริษัทเดิน อากาศไทยจำกัด มีเที่ยวบินจากกรุงเทพฯ ไปอุดรธานีสัปดาห์ละ ๕ วัน ยกเว้นวันอังคารกับวันพฤหัส ออกจากกรุงเทพฯ เวลา ๐๗.๔๕ นาฬิกา ถึงอุดรธานีเวลา ๐๙.๓๕ อัตราค่าโดยสารกรุงเทพฯ – อุดรธานี ๖๕๐ บาท

|  | daily departure time(s) | approx. duration | cost |
|---|---|---|---|
| bus |  |  |  |
| train |  |  |  |
| plane |  |  |  |

# 14

## mee hôrng wâhng mái?

—— *Do you have any vacancies?* ——

## มีห้องว่างไหม

### *In this unit you will learn*

- how to book a hotel room
- ... rěu bplào? questions
- days, months, years
- dates
- seasons
- another use of hâi

### 🔊 —— bòt sǒn-ta-nah    บทสนทนา ——

Peter and Sue have arrived at a small hotel in the provincial capital of Nakhorn Phanom.

| 📟 **Peter** | mee hôrng wâhng mái krúp? | มีห้องว่างไหมครับ |
|---|---|---|
| **Clerk** | mee krúp. | มีครับ |
| | ja pùk yòo gèe wun? | จะพักอยู่กี่วัน |
| **Peter** | yung mâi nâir krúp. | ยังไม่แน่ครับ |

—— **199** ——

| | | |
|---|---|---|
| | àht ja yòo jon těung wun sǎo | อาจจะอยู่จนถึงวันเสาร์ |
| | rěu wun ah-tít. | หรือวันอาทิตย์ |
| | hôrng dtìt air rěu bplào? | ห้องติดแอร์หรือเปล่า |
| **Clerk** | krúp dtìt air. | ครับติดแอร์ |
| **Peter** | kâh hôrng wun la tâo-rài krúp? | ค่าห้องวันละเท่าไรครับ |
| **Clerk** | wun la sǎhm-róy-hâh-sìp krúp. | วันละสามร้อยห้าสิบครับ |
| | tâh yòo ah-tít nèung | ถ้าอยู่อาทิตย์หนึ่ง |
| | ja lót hâi sìp bper– sen. | จะลดให้สิบเปอร์เซ็นต์ |
| **Peter** | kǒr doo hôrng gòrn dâi mái? | ขอดูห้องก่อนได้ไหม |
| **Clerk** | dâi krúp. chern tahng née krúp. | ได้ครับ เชิญทางนี้ครับ |
| **Peter** | mÓOng lôo-ut mun sěe-a. | มุ้งลวดมันเสีย |
| | chôo-ay gâir hâi nòy dâi mái? | ช่วยแก้ให้หน่อยได้ไหม |
| **Clerk** | dâi krúp. děe-o ja sôrm | ได้ครับ เดี๋ยวจะซ่อม |
| **Peter** | chôo-ay chèet yah gun yOOng | ช่วยฉีดยากันยุง |
| | dôo-ay dâi mái? | ด้วยได้ไหม |

| | | |
|---|---|---|
| **púk** | *to stay* | พัก |
| **nâir** | *to be certain* | แน่ |
| **àht (ja)** | *may* | อาจ (จะ) |
| **jon těung** | *until* | จนถึง |
| **wun sǎo** | *Saturday* | วันเสาร์ |
| **wun ah-tít** | *Sunday* | วันอาทิตย์ |
| **... rěu bplào?** | *... or not?* | ... หรือเปล่า |
| **dtìt air** | *to be air-conditioned* | ติดแอร์ |
| **(wun) la** | *per (day)* | (วัน) ละ |
| **ah-tít** | *week* | อาทิตย์ |

| hâi | for | ให้ |
| bper–sen | per cent | เปอร์เซ็นต์ |
| mÓOng lôo-ut | mosquito screen | มุ้งลวด |
| sěe-a | to be broken | เสีย |
| gâir | to fix, repair, mend | แก้ |
| sôrm | to repair, mend | ซ่อม |
| chèet | to spray, inject | ฉีด |
| yah gun yOOng | insecticide | ยากันยุง |

Peter and Sue have agreed to take the room and are now going out for a meal ...

| Clerk | bpai nǎi krúp? | ไปไหนครับ |
| Peter | bpai tahn kâo. | ไปทานข้าว |
| | kǒr-tôht | ขอโทษ |
| | kǒr fàhk kǒrng têe-nêe dâi mái? | ขอฝากของที่นี่ได้ไหม |
| Clerk | kǒrng a-rai krúp? | ของอะไรครับ |

| Peter | glôrng tài rôop láir | กล้องถ่ายรูปและ |
| | glôrng tai wee-dee-oh. | กล้องถ่ายวีดีโอ |
| Clerk | dâi krúp. | ได้ครับ |
| | fàhk têe-nêe bplòrt-pai. | ฝากที่นี่ปลอดภัย |
| | pǒm ja gèp wái nai dtôo sayf. | ผมจะเก็บไว้ในตู้เซฟ |
| Peter | kòrp-kOOn mâhk krúp. | ขอบคุณมากครับ |
| | kǒr fàhk gOOn-jair hôrng dôo-ay. | ขอฝากกุญแจห้องด้วย |

| | | |
|---|---|---|
| fàhk | *to deposit* | ฝาก |
| kǒrng | *things* | ของ |
| glôrng tài rôop | *camera* | กล้องถ่ายรูป |
| glôrng tài wee-dee-oh | *video camera* | กล้องถ่ายวีดีโอ |
| bplòrt-pai | *safe* (adjective) | ปลอดภัย |
| gèp wái | *to keep* | เก็บไว้ |
| dtôo sayf | *safe* (noun) | ตู้เซฟ |
| gOOn-jair | *key* | กุญแจ |

But some things defy a quick fix and a short, sharp spray, and the only solution is to change rooms.

| John | kǒr bplèe-un hôrng dâi mái krúp? | ขอเปลี่ยนห้องได้ไหมครับ |
|---|---|---|
| Clerk | tum-mai lâ krúp? | ทำไมละ่ครับ |
| John | krêu-ung bprùp ah-gàht | เครื่องปรับอากาศ |
| | mun sěe-a. | มันเสีย |
| Clerk | děe-o ja kêun bpai doo. | เดี๋ยวจะขึ้นไปดู |
| John | mâi dtôrng krúp. | ไม่ต้องครับ |
| | hôrng náhm chái mâi dâi dôo-ay. | ห้องน้ำใช้ไม่ได้ด้วย |
| | mâi mee náhm. | ไม่มีน้ำ |
| | yàhk bplèe-un hôrng dee gwàh. | อยากเปลี่ยนห้องดีกว่า |
| Clerk | bplèe-un mâi dâi krúp. | เปลี่ยนไม่ได้ครับ |
| | mâi mee hôrng èun. | ไม่มีห้องอื่น |

| | | |
|---|---|---|
| bplèe-un | *to change* | เปลี่ยน |
| tum-mai lâ? | *why?* | ทำไมละ่ |
| krêu-ung bprùp ah-gàht | *air-conditioning* | เครื่องปรับอากาศ |

| | | |
|---|---|---|
| **kêun** | *to go up* | ขึ้น |
| **hôrng náhm** | *toilet, bathroom* | ห้องน้ำ |
| **èun** | *other* | อื่น |

## Comprehension

1  How long are Peter and Sue thinking of staying at the hotel?
2  Do they want an air-conditioned room or a room with a fan?
3  How much is the room per night?
4  What inducement does the clerk offer the couple to stay longer?
5  What valuables do they want to leave in the hotel safe?
6  Why does John want to change rooms?
7  Why can't he?

# —pah-sǎh láir sǔng-kom    ภาษาและสังคม —

If you are staying in a large hotel in Bangkok you will find that most of the staff speak English. Since their English will be considerably better than your Thai at this stage, it is more appropriate for you to stick to English when speaking to them. However, in cheaper hotels and guest houses, especially in provincial areas, you may find it necessary to use Thai to book your room.

Hotel rooms will either be air-conditioned or have a ceiling fan (**pút lom** พัดลม). A room with a double-bed is confusingly described as a 'single room' (**hôrng dèe-o** ห้องเดี่ยว) while a 'double room' (**hôrng kôo** ห้องคู่) has two single beds. Rooms in modern hotels will include a western-style toilet, shower and wash basin, although in provincial areas you may find a Thai-style toilet and a large earthenware water jar, with a small bowl for scooping up the water and pouring over yourself. If your room has a water jar, you will probably find mosquitoes congregating there, and it is well worth being equipped with your own insecticide (**yah gun yOOng** ยากันยุง). And while on the subject of mosquitoes (**yOOng** ยุง), check that the mosquito screens (**mÓOng lôo-ut** มุ้งลวด) on the windows are in good condition, and if not insist on changing rooms.

The Thai word for hotel (**rohng rairm** โรงแรม) is also a euphemism for brothel, and many of the cheaper hotels that are not brothels are used primarily for illicit liaisons. If you find you get odd looks when you arrive alone and try to book in for a week, you may be at the wrong kind of establishment. If in doubt, consult an official government list of recommended hotels which is readily available from the Thai Tourist Authority.

—————— **sǔm-noo-un** สำนวน ——————

How to:

● ask if there are any free rooms

mee hôrng wâhng mái?      มีห้องว่างไหม

● say you will stay until Saturday

ja yòo jon těung wun sǎo      จะอยู่จนถึงวันเสาร์

● ask whether the room has air-conditioning

hôrng dtìt air rěu bplào?      ห้องติดแอร์หรือเปล่า

● ask what the daily rate is

kâh hôrng wun la tâo-rài?      ค่าห้องวันละเท่าไร

● ask to see the room

kǒr doo hôrng gòrn dâi mái?      ขอดูห้องก่อนได้ไหม

● say X is broken and ask for it to be fixed

X sěe-a      X เสีย

chôo-ay gâir hâi nòy dâi mái?      ช่วยแก้ให้หน่อยได้ไหม

- ask someone to spray insect repellent

  chôo-ay chèet yah gun yOOng dâi mái?    ช่วยฉีดยากันยุงได้ไหม

- ask to leave something

  kŏr fàhk kŏrng têe-nêe dâi mái?    ขอฝากของที่นี่ได้ไหม

- ask to change rooms

  kŏr bplèe-un hôrng dâi mái?    ขอเปลี่ยนห้องได้ไหม


🔲 ————— **kum ùt-tí-bai**    คำอธิบาย —————

## 1 ... rĕu bplào? ... หรือเปล่า questions

... **rĕu bplào?** literally means ... *or not?* although the English translation makes this question form sound rather more abrupt than it is in Thai. In fact, there is nothing impolite about asking ... **rĕu bplào?** questions; it is a way of showing that you need a straight answer.

bpai rĕu bplào?                 *Are you going (or not)?*
hôrng dtìt air rĕu bplào?       *Does the room have air-conditioning
                                 (or not)?*

## 🔲 2 Days

| | | |
|---|---|---|
| wun jun | *Monday* | วันจันทร์ |
| wun ung-kahn | *Tuesday* | วันอังคาร |
| wun pÓOt | *Wednesday* | วันพุธ |
| wun pá-réu-hùt | *Thursday* | วันพฤหัส |
| wun sÒOk | *Friday* | วันศุกร์ |

| | | |
|---|---|---|
| wun sǎo | *Saturday* | วันเสาร์ |
| wun ah-tít | *Sunday* | วันอาทิตย์ |

## 3 *Months* เดือน

| | | |
|---|---|---|
| mók-ga-rah-kom | *January* | มกราคม |
| gOOm-pah-pun | *February* | กุมภาพันธ์ |
| mee-nah-kom | *March* | มีนาคม |
| may-sǎh-yon | *April* | เมษายน |
| préut-sa-pah-kom | *May* | พฤษภาคม |
| mí-tOO-nah-yon | *June* | มิถุนายน |
| ga-rúk-ga-dah-kom | *July* | กรกฎาคม |
| sǐng-hǎh-kom | *August* | สิงหาคม |
| gun-yah-yon | *September* | กันยายน |
| dtOO-lah-kom | *October* | ตุลาคม |
| préut-sa-jìk-gah-yon | *November* | พฤศจิกายน |
| tun-wah-kom | *December* | ธันวาคม |

Notice that the final syllable is **kom** for months with 31 days, **yon** for 30 days and **pun** for the shortest month, February. In normal speech, the word **deu-un** is often prefixed and the final syllable omitted:

| | |
|---|---|
| bpai deu-un sǐng-hǎh | *I'm going in August.* |
| glùp deu-un tun-wah | *He's coming back in December.* |

## 4 *Dates*

Ordinal numbers in Thai are formed by adding **têe** (ที่) in front of the number:

| | | |
|---|---|---|
| têe nèung | *first* | ที่หนึ่ง |
| têe sǒrng | *second* | ที่สอง |

| | | |
|---|---|---|
| têe săhm | *third* | ที่สาม |

Dates are expressed using the pattern **wun** + ordinal number + month:

| | |
|---|---|
| wun têe sìp tun-wah-kom | *10th December* |
| wun têe yêe-sìp may-săh-yon | *20th April* |

## 5 Years ปี

The year **(bpee)** is normally counted according to the Buddhist Era (B.E.) (**pÓOt-ta-sùk-ka-râht** or **por sŏr** (พ.ศ.) for short ) which began with the birth of the Buddha, 543 years before the birth of Christ. To convert Thai years to A.D. (**kor sŏr** (ค.ศ.) for short), you simply subtract 543 years. Thus, 2500 B.E. is 1957 A.D.

## 6 Seasons

There are three seasons in Thailand, the cool season (November to February), the hot season (March to June) and the rainy season (July to October). The formal Thai word for *season* is **reu-doo** (ฤดู) but **nâh** (หน้า) is more commonly used in speech.

| | | |
|---|---|---|
| nâh năo | *cool season* | หน้าหนาว |
| nâh rórn | *hot season* | หน้าร้อน |
| nâh fŏn | *rainy season* | หน้าฝน |

## 7 hâi ให้

You met the word **hâi** in Unit 10 meaning *to get someone to do something* (**hâi kOOn Cha-ní-dah sùng dee gwàh**). **hâi** also means *to give* and *for*. In this Unit you will find two examples of **hâi** meaning *for*. Notice that the pronoun, given in brackets in the example, is commonly omitted in speech.

| | |
|---|---|
| ja lót hâi (kOOn) sìp bper-sen | *I'll give you a 10% discount.* |
| pǒm ja gâir hâi (kOOn) | *I'll repair it for you.* |
| káo ja séu hâi (rao) | *He'll buy it for us.* |

## 8  tum-mai lâ? ทำไมล่ะ

When Thais ask *why?* in response to a statement, they frequently add
the particle **lâ** after **tum-mai.**

| | |
|---|---|
| prÔOng née chún mâi bpai | *I'm not going tomorrow.* |
| – tum-mai lâ? | *– Why?* |

## 9  'air-conditioned'

Although the English word **air** is frequently used to mean *air-conditioned* (e.g. in expressions like **dtìt air** *(air-conditioned)*, **hôrng air** *(air-conditioned room)*, **rót air** *(air-conditioned bus)*, the more formal Thai term is **bprùp ah-gàht** (ปรับอากาศ) which literally means *'adjust air'*. An air-conditioner is **krêu-ung** *(machine)* **bprùp ah-gàht** (เครื่องปรับอากาศ).

☑ ———— **bàirp fèuk hùt**   แบบฝึกหัด ————

1  Simon is booking into a hotel. He wants an air-conditioned room for five days. He also wants to know the price and to see the room first. Complete the dialogue.

| | | |
|---|---|---|
| **Simon** | ............................... | ............................... |
| **Clerk** | mee krúp. | มีครับ |
| | ao hôrng dtìt air châi mái krúp? | เอาห้องติดแอร์ใช่ไหมครับ |
| **Simon** | ............................... | ............................... |
| **Clerk** | kít ja yòo gèe wun krúp? | คิดจะอยู่กี่วันครับ |

| | | |
|---|---|---|
| **Simon** | ..................................... | ..................................... |
| | ..........................? | ..........................? |
| **Clerk** | wun la săhm róy bàht. | วันละสามร้อยบาท |
| **Simon** | ..........................? | ..................................... |
| **Clerk** | dâi krúp. chern tahng née. | ได้ครับ เชิญทางนี้ |

**2**  How would you ask to leave the following articles in the hotel safe?

(a) glôrng tài rôop  (b) gra-bpăo  (c) gOOn-jair  (d) núng-sĕu dern-tahng

กล้องถ่ายรูป        กระเป๋า        กุญแจ        หนังสือเดินทาง

**3**  How would you say the following dates?

(a)  9th January
(b)  19th June
(c)  31st August
(d)  5th November

# ☑ ——— **bàirp fèuk àhn**   แบบฝึกอ่าน ———

Here is Noi, a Thai hotel worker talking about her work. Answer the
questions which follow.

ฉันทำงานอยู่ที่นี่เกือบ ๒๐ ปีแล้วค่ะ

ทำงานอยู่ที่นี่สบาย ทำความสะอาดห้อง และ

ซักรีดเสื้อผ้า มาทำงานเวลา ๒ โมงเช้าแล้ว

กลับบ้านบ่าย ๔ โมง แขกที่นี่ส่วนมากเป็น

ชาวต่างประเทศ ฝรั่งก็มี จีนก็มี ญี่ปุ่นก็มี

บางคนก็ใจดีมาก ให้ทิปเป็นร้อยกว่าบาท

แต่ตอนนี้เป็นหน้าฝน ไม่ค่อยมีแขกมาก

งานก็ไม่ค่อยมีมากเหมือนกัน ฉันก็นั่งอยู่

คุยกับเพื่อนทั้งวัน

| เกือบ | almost |
|---|---|
| สบาย | to be happy, well, comfortable |
| ความสะอาด | cleaning |
| ซัก | to wash |
| รีด | to iron |
| เสื้อผ้า | clothes |
| แขก | guest |
| ส่วนมาก | mostly, for the most part |
| ชาวต่างประเทศ | foreigners |
| ใจดี | to be kind |
| ให้ | to give |
| ทิป | tip |
| หน้าฝน | rainy season |

| เหมือนกัน | *likewise* |
| นั่ง | *to sit* |
| คุย | *to chat* |
| ทั้งวัน | *all day* |

## Questions :

๑ น้อยทำงานอยู่ที่โรงแรมกี่ปีแล้ว

๒ ที่โรงแรมน้อยทำอะไรบ้าง

๓ น้อยชอบทำงานที่โรงแรมไหม

๔ น้อยมาทำงานกี่โมง

๕ แขกที่โรงแรมส่วนมากเป็นชาวอะไร

๖ หน้าฝนมีแขกมากไหม

๗ ถ้า (if) ไม่มีงานทำมาก น้อยจะทำอะไร

## bòt àhn  บทอ่าน

เล่มที่ 56

บริษัท รีโนโฮเต็ล จำกัด
**RENO HOTEL**

เลขที่ 42

40 ซอยเกษมสันต์ 1 ถนนพระราม 1 ต. วังใหม่ อ. ปทุมวัน กรุงเทพฯ
40 (So Kasem san 1) Rama 1 Road Pratumwan Bangkok

ใบเสร็จรับเงิน
RECEIPT

☎ 2150026 2150027 FAX: (662) 2153430

ทะเบียนการค้าเลขที่
10 41 4897

วันที่ 22/9/36
Date

ได้รับเงินจาก MR. SMITH DAVID
Received From

ห้องเลขที่ 204
Room No.

ชำระค่าห้องจาก 14/9/36
For Room From

ถึง 24/9/36
To

รวม 10½
Total

วัน
Day

20,004

รวมเป็นเงิน — 5,775 —
Total

บาท
Baht

ลงนาม

ผู้รับเงิน
Cashier

# 15

## prÔOng née bpai têe-o têe-nǎi?

*Where are you going tomorrow?*

## พรุ่งนี้ไปเที่ยวที่ไหน

## *In this unit you will learn*

- how to ask for permission
- how to make suggestions and give advice
- how to politely avoid committing yourself
- two words for *visit*
- **sa-nÒOk**

## bòt sǒn-ta-nah บทสนทนา

Peter and Sue are wondering how best to get to see the famous temple of Wat That Phanom which is some way out of the provincial capital where their hotel is.

| Clerk | prÔOng née bpai têe-o têe-nǎi krúp? | พรุ่งนี้ไปเที่ยวที่ไหนครับ |
|-------|-------------------------------------|--------------------------|
| Sue | yung mâi nâir kâ. | ยังไม่แน่ค่ะ |
| Clerk | kOOn koo-un ja bpai têe-o | คุณควรจะไปเที่ยว |
| | wút tâht pa-nom. | วัดธาตุพนม |

|  | mee chêu sěe-ung mâhk. | มีชื่อเสียงมาก |
|---|---|---|
|  | fa-rùng chôrp bpai doo. | ฝรั่งชอบไปดู |
| **Sue** | kâ rao yàhk ja bpai têe-o. | ค่ะ เราอยากจะไปเที่ยว |
|  | pêu-un bòrk wâh soo-ay mâhk. | เพื่อนบอกว่าสวยมาก |
|  | dtàir mâi sâhp wâh | แต่ไม่ทราบว่า |
|  | ja bpai yung-ngai. | จะไปอย่างไร |
| **Clerk** | pǒm wâh bpai gùp too-a dee gwàh. | ผมว่าไปกับทัวร์ดีกว่า |
|  | mee rót air bpai tÓOk cháo glùp yen. | มีรถแอร์ไปทุกเช้ากลับเย็น |
| **Peter** | lěr krúp? | หรือครับ |
|  | kâh too-a tâo-rài krúp? | ค่าทัวร์เท่าไรครับ |
| **Clerk** | kon la sǒrng róy jèt-sìp krúp. | คนละสองร้อยเจ็ดสิบครับ |
| **Peter** | laír-o jorng têe-nǎi? | แล้วจองที่ไหน |
| **Clerk** | mâi mee bpun-hǎh krúp. | ไม่มีปัญหาครับ |
|  | pǒm ja jorng hâi gôr dâi. | ผมจะจองให้ก็ได้ |
| **Sue** | rót òrk gèe mohng ká? | รถออกกี่โมงคะ |
| **Clerk** | sǒrng mohng cháo. | สองโมงเช้า |
|  | òrk jàhk nâh rohng rairm nêe eng. | ออกจากหน้าโรงแรมนี่เอง |
|  | bpai rěu bplào? | ไปหรือเปล่า |
| **Peter** | děe-o, rao kít doo gòrn krúp. | เดี๋ยว เราคิดดูก่อนครับ |
|  | mâi sâhp wâh mee too-a bpai | ไม่ทราบว่า มีทัวร์ไป |
|  | bpra-tâyt lao dôo-ay rěu bplào? | ประเทศลาวด้วยหรือเปล่า |
| **Clerk** | dtorn née yung mâi mee krúp. | ตอนนี้ยังไม่มีครับ |
|  | tâh yàhk bpai lao gôr dtôrng | ถ้าอยากไปลาวก็ต้อง |
|  | bpai jung-wùt nǒrng-kai. | ไปจังหวัดหนองคาย |

| | | |
|---|---|---|
| **têe-o** | *to visit, go out* | เที่ยว |
| **yung** | *still* | ยัง |
| **koo-un** | *should, ought to* | ควร |
| **wút tâht pa-nom** | *Wat That Phanom* | วัดธาตุพนม |
| **mee chêu sěe-ung** | *to be famous* | มีชื่อเสียง |
| **too-a** | *tour* | ทัวร์ |
| **air** | *air-conditioned* | แอร์ |
| **bpun-hǎh** | *problem* | ปัญหา |
| **nêe eng** | *this very ...* | นี่เอง |
| **kít doo** | *to think about, consider* | คิดดู |
| **bpra-tâyt lao** | *Laos* | ประเทศลาว |
| **jung-wùt** | *province* | จังหวัด |
| **nǒrng-kai** | *Nongkhai* | หนองคาย |

Earlier Malee and Sue discussed a visit Sue had made to the seaside ...

| | | |
|---|---|---|
| **Malee** | kOOn Susan ker-ee bpai têe-o chai ta-lay têe meu-ung tai mái? | คุณ Susan เคยไปเที่ยวชายทะเลที่เมืองไทยไหม |
| **Sue** | ker-ee. | เคย |
| | ker-ee bpai pút-ta-yah | เคยไปพัทยา |
| | krúng nèung mêu-a sǒrng | ครั้งหนึ่งเมื่อสอง |
| | sǎhm deu-un gòrn. | สามเดือนก่อน |
| **Malee** | sa-nÒOk mái? | สนุกไหม |
| **Sue** | gôr ... kwahm jing mâi kôy sa-nÒOk tâo-rài. mee kon yér-yáir. | ก็ ... ความจริงไม่ค่อยสนุกเท่าไร มีคนเยอะแยะ |

| | | |
|---|---|---|
| | mâi chôrp. láir náhm ta-lay | ไม่ชอบ และน้ำทะเล |
| | man mâi kôy sa-àht. | มันไม่ค่อยสะอาด |
| **Malee** | tâh bpai chai ta-lay koo-un ja bpai | ถ้าไปชายทะเล ควรจะไป |
| | hŏo-a hĭn dee gwàh. | หัวหินดีกว่า |
| | ker-ee bpai mái? | เคยไปไหม |
| **Sue** | mâi ker-ee. | ไม่เคย |
| **Malee** | hŏo-a hĭn ngêe-up gwàh pút-ta-yah. | หัวหินเงียบกว่าพัทยา |
| | mee núk tôrng têe-o nóy gwàh. | มีนักท่องเที่ยวน้อยกว่า |
| | láir kít wâh náhm ta-lay sa-àht | และคิดว่าน้ำทะเลสะอาด |
| | gwàh dôo-ay. | กว่าด้วย |
| | chún ker-ee bpai gùp pêu-un | ฉันเคยไปกับเพื่อนๆ |
| | pêu-un. púk yòo bung-ga-loh. | พักอยู่บังกะโล |
| | mâi kôy pairng tâo-rài. | ไม่ค่อยแพงเท่าไร |

| | | |
|---|---|---|
| **wun sǎo wun ah-tít** | *weekend* | วันเสาร์วันอาทิตย์ |
| **chai ta-lay** | *seaside* | ชายทะเล |
| **pút-ta-yah** | *Pattaya* | พัทยา |
| **yér-yáir** | *lots* | เยอะแยะ |
| **ta-lay** | *sea* | ทะเล |
| **hŏo-a hĭn** | *Hua Hin* | หัวหิน |
| **ngêe-up** | *quiet calm* | เงียบ |
| **bung-ga-loh** | *bungalow* | บังกะโล |

Peter and Sue are now at Wat That Phanom and wondering whether there are any restrictions on taking photographs.

| | | |
|---|---|---|
| **Sue** | kŏr-tôht kâ. | ขอโทษค่ะ |
| | têe-nêe hâhm tài rôop rĕu bplào? | ที่นี่ห้ามถ่ายรูปหรือเปล่า |

| **Thai** | kít wâh mâi hâhm krúp. | คิดว่าไม่ห้ามครับ |
| | dtair ja bpai tǎhm jâo-nâh-têe hâi. | แต่จะไปถามเจ้าหน้าที่ให้ |
| | ... kǒr-tôht krúp | ... ขอโทษครับ |
| | têe-nêe tài rôop dâi châi mái? | ที่นี่ถ่ายรูปได้ใช่ไหม |
| **Official** | têe-nêe dâi krúp. | ที่นี่ได้ครับ |
| | dtàir kâhng nai hâhm tài. | แต่ข้างในห้ามถ่าย 🍃 |
| | chôo-ay bòrk fa-rùng wâh dtôrng | ช่วยบอกฝรั่งว่าต้อง |
| | tòrt rorng táo kâhng nai dôo-ay. | ถอดรองเท้าข้างในด้วย |

| **hâhm** | *to forbid* | ห้าม |
| **tài rôop** | *to take a photograph* | ถ่ายรูป |
| **tǎhm** | *to ask* | ถาม |
| **jâo-nâh-têe** | *official* | เจ้าหน้าที่ |
| **tòrt** | *to take off* | ถอด |
| **rorng táo** | *shoes* | รองเท้า |

## *Comprehension*

1 What advice does the hotel clerk have for getting to Wat That Phanom?

2 How much will it cost?

3 What favour does the clerk offer to do for Peter and Sue?

4 If Peter and Sue want to visit Laos, where should they book their tour from?

5 Has Sue ever been to the seaside in Thailand?

6 When did she go to Pattaya?

7 What didn't she like about Pattaya?

8 What would be a better coastal resort to visit, according to Malee?

9 Where did Malee stay when she went to Hua Hin?

10 What message did the offical wish to convey to Peter and Sue?

# — pah-sǎh láir sǔng-kom ภาษาและสังคม —

Tourism has for many years been one of Thailand's major industries. By the early 1990s there were more than five million foreigners visiting the country each year. Cheap package tours involving a few days in Bangkok followed by short stays in either the northern province of Chiangmai or at one of the seaside resorts such as Pattaya, Phuket or Hua Hin became increasingly popular with foreign tourists from the mid 1970's. The domestic tourist market also expanded as the rapidly growing and increasingly affluent middle class sought to escape the noise and pollution of Bangkok at weekends. To the alarm of many environmentalists, it is not only modern hotels that have sprung up in once remote provinces but also golf courses which take a huge toll on local water resources.

# ———— sǔm-noo-un สำนวน ————

How to:

- advise someone to do something
  kOOn koo-un ja ...                    คุณควรจะ ...

- say that you don't know how to do something
  mâi sâhp wâh ja tum yung-ngai     ไม่ทราบว่าจะทำอย่างไร

- tell someone you think ... would be better
  pǒm (chún) wâh ... dee gwàh        ผม(ฉัน)ว่า ... ดีกว่า

- politely avoid committing yourself
  děe-o, kít doo gòrn                   เดี๋ยว คิดดูก่อน

- ask whether something is fun
  ... sa-nÒOk mái?                      ... สนุกไหม

- ask whether something is allowed

  ... dâi mái?                          ... ได้ไหม

- ask whether something is forbidden

  hâhm ... rĕu bplào?              ห้าม ... หรือเปล่า

---

# kum ùt-tí-bai  คำอธิบาย

## 1 têe-o  เที่ยว

**têe-o** means *to visit (places)*. It occurs also in the expression **bpai têe-o** (*I'm going out*), a deliberately vague response to the informal greeting **bpai nai?** (*Where are you going?*) and **têe-o póo-ying**, a common euphemism meaning *to visit the brothel*. A different verb, **yêe-um** (เยี่ยม) is used for visiting people, or home.

## 2 ... kít doo gòrn  คิดดูก่อน

It is very easy, if you are a foreign visitor to Thailand, to be swept along by offers to take you to places, show you things and sell you things which you perhaps don't really want to see or buy. **dĕe-o kít doo gòrn** (*Wait a minute, I'll think about it*) should be enough to politely discourage the over-persistent.

## 3 mâi sâhp wâh ...  ไม่ทราบว่า ...?

The expression **mâi sâhp wâh ...** (*I don't know ...*) occurs twice in the conversations at the start of this unit. In the first instance, it is a straightforward statement – **mâi sâhp wâh ja bpai yung-ngai** (*I don't know how I'm going to go*). In the second example, however, it is a rather tentative way of posing a question – **mâi sâhp wâh mee too-a bpai bpra-tâyt lao dôo-ay rĕu bplào?** (*I don't know whether you have any tours to Laos, too, or not?*). As your Thai improves, listen for this way of posing a question in television and radio interviews.

# 4 sa-nÒOk สนุก

**sa-nÒOk** is usually translated as *fun*, although it is much more commonly used in Thai than its English equivalent. It is quite reasonable to ask **sa-nÒOk mái?** not just about parties or visits to the cinema but also business trips and conferences. Many Thais see a love of 'sanuk' (as it is usually written in western books on Thailand) as an essential part of 'Thainess'.

# 5 mâi ker-ee ... ไม่เคย ... *and* mâi kôy ... ไม่ค่อย ...

You have already met **mâi ker-ee ...** *(to have never ...)* in Unit 11 and **mâi kôy ...** *(not very ...)* in Unit 9. Although their meanings are quite distinct, they can sound similar to the beginner's ears and are often confused. Here are a few examples to refresh your memory:

| | |
|---|---|
| mâi ker-ee bpai | *I have never been there.* |
| mâi ker-ee gin | *I have never eaten it.* |
| mâi ker-ee tum | *I have never done it.* |
| mâi kôy chôrp | *I don't like it very much.* |
| mâi kôy pairng | *It's not very expensive.* |
| mâi kôy sa-nÒOk | *It wasn't much fun.* |

# 6 *Reduplication of nouns*

While **pêu-un** can mean *friend* or *friends*, it is quite often reduplicated to clarify that a plural meaning is intended. It should not be assumed, however, that all nouns can be reduplicated in this way; in fact, the vast majority cannot.

| | |
|---|---|
| ย ทัวร์ | Far East Tours |
| ัวร์ | package tour |
| | by |
| | aeroplane |
| | coach |
| องเที่ยว | itinerary |
| เรม) | hotel |
| ร์ | weekend tour |
| | evening |

## bàirp fèuk hùt  แบบฝึกหัด

1  'I think it would be better to ...' A friend is always trying to organise your life by telling you what you should do. Resist the suggestion and, using the prompt in brackets, point out you have a better idea.

*Example :*

**Friend**  kOOn koo-un ja bpai têe-o pút-ta-yah (poo-gèt)
**You**  kít wâh bpai têe-o poo-gèt dee gwàh

(a)  kOOn koo-un ja bpai dtorn yen (dtorn cháo)
(b)  kOOn koo-un ja bpai táirk-sêe (rót-may)
(c)  kOOn koo-un ja púk yòo têe bâhn rao (rohng-rairm)
(d)  kOOn koo-un ja sùng ah-hǎhn fa-rùng (ah-hǎhn tai)

2  What would you say if you did not know how to:

(a)  do something?
(b)  get somewhere?

พิพิธภัณฑ์สถานแห่งชาติ

(c) eat something?
(d) read something?
(e) use something?
(f) repair something?

3 Here are some 'forbidden' notices. Match the Thai script with the translation.

(a) ห้ามถ่ายรูป      (i) No Parking

(b) ห้ามจอดรถ      (ii) Sale Prohibited

(c) ห้ามสูบบุหรี่      (iii) No Entry

(d) ห้ามเข้า      (iv) No Smoking

(e) ห้ามขาย      (v) Photography Forbidden

## bòt àhn บทอ่าน

A friend from England is planning to make a trip to Phuket. Using the advertisement on the following page, make a note of possible options, including method of travel, length of stay, day of departure and cost. Make a note also of the name, address and telephone number of the company.

Notice the large number of English words used in the advertisement on the following page. This is common in advertising. You will find the vocabulary for the advertisement on page 224.

ฟาร์อีสท์ฯ ทัวร์

๑๘๙๒-๔ ถนนเพชรบุรีตัดใหม่

โทร. ๓๙๑-๖๑๐๑-๓

แพ็คเก็จทัวร์ ออกเดินทางทุกวั

เครื่องบิน ๓ วัน

รายการท่องเที่ยว

*เชียงใหม่     ดอยอินทนน
สันกำแพง ท
พักโรงแรมช

*ภูเก็ต     เกาะพีพี หา
อ่าวพังงา
พัก ร.ร. หา

วีคเอนทัวร์ออกเดินทางทุกคื
วันอาทิตย์ หรือเช้าวันจันทร์

* เชียงใหม่     ดอยสุเทพ
หมู่บ้านชา
พัก ร.ร. เ

* ภูเก็ต     เกาะพีพี
พัก ร.ร. ำ
(กลับเช้า

ฟาร์อีสท์
แพ็คเก็จ
โดย
เครื่องบิ
รถโค้ช
รายการ
ร.ร. (โร
วีคเอนทั
ค่ำ

The Royal Palace, Bangkok

# KEY TO
## THE EXERCISES

## Unit 1

**bàirp fèuk hùt** **1** (*a*) (káo) chêu Peter. (*b*) (káo) nahm sa-gOOn
Green. (*c*) (káo) bpen kon ung-grìt. (*d*) (káo) bpen núk tÓO-rá-gìt.
(*e*) (káo) chêu Malee. (*f*) (káo) bpen kon tai. (*g*) châi. **2** (*a*) (pǒm
(dee-chún) chêu ... (*b*) nǎhm sa-gOOn ... (*c*) bpen kon ... (*d*) bpen ...
/ tum ngahn gùp ... **3** (*a*) (ii) (*b*) (iv) (*c*) (i) (*d*) (iii) **4** (*b*) káo chêu
John. nahm sa-gOOn Stevens. bpen kon a-may-ri-gun. mah jàhk
Florida. bpen núk sèuk-sǎh. (*c*) káo chêu Makoto. nahm sa-gOOn
Iwasaki. bpen kon yêe-bpÒOn. mah jàhk Tokyo. bpen núk
tÓO-rá-gìt. (*d*) káo chêu Paula. nahm sa-gOOn Besson. bpen kon
fa-rùng-sàyt. mah jàhk Paris. bpen kroo. **5** (*a*) kǒr-tôht krúp (kâ)
kOOn chêu a-rai? (*b*) káo chêu Sǒm-chai châi mái? (*c*) káo
nahm sa-gOOn a-rai? (*d*) káo bpen kon tai châi mái? (*e*) káo bpen
kroo châi mái?

**bàirp fèuk áhn** **2**

| | | | |
|---|---|---|---|
| mah | yaa | nahm | ngahn |
| wun | num | rum | ror |
| norn | rai | nai | yai |
| lao | yao | rao | yorm |

**3** yahm lao mah. ror nahn. nahng lah nai. yai rum nahn.
**4** (*a*) 236-4890 (*b*) 580-7359 (*c*) 225-7381 (*d*) 693-2145 (*e*) 371-9548

## Unit 2

**bàirp fèuk hùt** **1** (*b*) pairng bpai nòy krúp (kâ). hâh-sìp bàht dâi
mái? (*c*) pairng bpai nòy krúp (kâ). hòk-sìp bàht dâi mái?
(*d*) pairng bpai nòy krúp (kâ). yêe-sìp bàht dâi mái? (*e*) pairng bpai
nòy krúp (kâ). sǎhm-sìp bàht dâi mái? **2** (*a*) nêe tâo-rài krúp
(ká)? (*b*) pairng bpai nòy. (*c*) lót nòy dâi mái? (*d*) hâh-sìp bàht dâi
mái? (*e*) sěe dairng mâi sǒo-ay. (*f*) sěe kěe-o mee mái? **3** (*a*) sùp-
bpa-rót bai la tâo-rài? (*b*) sôm loh la tâo-rài? (*c*) glôo-ay wěe la tâo-rài?
(*d*) ma-la-gor bai la tâo-rài? (*e*) ma-môo-ung bai la tâo-rài?
(*f*) dtairng-moh bai la tâo-rài? (*g*) nòy-nàh loh la tâo-rài? **4** nêe (rêe-

uk wâh) a-rai? / a-rai ná? / ma-môo-ung châi mái krúp? / bai la tâo-
rài? / lót nòy dâi mái?

**bàirp fèuk áhn 2**

| | | | |
|---|---|---|---|
| gin | gun | jai | doo |
| dee | dtah | dtee | bin |
| bai | bpai | bpee | mohng |
| bpoo | rohng | yOOng | un |

**4** (a) yOOng bin bpai bin mah. (b) lOOng yin dee mah doo. (c) nai
nah mee bpoo dum (d) yahm lao dtee ngoo dtai. (e) ror doo nahng
ngahm dung. **5** (a) (iii) (b) (v) (c) (i) (d) (ii) (e) (iv)

# Unit 3

**bàirp fèuk hùt** **1** (a) bpai sa-yǎhm sa-kwair mái? (b) bpai ta-nǒn
sÒO-kǒOm-wít soy sǎhm-sìp gâo mái? (c) bpai wút prá-gâir-o mái?
(d) bpai sa-nǎhm bin dorn meu-ung mái? (e) bpai rohng-rairm
ree-yen mái? **2** (a) (v) B (b) (iii) E (c) (iv) A (d) (i) C (e) (ii) D **3** bpai
ta-nǒn sÒO-kǒOm-wít soy hâh-sìp sǎhm mái? / kâo krúp. bpai
sÒOt soy. / châi krúp. bpai tâo-rài? / pairng bpai nòy krúp. / hâh-sìp
bàht dâi mái? **4** (a) těung sèe-yâirk láir-o lée-o sái. (b) jòrt
têe-nôhn. (c) ler-ee bpai èek nít nèung. (d) bpai sÒOt soy (e) lée-o
kwǎh dtrong née

**bàirp fèuk áhn** **1** (live syllables marked in bold)

| **bpai** | èek | nít | jòrt | mâhk |
|---|---|---|---|---|
| **gun** | **dee** | **ree-noh** | dtìt | **rohng** |

**2**

| bèep | nahng | gùt | jÒOt | nút |
|---|---|---|---|---|
| bpee | dàap | jahn | jàhk | dtai |
| lâhp | rao | mêet | rôrp | bpàhk |

**3**

| yâhk | mee | nút | gùp |
|---|---|---|---|
| ngahn | yOOng | gùt | mâhk |
| jàhk | rêep | ai | norn |
| yorm | lôok | bpai | jòrt |

# Unit 4

**bàirp fèuk hùt** **1** (a) (iii) (b) (v) (c) (i) (d) (ii) (e) (iv) **2** (a) kǒr
doo may-noo nòy. (b) ao ba-mèe náhm sǒrng chahm (c) ao kâo pùt
gài sǎhm jahn. (d) ao núm kǎirng bplào hâh gâir-o. (e) chék bin

krúp (kâ) **3** They wanted two plates of shrimp fried rice, a Pepsi and a large Singha beer. They ended up with a plate of chicken fried rice, a plate of pork fried rice, a Coke and a small Singha beer.

**bàirp fèuk áhn 1**

| | | | | |
|---|---|---|---|---|
| chai | soy | bàht | kum | chôrp |
| tahng | pah | púk | tum | tÓOk |
| keun | deung | dtèuk | keu | ker-ee |
| ler-ee | pairng | dairng | kon | long |
| yen | lék | bpen | jèt | gôr |

**3** (*a*) (i) (*b*) (iii)

# Unit 5

**bàirp fèuk hùt 1** (*b*) Eddie, Nikki láir-o gôr Nuan yòo kâhng nôrk. (*c*) Sue láir Tom yòo kâhng bon. (*d*) Peter yòo kâhng lâhng. (*e*) Nikki láir Eddie yòo kâhng nâh. (*f*) Nuan yòo kâhng lǔng. **2** (*a*) tǎir-o née mee dtôo toh-ra-sùp mái? (*b*) tǎir-o née mee bor-ri-gahn tài àyk-ga-sǎhn mái? (*c*) tǎir-o née mee hôrng náhm mái? (*d*) tǎir-o née mee rohng pa-yah-bahn mái? (*e*) tǎir-o née mee ta-nah-kahn mái? **3** (*a*) sa-nǎhm gee-lah. (*b*) ráhn ah-hǎhn kwǔn-jai. (*c*) dtôo toh-ra-sùp

**bàirp fèuk áhn 1**

| | | | |
|---|---|---|---|
| kǎi | kǒr | kùp | chèet |
| tǎhm | tòok | pìt | fàhk |
| sěe | sÒOt | sǒrn | sǎo |
| sùk | sìp | hùk | hǎh |
| lǔng | wùt | lǎi | nǒo |

**3** (i) (*f*) (ii) (*d*) (iii) (*b*) (iv) (*e*) (v) (*a*) (vi) (*c*)

# Unit 6

**bàirp fèuk hùt 1** (*a*) To send something by registered air-mail to Japan; 95 baht. (*b*) Three aerogrammes and four 5-baht stamps; 56 baht. (*c*) Three 9-baht stamps and an aerogramme; 39 baht. **2** (*a*) sòng bpóht-gáht bpai a-may-ri-gah tâo-rài? (*b*) sòng bpai tahng ah-gàht tâo-rài? (*c*) dtôrng-gahn (ao) sa-dtairm gâo bàht hâh doo-ung. (*d*) dtôrng-gahn (ao) jòt-mǎi ah-gàht sèe pàirn (*e*) túng mòt tâo-rài? **3** (*a*)doo-ung (*b*) tôo-ay (*c*) kon (*d*) chahm (*e*) kòo-ut (or gâir-o) (*f*) pàirn (*g*) jahn

**bàirp fèuk áhn   1**

| | | | |
|---|---|---|---|
| jai | pôot | tai | nahn |
| tum | bpai | púk | tǎir-o |
| mái | kǒr-tôht | jàhk | kǒrng |
| bpen | bpàirt | bàht | pairng |
| hòk | jòrt | mee | mǒo |
| lék | nǎo | yen | sěe |

**bòt àhn**   Yupha is Thai. She comes from Loei. Somchai is Yupha's husband. Somchai comes from Tak. Yupha and Somchai have five children. They have two sons and three daughters.

# Unit 7

**bàirp fèuk hùt   1**   kǒr pôot gùp kOOn Peter nòy, dâi mái ká? / káo ja glùp mêu-rai? / kâ. kòrp-kOOn kâ. sa-wùt dee kâ.   **2**   (*a*) kǒr pôot gùp kOOn Marisa nòy dâi mái krúp (ká)? (*b*) krai pôot krúp (ká)? (*c*) kǒr dtòr ber sǎhm-hâh-gâo. (*d*) ror sùk krôo ná krúp (ká). (*e*) kOOn Araya ja glùp mêu-rai? (*f*) (chôo-ay) pôot dung dung nòy dâi mái?   **3**   (*b*) kOOn Cha-nít mâi yòo krúp (kâ). òrk bpai tahn kâo. kít wâh ja glùp dtorn bài. (*c*) kOOn Wít-ta-yah mâi yòo krúp (kâ). òrk bpai tOO-rá. kít wâh ja glùp dtorn yen.

**bàirp fèuk áhn   1**

| | | | |
|---|---|---|---|
| mâi | nêe | pôr | mâir |
| dtèun | kôo | kài | gài |
| dtàir | sùng | sài | dtòr |
| chêu | châi | pêe | têe |
| nèung | lòr | nòy | mùn |

**2**   (from left to right) châi mái?; mâi châi; nêe tâo-rai?; pairng bpai nòy; mâi pairng ròrk; yêe-sìp bàht; těung sèe-yâirk; jòrt têe-nêe; yòo têe-nôhn; mâi bpen rai; sòng bpai tahng ah-gàht; jòt-mǎi ah-gàht sǒrng pàirn   **3**   (*a*) Soi 33 (*b*) 80 baht (*c*) It is too expensive. (*d*) The traffic is badly jammed.

# Unit 8

**bàirp fèuk hùt   1**   (*a*) sa-bai dee krúp (kâ). (*b*) bpen nít-nòy krúp (kâ). (*c*) nahn (mâi nahn) krúp (kâ). (*d*) mâi gèng krúp (kâ). (*e*) kòrp-kOOn krúp (kâ). (*f*) mee (mâi mee) krúp (kâ). (*g*) dtàirng ngahn láir-o (yung mâi dtàirng ngahn) krúp (kâ).   **2**   kOOn chêu a-rai ká? / ah-yÓO tâo-rài? / yòo meu-ung tai nahn mái? / dtàirng ngahn láir-o rěu yung? /

mee lôok láir-o rěu yung? / lôok ah-yÓO tâo-rài? **3** (*a*) sa-wùt dee
krúp (kâ) kOOn Sunisa. sa-bai dee lěr krúp (ká)? (*b*) chern kâhng nai
ná krúp (kâ). (*c*) yòo (meu-ung) ung-grìt nahn mái? (*d*) pêe-sǎo pôot
ung-grìt gèng. (*e*) mee pêe-nórng gèe kon? (*f*) nórng-chai ah-yÓO
tâo-rài?

**bàirp fèuk áhn 1**

| | | | |
|---|---|---|---|
| dtôrng | tíng | bâhn | hâi |
| róo | kêun | née | tâh |
| gâo | náhm* | láir-o | gÔOng |
| rórn | hôrng | séu | bpâi |
| nóhn | gâir-o | nâh | dâi |

(* pronounced with a long vowel when it occurs in isolation)
**2** (from left to right) dâi mái?; mâi dâi; sǎhm-sìp-hâh; kâo soy
mái?; róo-jùk mái?; gôr láir-o gun; kâo pùt gOOng; gâir-o nèung; kâo
nâh gài; tǎir-o née; ráhn ah-hǎn; túng mòt hâh-sìp bàht; sǒrng
róy bGaht. **4** (*a*) Two plates of shrimp fried rice and one plate of
duck rice (*b*) Duck rice (*c*) Red pork rice (*d*) Pepsi (*e*) Orange
juice

# Unit 9

**bàirp fèuk hùt 1** (*b*) bèu-a. mâi kôy chôrp bpen ta-hǎhn. yàhk
bpen kroo mâhk gwàh. (*c*) bèu-a. mâi kôy chôrp bpen kroo. yàhk
bpen mǒr mâhk gwàh. (*d*) bèu-a. mâi kôy chôrp bpen mǒr. yàhk
bpen lay-kǎh-nOO-gahn mâhk gwàh. (*e*) bèu-a. mâi kôy chôrp bpen
lay-kǎh-nOO-gahn. yàhk bpen núk tÓO-rá-gìt mâhk gwàh. (*f*) bèu-a.
mâi kôy chôrp bpen núk tÓO-rá-git. yàhk bpen núk núng-sěu pim
mâhk gwàh. (*g*) bèu-a. mâi kôy chôrp bpen nák núng-sěu pim. yàhk
bpen mâir bâhn mâhk gwàh. (*h*) bèu-a. mâi kôy chôrp bpen mâir
bâhn. yàhk bpen sàyt-tǎe mâhk gwàh. **2** (*a*) (ii), (iii), (iv), (vi),
(viii) (*b*) (i), (v), (vii), (ix), (x) **3** (*a*) (iii) (*b*) (ii) (*c*) (i) (*d*) (iii) (*e*) (iv)
(*f*) (ii)

**bàirp fèuk áhn 1**

| | | | |
|---|---|---|---|
| měu-un | ngern | deu-un | bèu-a |
| sěe-a | chôo-a-mohng | ná | sa-àht |
| kOOn | ká | mêu-a | sǒo-ay |
| pâhk | gèrt | poo-gèt | |

**2** kOOn chêu a-rai? sěe dairng sǒo-ay mâhk; rêe-uk wâh nóy-nàh; loh
la tâo-rài?; lée-o sái têe-nêe; ao náhm a-arai ká?; kǒr bpép-sêe kòo-
ut nèung; ao kòo-ut yài; yàhk ja long ta-bee-un dôo-ay; pôot pah-sǎh

The Royal Palace, Bangkok

# KEY TO THE EXERCISES

## Unit 1

**bàirp fèuk hùt** **1** (*a*) (káo) chêu Peter. (*b*) (káo) nahm sa-gOOn Green. (*c*) (káo) bpen kon ung-grìt. (*d*) (káo) bpen núk tÓO-rá-gìt. (*e*) (káo) chêu Malee. (*f*) (káo) bpen kon tai. (*g*) châi. **2** (*a*) (pǒm (dee-chún) chêu ... (*b*) nǎhm sa-gOOn ... (*c*) bpen kon ... (*d*) bpen ... / tum ngahn gùp ... **3** (*a*) (ii) (*b*) (iv) (*c*) (i) (*d*) (iii) **4** (*b*) káo chêu John. nahm sa-gOOn Stevens. bpen kon a-may-ri-gun. mah jàhk Florida. bpen núk sèuk-sǎh. (*c*) káo chêu Makoto. nahm sa-gOOn Iwasaki. bpen kon yêe-bpÒOn. mah jàhk Tokyo. bpen núk tÓO-rá-gìt. (*d*) káo chêu Paula. nahm sa-gOOn Besson. bpen kon fa-rùng-sàyt. mah jàhk Paris. bpen kroo. **5** (*a*) kǒr-tôht krúp (kâ) kOOn chêu a-rai? (*b*) káo chêu Sǒm-chai châi mái? (*c*) káo nahm sa-gOOn a-rai? (*d*) káo bpen kon tai châi mái? (*e*) káo bpen kroo châi mái?

**bàirp fèuk áhn** **2**

| | | | |
|---|---|---|---|
| mah | yaa | nahm | ngahn |
| wun | num | rum | ror |
| norn | rai | nai | yai |
| lao | yao | rao | yorm |

**3** yahm lao mah. ror nahn. nahng lah nai. yai rum nahn.

**4** (*a*) 236-4890 (*b*) 580-7359 (*c*) 225-7381 (*d*) 693-2145 (*e*) 371-9548

## Unit 2

**bàirp fèuk hùt** **1** (*b*) pairng bpai nòy krúp (kâ). hâh-sìp bàht dâi mái? (*c*) pairng bpai nòy krúp (kâ). hòk-sìp bàht dâi mái? (*d*) pairng bpai nòy krúp (kâ). yêe-sìp bàht dâi mái? (*e*) pairng bpai nòy krúp (kâ). sǎhm-sìp bàht dâi mái? **2** (*a*) nêe tâo-rài krúp (ká)? (*b*) pairng bpai nòy. (*c*) lót nòy dâi mái? (*d*) hâh-sìp bàht dâi mái? (*e*) sěe dairng mâi sǒo-ay. (*f*) sěe kěe-o mee mái? **3** (*a*) sùp-bpa-rót bai la tâo-rài? (*b*) sôm loh la tâo-rài? (*c*) glôo-ay wěe la tâo-rài? (*d*) ma-la-gor bai la tâo-rài? (*e*) ma-môo-ung bai la tâo-rài? (*f*) dtairng-moh bai la tâo-rài? (*g*) nòy-nàh loh la tâo-rài? **4** nêe (rêe-uk wâh) a-rai? / a-rai ná? / ma-môo-ung châi mái krúp? / bai la tâo-rài? / lót nòy dâi mái?

**bàirp fèuk áhn 2**

| gin | gun | jai | doo |
|-----|-----|-----|-----|
| dee | dtah | dtee | bin |
| bai | bpai | bpee | mohng |
| bpoo | rohng | yOOng | un |

4 (*a*) yOOng bin bpai bin mah. (*b*) lOOng yin dee mah doo. (*c*) nai nah mee bpoo dum (*d*) yahm lao dtee ngoo dtai. (*e*) ror doo nahng ngahm dung. 5 (*a*) (iii) (*b*) (v) (*c*) (i) (*d*) (ii) (*e*) (iv)

# Unit 3

**bàirp fèuk hùt** 1 (*a*) bpai sa-yǎhm sa-kwair mái? (*b*) bpai ta-nǒn sÒO-kǑOm-wít soy sǎhm-sìp gâo mái? (*c*) bpai wút prá-gâir-o mái? (*d*) bpai sa-nǎhm bin dorn meu-ung mái? (*e*) bpai rohng-rairm ree-yen mái? 2 (*a*) (v) B (*b*) (iii) E (*c*) (iv) A (*d*) (i) C (*e*) (ii) D 3 bpai ta-nǒn sÒO-kǑOm-wít soy hâh-sìp sǎhm mái? / kâo krúp. bpai sÒOt soy. / châi krúp. bpai tâo-rài? / pairng bpai nòy krúp. / hâh-sìp bàht dâi mái? 4 (*a*) tǔung sèe-yâirk láir-o lée-o sái. (*b*) jòrt têe-nôhn. (*c*) ler-ee bpai èek nít nèung. (*d*) bpai sÒOt soy (*e*) lée-o kwǎh dtrong née

**bàirp fèuk áhn** 1 (live syllables marked in bold)

| **bpai** | èek | nít | jòrt | mâhk |
|----------|-----|-----|------|------|
| **gun** | **dee** | **ree-noh** | dtìt | **rohng** |

**2**

| bèep | nahng | gùt | jÒOt | nút |
|------|-------|-----|------|-----|
| bpee | dàap | jahn | jàhk | dtai |
| lâhp | rao | mêet | rôrp | bpàhk |

**3**

| yâhk | mee | nút | gùp |
|------|-----|-----|-----|
| ngahn | yOOng | gùt | mâhk |
| jàhk | rêep | ai | norn |
| yorm | lôok | bpai | jòrt |

# Unit 4

**bàirp fèuk hùt** 1 (*a*) (iii) (*b*) (v) (*c*) (i) (*d*) (ii) (*e*) (iv) 2 (*a*) kǒr doo may-noo nòy. (*b*) ao ba-mèe náhm sǒrng chahm (*c*) ao kâo pùt gài sǎhm jahn. (*d*) ao núm kǎirng bplào hâh gâir-o. (*e*) chék bin krúp (kâ)   **3**   They wanted two plates of shrimp fried rice, a Pepsi and a large Singha beer. They ended up with a plate of chicken fried rice, a plate of pork fried rice, a Coke and a small Singha beer.

**bàirp fèuk áhn**   **1**

| chai | soy | bàht | kum | chôrp |
| tahng | pah | púk | tum | tÓOk |
| keun | deung | dtèuk | keu | ker-ee |
| ler-ee | pairng | dairng | kon | long |
| yen | lék | bpen | jèt | gôr |

**3**   (*a*) (i) (*b*) (iii)

# Unit 5

**bàirp fèuk hùt**   **1**   (*b*) Eddie, Nikki láir-o gôr Nuan yòo kâhng nôrk. (*c*) Sue láir Tom yòo kâhng bon. (*d*) Peter yòo kâhng lâhng. (*e*) Nikki láir Eddie yòo kâhng nâh. (*f*) Nuan yòo kâhng lǔng. **2**   (*a*) tǎir-o née mee dtôo toh-ra-sùp mái? (*b*) tǎir-o née mee bor-ri-gahn tài àyk-ga-sǎhn mái? (*c*) tǎir-o née mee hôrng náhm mái? (*d*) tǎir-o née mee rohng pa-yah-bahn mái? (*e*) tǎir-o née mee ta-nah-kahn mái?   **3**   (*a*) sa-nǎhm gee-lah. (*b*) ráhn ah-hǎhn kwǔn-jai. (*c*) dtôo toh-ra-sùp

**bàirp fèuk áhn**   **1**

| kǎi | kǒr | kùp | chèet |
| tǎhm | tòok | pìt | fàhk |
| sěe | sÒOt | sǒrn | sǎo |
| sùk | sìp | hùk | hǎh |
| lǔng | wùt | lǎi | nǒo |

**3**   (i) (*f*) (ii) (*d*) (iii) (*b*) (iv) (*e*) (v) (*a*) (vi) (*c*)

# Unit 6

**bàirp fèuk hùt**   **1**   (*a*) To send something by registered air-mail to Japan; 95 baht. (*b*) Three aerogrammes and four 5-baht stamps; 56 baht. (*c*) Three 9-baht stamps and an aerogramme; 39 baht. **2**   (*a*) sòng bpóht-gáht bpai a-may-ri-gah tâo-rài? (*b*) sòng bpai tahng ah-gàht tâo-rài? (*c*) dtôrng-gahn (ao) sa-dtairm gâo bàht hâh doo-ung. (*d*) dtôrng-gahn (ao) jòt-mǎi ah-gàht sèe pàirn (*e*) túng mòt tâo-rài?   **3**   (*a*) doo-ung (*b*) tôo-ay (*c*) kon (*d*) chahm (*e*) kòo-ut   (or gâir-o) (*f*) pàirn (*g*) jahn

**bàirp fèuk áhn  1**

| | | | |
|---|---|---|---|
| jai | pôot | tai | nahn |
| tum | bpai | púk | tǎir-o |
| mái | kǒr-tôht | jàhk | kǒrng |
| bpen | bpàirt | bàht | pairng |
| hòk | jòrt | mee | mǒo |
| lék | nǎo | yen | sěe |

**bòt àhn**  Yupha is Thai. She comes from Loei. Somchai is Yupha's husband. Somchai comes from Tak. Yupha and Somchai have five children. They have two sons and three daughters.

# Unit 7

**bàirp fèuk hùt  1**  kǒr pôot gùp kOOn Peter nòy, dâi mái ká? / káo ja glùp mêu-rai? / kâ. kòrp-kOOn kâ. sa-wùt dee kâ.  **2**  (a) kǒr pôot gùp kOOn Marisa nòy dâi mái krúp (ká)? (b) krai pôot krúp (ká)? (c) kǒr dtòr ber sǎhm-hâh-gâo. (d) ror sùk krôo ná krúp (ká). (e) kOOn Araya ja glùp mêu-rai? (f) (chôo-ay) pôot dung dung nòy dâi mái?  **3**  (b) kOOn Cha-nít mâi yòo krúp (kâ). òrk bpai tahn kâo. kít wâh ja glùp dtorn bài. (c) kOOn Wít-ta-yah mâi yòo krúp (kâ). òrk bpai tOO-rá. kít wâh ja glùp dtorn yen.

**bàirp fèuk áhn  1**

| | | | |
|---|---|---|---|
| mâi | nêe | pôr | mâir |
| dtèun | kôo | kài | gài |
| dtàir | sùng | sài | dtòr |
| chêu | châi | pêe | têe |
| nèung | lòr | nòy | mùn |

**2**  (from left to right) châi mái?; mâi châi; nêe tâo-rai?; pairng bpai nòy; mâi pairng ròrk; yêe-sìp bàht; těung sèe-yâirk; jòrt têe-nêe; yòo têe-nôhn; mâi bpen rai; sòng bpai tahng ah-gàht; jòt-mǎi ah-gàht sǒrng pàirn  **3**  (a) Soi 33 (b) 80 baht (c) It is too expensive. (d) The traffic is badly jammed.

# Unit 8

**bàirp fèuk hùt  1**  (a) sa-bai dee krúp (kâ). (b) bpen nít-nòy krúp (kâ). (c) nahn (mâi nahn) krúp (kâ). (d) mâi gèng krúp (kâ). (e) kòrp-kOOn krúp (kâ). (f) mee (mâi mee) krúp (kâ). (g) dtàirng ngahn láir-o (yung mâi dtàirng ngahn) krúp (kâ).  **2**  kOOn chêu a-rai ká? / ah-yÓO tâo-rài? / yòo meu-ung tai nahn mái?/ dtàirng ngahn láir-o rěu yung? /

mee lôok láir-o rĕu yung? / lôok ah-yÓO tâo-rài?   **3**   (*a*) sa-wùt dee
krúp (kâ) kOOn Sunisa. sa-bai dee lĕr krúp (ká)? (*b*) chern kâhng nai
ná krúp (kâ). (*c*) yòo (meu-ung) ung-grìt nahn mái? (*d*) pêe-sǎo pôot
ung-grìt gèng. (*e*) mee pêe-nórng gèe kon?   (*f*) nórng-chai ah-yÓO
tâo-rài?

**bàirp fèuk áhn**   **1**

| dtôrng | tíng | bâhn | hâi |
|--------|------|------|-----|
| róo | kêun | née | tâh |
| gâo | náhm* | láir-o | gÔOng |
| rórn | hôrng | séu | bpâi |
| nóhn | gâir-o | nâh | dâi |

(* pronounced with a long vowel when it occurs in isolation)
**2**      (from left to right) dâi mái?; mâi dâi; sǎhm-sìp-hâh; kâo soy
mái?; róo-jùk mái?; gôr láir-o gun; kâo pùt gOOng; gâir-o nèung; kâo
nâh gài; tǎir-o née; ráhn ah-hǎn; túng mòt hâh-sìp bàht; sŏrng
róy bGaht.   **4**   (*a*) Two plates of shrimp fried rice and one plate of
duck rice (*b*) Duck rice (*c*) Red pork rice (*d*) Pepsi (*e*) Orange
juice

# Unit 9

**bàirp fèuk hùt**   **1**    (*b*) bèu-a. mâi kôy chôrp bpen ta-hǎhn. yàhk
bpen kroo mâhk gwàh. (*c*) bèu-a. mâi kôy chôrp bpen kroo. yàhk
bpen mŏr mâhk gwàh. (*d*) bèu-a. mâi kôy chôrp bpen mŏr. yàhk
bpen lay-kǎh-nOO-gahn mâhk gwàh. (*e*) bèu-a. mâi kôy chôrp bpen
lay-kǎh-nOO-gahn. yàhk bpen núk tÓO-rá-gìt mâhk gwàh. (*f*) bèu-a.
mâi kôy chôrp bpen núk tÓO-rá-git. yàhk bpen núk núng-sĕu pim
mâhk gwàh. (*g*) bèu-a. mâi kôy chôrp bpen nák núng-sĕu pim. yàhk
bpen mâir bâhn mâhk gwàh. (*h*) bèu-a. mâi kôy chôrp bpen mâir
bâhn. yàhk bpen sàyt-tĕe mâhk gwàh.   **2**      (*a*) (ii), (iii), (iv), (vi),
(viii) (*b*) (i), (v), (vii), (ix), (x)   **3**   (*a*) (iii) (*b*) (ii) (*c*) (i) (*d*) (iii) (*e*) (iv)
(*f*) (ii)

**bàirp fèuk áhn**   **1**

| mĕu-un | ngern | deu-un | bèu-a |
|--------|-------|--------|-------|
| sĕe-a | chôo-a-mohng | ná | sa-àht |
| kOOn | ká | mêu-a | sŏo-ay |
| pâhk | gèrt | poo-gèt | |

**2** kOOn chêu a-rai? sĕe dairng sŏo-ay mâhk; rêe-uk wâh nóy-nàh; loh
la tâo-rài?; lée-o sái têe-née; ao náhm a-arai ká?; kŏr bpép-sêe kòo-
ut nèung; ao kòo-ut yài; yàhk ja long ta-bee-un dôo-ay; pôot pah-sǎh

——— **bàirp fèuk hùt** แบบฝึกหัด ———

1 'I think it would be better to ...' A friend is always trying to organise your life by telling you what you should do. Resist the suggestion and, using the prompt in brackets, point out you have a better idea.

*Example:*

**Friend** kOOn koo-un ja bpai têe-o pút-ta-yah (poo-gèt)
**You** kít wâh bpai têe-o poo-gèt dee gwàh

(a) kOOn koo-un ja bpai dtorn yen (dtorn cháo)
(b) kOOn koo-un ja bpai táirk-sêe (rót-may)
(c) kOOn koo-un ja púk yòo têe bâhn rao (rohng-rairm)
(d) kOOn koo-un ja sùng ah-hǎhn fa-rùng (ah-hǎhn tai)

2 What would you say if you did not know how to:

(a) do something?
(b) get somewhere?

— 221 —

(c) eat something?
(d) read something?
(e) use something?
(f) repair something?

3 Here are some 'forbidden' notices. Match the Thai script with
  the translation.

(a) ห้ามถ่ายรูป      (i)   No Parking

(b) ห้ามจอดรถ      (ii)   Sale Prohibited

(c) ห้ามสูบบุหรี่    (iii)   No Entry

(d) ห้ามเข้า       (iv)   No Smoking

(e) ห้ามขาย      (v)   Photography Forbidden

―――――――― **bòt àhn** บทอ่าน ――――――――

A friend from England is planning to make a trip to Phuket.
Using the advertisement on the following page, make a note
of possible options, including method of travel, length of stay,
day of departure and cost. Make a note also of the name, address
and telephone number of the company.

Notice the large number of English words used in the advertisement
on the following page. This is common in advertising. You will find
the vocabulary for the advertisement on page 224.

## ฟาร์อีสท์ฯ ทัวร์

๑๘๙๒-๔ ถนนเพชรบุรีตัดใหม่ กรุงเทพฯ ๑๐๓๑๐
โทร. ๓๙๑-๖๑๐๑-๓

---

แพ็คเก็จทัวร์ ออกเดินทางทุกวันโดยเครื่องบิน หรือรถโค้ชปรับอากาศ

---

เครื่องบิน ๓ วัน ๒ คืน, รถโค้ช ๓ วัน ๔ คืน

| รายการท่องเที่ยว | | รถโค้ช | เครื่องบิน |
|---|---|---|---|
| *เชียงใหม่ | ดอยอินทนนท์ ดอยสุเทพ สันกำแพง หมู่บ้านชาวแม้ว พักโรงแรมช้างเผือก | ๓,๑๕๐ | ๕,๔๐๐ |
| *ภูเก็ต | เกาะพีพี หาดราไวย์ อ่าวพังงา พัก ร.ร. หาดป่าตอง | ๓,๖๐๐ | ๖,๔๐๐ |

---

วีคเอนทัวร์ออกเดินทางทุกคืนวันศุกร์ โดยรถโค้ชปรับอากาศ กลับค่ำวันอาทิตย์ หรือเช้าวันจันทร์

---

| | | |
|---|---|---|
| * เชียงใหม่ | ดอยสุเทพ สันกำแพง หมู่บ้านชาวแม้ว พัก ร.ร. เชียงใหม่ภูคำ | ๒,๒๐๐ |
| * ภูเก็ต | เกาะพีพี หาดราไวย์ พัก ร.ร. หาดป่าตอง (กลับเช้าวันจันทร์) | ๓,๑๐๐ |

---

| | |
|---|---|
| ฟาร์อีสท์ฯ ทัวร์ | *Far East Tours* |
| แพ็คเก็จทัวร์ | *package tour* |
| โดย | *by* |
| เครื่องบิน | *aeroplane* |
| รถโค้ช | *coach* |
| รายการท่องเที่ยว | *itinerary* |
| ร.ร. (โรงแรม) | *hotel* |
| วีคเอนทัวร์ | *weekend tour* |
| ค่ำ | *evening* |

tai bpen mái?; lôok chai ah-yÓO săhm kòo-up; ja lâirk   bplèe-un
sŏrng róy   **3**   (a) Chiangmai (b) 30 years (c) The air is cleaner in
Chiangmai and there is less traffic.

**bòt àhn**   Khun Chanida is from the South. She was born in Phuket.
Her father was a policeman and her mother a housewife. They
had five children. Chanida's parents and her brothers and sisters
moved here when Chanida was five years old. Chanida's older
brother's name is Wit. He did well at school. He said he wanted
to be a doctor.

# Unit 10

**bàirp fèuk hùt**   **1**   (a) bpen. (b) pèt. (c) bpen. (d) a-ròy. (e) mâi bpen.
(f) mâi sòop.   **2**   ao gairng néu-a, bplah bprêe-o wăhn, gài pùt kǐng
láir-o gôr dtôm yum gÔOng.   **3**   (a) dtôm yum mai ao pèt mâhk ná.
(b) gairng néu-a-pèt (mâhk) mái? (c) gài pùt kǐng a-ròy mâhk ná.
(d) mee pǒn-la-mái a-rai bâhng? (e) ka-nǒm tai wǎhn gern bpai.
mee ai dtim mái?

**bàirp fèuk áhn 1**

| | | | | |
|---|---|---|---|---|
| gwàh | kwǎh | grOOng | bpra-dtoo | bplah |
| bplào | dtrong | glai | glâi | glùp |
| krai | klái | bpra-dtâyt | prá | ta-nǒn |
| ka-nàht | sa-nÒOk | sa-tǎhn | sa-bai | bor-ri-sùt |

**2**   (i) (b); (ii) (c) ;(iii) (d) ;(iv) (a)   **3**   (2) and (4)   **4**   The waiter got
two dishes right. He brought sweet and sour *pork* (instead of *fish*)
and *crab* (instead of *shrimp*) 'tom yam'.

**bòt àhn**   (a) There's hardly any work apart from rice farming.
(b) She doesn't like farming. It's hard. (c) Washing up (d) No,
sometimes she thinks it's boring. (e) Because she hasn't got
enough money.

# Unit 11

**bàirp fèuk hùt**   **1**   (a) mâi gèng ròrk krúp (kâ). (b) ker-ee krúp (kâ).
(c) mâi nahn krúp (kâ). (d) ree-un têe ... krúp (kâ). (e) dâi nít-nòy
krúp (kâ). (f) bpen nít-nòy krúp (kâ). (g) yâhk měu-un gun krúp (kâ).
**2**   Paula pôot pah-sǎh jeen gèng. Nicola pôot pah-sǎh jeen dâi
nít-nòy. Kevin pôot pah-sǎh yêe-bpÒOn dâi klôrng. Stephen pôot
pah-sǎh yêe-bpÒOn gèng. Sarah pôot pah-sǎh yêe-bpÒOn dâi nít-nòy.
Sharon pôot pah-sǎh gâo-lěe dâi klôrng. Sarah pôot pah-sǎh gâo-lěe

gèng. Kevin pôot pah-săh gâo-lĕe dâi nít-nòy. Nicola pôot pah-săh wêe-ut-nahm dâi klôrng. Kathy pôot pah-săh wêe-ut-nahm gèng. Paula pôot pah-săh wêe-ut-nahm dâi nít-nòy.

**bàirp fèuk áhn**   1   mâi kôy gèng tâo-rài; mâi kôy a-ròy tâo-rài; mâi kôy pairng tâo-rài; tum-mai pôot tai chút; tum-mai mâi chôrp; tum-mai mâi gin; prór wâh mâir bpen kon tai; prór wâh mâi sŏo-ay; prór wâh mâi a-ròy; ker-ee bpai mái?; ker-ee doo mái?; ker-ee gin mái?   2   (a) Sukanya Saengjan (b) 22 (c) Fluently (d) She cannot read or write Cambodian.
3

## Application for Temporary Position

**Forename** Mr Wichai          **Surname** Saitorng

**Date of birth** 8   **Month** December   **B.E.** 2496

**Address** 21 / 3   **Soi** Aree   **Road** Phaholyothin

**Tambol** ....... **Amphoe** Phaya Thai   **Province** Bangkok

**Nationality** Thai

**Present position** Civil servant   **Monthly salary** 14,500 baht

**Educational background**

2518 Graduated with Bachelor's degree from Ramkhamhaeng University

**Work experience**

2518 – 2525   Worked with UNHCR in Aranyaprathet, Prachinburi.

2525 – present   Working at the Ministry of Foreign Affairs

**Knowledge of Cambodian**

|              | speaking | reading | writing |
|--------------|----------|---------|---------|
| **fluent**   | ✓        |         |         |
| **good**     |          | ✓       |         |
| **a little** |          |         | ✓       |

**bòt àhn**   (a) About six months (b) He studied on his own. (c) He used a textbook and tapes. (d) He can read a little, if they are easy words. But he can't really write the language.

# Unit 12

**bàirp fèuk hùt** **1** (a) bplair wâh 'mee-a'. (b) bplair wâh 'gin'. (c) bplair wâh 'róo'. (d) bplair wâh 'ao-a-rai'? **2** a-rai ná? / pôot cháh cháh nòy dâi mái? / 'nǔng' bplair wâh a-rai? / kâo jai (láir-o).

**bàirp fèuk áhn** **1** a-rai ná?; pôot èek tee dâi mái?; pôot cháh cháh nòy dâi mái?; bplair wâh a-rai?; mâi kâo jai; sa-gòt yung-ngai?; kěe-un yung-ngai?; fung róo rêu-ung; mâi róo rêu-ung. **2** soy ga-sǎym-sǔn; bee-a sǐng; gèp sa-dtung; bprai-sa-nee; bpóht-gáht; sa-dtairm **3** (a) (iv), (b) (v), (c) (vi), (d) (vii), (e) (iii), (f) (ii), (g) (i)

**bòt àhn** (a) Because her husband is English. (b) For three years. (c) She didn't want to come because she could hardly speak English. She had studied it at school but wasn't very good. When English people ·spoke she couldn't understand a thing. (d) She studied English at a local school. She studied for two or three hours every day. (e) Her English really improved a lot.

# Unit 13

**bàirp fèuk hùt** **1** (a) sǎhm mohng krêung. (b) bài sǒrng mohng yêe-sìp nah-tee (c) hâh mohng yen (d) èek sìp-hâh nah-tee sèe tÔOm. **2** (a) (iii) (b) (iv) (c) (ii) (d) (i) **3** (a) bpai chee-ung-mài jorng dtǒo-a têe-nǎi? (b) bpai sǒng-klǎh séu dtǒo-a têe-nǎi? (c) bpai na-korn pa-nom kêun rót-may têe-nǎi? (d) rót-may bpai kǒrn-gàirn òrk jàhk têe-nǎi? (e) rót-may bpai chee-ung-mài òrk gèe mohng? (f) chái way-lah dern tahng gèe chôo-a-mohng?

**bàirp fèuk áhn** **1** (a) (iv) (b) (vi) (c) (ii) (d) (ix) (e) (vii) (f) (xi) (g) (i) (h) (x) (i) (xiii) (j) (v) (k) (iii) (l) (viii) (m) (xii) **2** (a) หนองคายอยู่ ห่างจากกรุงเทพฯ ๖๑๔ กิโลเมตร (b) บริษัท วี ไอ พี จำกัด มีรถไปหนองคายวันละ ๒ เที่ยว (c) รถไปหนองคายออกเวลา ๐๘.๐๐ และ ๒๑.๓๐ นาฬิกา (d) ใช้เวลาเดินทางประมาณ ๑๐ ชั่วโมง (e) ค่า โดยสารคนละ ๓๘๐ บาท

# Unit 14

**bàirp fèuk hùt** **1** mee hôrng wâhng mái krúp? / châi krúp. / hâh wun krúp. kâh hôrng wun la tâo-rài krúp? / kǒr doo hôrng gòrn dâi mái? **2** (a) kǒr fàhk glôrng tài rôop nai dtôo sáyf dâi mái? (b) kǒr fàhk gra-bpǎo nai dtôo sáyf dâi mái? (c) kǒr fàhk gOOn-jair nai dtôo sáyf dâi mái? (d) kǒr fàhk núng-sěu dern-tahng nai dtôo sáyf dâi mái? **3** (a) wun têe gâo mók-ga-rah (b) wun têe sìp-gâo mí-tOO-nah (c) wun têe sǎhm-sìp-èt sǐng-hǎh (d) wun têe hâh préut-sa-jìk-gah-yon

**bàirp fèuk áhn** I've worked here nearly 20 years. It's alright working here. I clean the rooms and do the laundry. I come to work at 8 a.m. and go home at 4 p.m. Most of the guests here are foreigners. There are farangs, Chinese and Japanese too. Some are very kind. They give tips of over 100 baht. But it's the rainy season now. There aren't many guests. There's not much work either. So I sit chatting with my friends all day.·

# Unit 15

**bàirp fèuk hùt** **1** (a) kít wâh bpai dtorn cháo dee gwàh. (b) kít wâh bpai rót-may dee gwàh. (c) kít wâh púk yoo rohng rairm dee gwàh. (d) kít wâh sùng ah-hǎhn tai dee gwàh. **2** (a) mâi sâhp wâh ja tum yung-ngai. (b) mâi sâhp wâh ja bpai yung-ngai. (c) mâi sâhp ·wâh ja gin yung-ngai. (d) mâi sâhp wâh ja àhn yung-ngai. (e) mâi sâhp wâh ja chái yung-ngai. (f) mâi sâhp wâh ja sôrm yung-ngai. **3** (a) (v) (b) (i) (c) (iv) (d) (iii) (e) (ii)

# APPENDICES

## Consonant classes

The chart below lists all the Thai consonants according to class
and gives the pronunciation for each consonant both at the
beginning of a word and at the end. Perhaps the easiest way
to remember the class of a consonant is to memorise the
shorter lists of mid class and high class consonants so
that everything not on those lists can be assumed to be
low class.

**Low class**

|         | น | ม | ง | ร | ล | ย | ว |
|---------|---|---|---|---|---|---|---|
| initial | n | m | ng | r | l | y | w |
| final   | n | m | ng | n | n | y | w |

|         | ค | ช | ซ | ท | พ | ฟ |
|---------|---|---|---|---|---|---|
| initial | k | ch | s | t | p | f |
| final   | k | t | t | t | p | p |

|         | ฆ | ฑ | ภ | ญ | ณ |
|---------|---|---|---|---|---|
| initial | k | t | p | y | n |
| final   | k | t | p | n | n |

|         | ฌ | ฒ | ฬ | ฬ | ฮ |
|---------|---|---|---|---|---|
| initial | ch | t | t | l | h |
| final   | – | t | t | n | – |

## Mid class

| | ก | จ | ด | ต | บ | ป | อ | ฎ | ฏ |
|---|---|---|---|---|---|---|---|---|---|
| initial | g | j | d | dt | b | bp | zero | d | dt |
| final | k | t | t | t | p | p | – | t | t |

## High class

| | ข | ฉ | ถ | ผ | ฝ | ศ,ส,ษ | ห | ฐ |
|---|---|---|---|---|---|---|---|---|
| initial | k | ch | t | p | f | s | h | t |
| final | k | t | t | p | p | t | – | t |

# ——— Vowels ———

## Long vowels

| –า | –อ | โ– | ◌ี | ◌ู | ◌ื | เ– | แ– | เ–ีย | เ–ือ | ◌ัว | เ–ิ |
|---|---|---|---|---|---|---|---|---|---|---|---|
| -ah | -or | -oh | -ee | -oo | -eu | -ay | -air | -ee-a | -eu-a | -oo-a | -er |

## Short vowels

| ◌ั | ไ– | ใ– | ◌ิ | ◌ุ | ◌ึ | เ◌ | แ◌ | เ–า | –ะ |
|---|---|---|---|---|---|---|---|---|---|
| -u | -ai | -ai | -i | **-oo** | -eu | -e | -air | -ao | -a |

# Summary of tone rules

## Words without tone marks

| *initial consonant class* | LIVE SYLLABLE | DEAD SYLLABLE | |
|---|---|---|---|
| | | SHORT VOWEL | LONG VOWEL |
| LOW CLASS | **MID TONE** | **HIGH TONE** | **FALLING TONE** |
| MID CLASS | **MID TONE** | **LOW TONE** | **LOW TONE** |
| HIGH CLASS | **RISING TONE** | **LOW TONE** | **LOW TONE** |

## Words with tone marks

| *initial consonant class* | mái àyk (-่) | mái toh (-้) | mái dtree (-๊) | mái jùt-dta-wah (-๋) |
|---|---|---|---|---|
| LOW CLASS | **FALLING** | **HIGH** | **HIGH** | **RISING** |
| MID CLASS | **LOW** | **FALLING** | **HIGH** | **RISING** |
| HIGH CLASS | **LOW** | **FALLING** | **HIGH** | **RISING** |

# —————— Dictionary order ——————

A *Thai-English Student's Dictionary* (Stanford) by Mary Haas is essential for any serious student of Thai. *Robertson's Practical English-Thai Dictionary* (Tuttle) is invaluable for the beginner.

## *Consonants*

| | | | | | |
|---|---|---|---|---|---|
| ก | g | ณ | n | ร | r |
| ข | k | ด | d | ฤ | reu |
| ค | k | ต | dt | ฤๅ | reu |
| ฆ | k | ถ | t | ล | l |
| ง | ng | ท | t | ฦ | leu |
| จ | j | ธ | t | ฦๅ | leu |
| ฉ | ch | น | n | ว | w |
| ช | ch | บ | b | ศ | s |
| ซ | s | ป | bp | ษ | s |
| ฌ | ch | ผ | p | ส | s |
| ญ | y | ฝ | f | ห | h |
| ฎ | d | พ | p | ฬ | l |
| ฏ | dt | ฟ | f | อ | zero |
| ฐ | t | ภ | p | ฮ | h |
| ฑ | t | ม | m | | |
| ฒ | t | ย | y | | |

# *Vowels*

| | | | |
|---|---|---|---|
| –อ | -or | เ–อะ | -er |
| –ะ | -a | เ–ะ | -e |
| ◌ุ | -u- | เ–า | -aw |
| –ัว | -oo-a | เ–าะ | -or |
| –า | -ah | เ–ื | -er |
| –ำ | -um | เ–ีย | -ee-a |
| ◌ิ | -i | เ–ียะ | -ee-a |
| ◌ี | -ee | เ–ือ | -eu-a |
| ◌ึ | -eu | แ– | -air |
| ◌ื | -eu | แ–ื | -air |
| ◌ู | **-oo** | แ–ะ | -air |
| ◌ู | -oo | โ– | -oh |
| เ– | -ay | โ–ะ | -o |
| เ–ื | -e | ไ– | -ai |
| เ–ย | -er-ee | ใ– | -ai |

# THAI – ENGLISH
## VOCABULARY.

Numbers given in brackets refer to the unit in which each word was first given.

| | | |
|---|---|---|
| **a-may-ri-gah (6)** | *America* | อเมริกา |
| **a-may-ri-gun (1)** | *American* | อเมริกัน |
| **a-rai? (1)** | *what?* | อะไร |
| **a-rai gôr dâi (10)** | *anything* | อะไรก็ได้ |
| **a-rai ná? (2)** | *pardon?* | อะไรนะ |
| **a-ròy (2)** | *to be tasty* | อร่อย |
| **ah-gàht (9)** | *weather, climate* | อากาศ |
| **ah-tít (14)** | *week* | อาทิตย์ |
| **ah-yÓO (8)** | *age* | อายุ |
| **àhn (11)** | *to read* | อ่าน |
| **àht (ja) (14)** | *may* | อาจ(จะ) |
| **ai dtim (10)** | *ice-cream* | ไอสครีม |
| **air (15)** | *air-conditioned* | แอร์ |
| **ao (4)** | *want* (verb) | เอา |
| **ao ... bpai (13)** | *to take* | เอา ... ไป |
| **ba-mèe (4)** | *egg noodles* | บะหมี่ |
| **ba-mèe náhm (4)** | *egg noodle soup* | บะหมี่น้ำ |
| **bâhn (9)** | *house, home* | บ้าน |
| **bahng (9)** | *some* | บาง |
| **... bâhng (10)** | (see **kum ùt-tì-bai,** Unit 10) | ... บ้าง |

| | | |
|---|---|---|
| **bàht (2)** | *baht* (unit of currency) | บาท |
| **bai (13)** | classifier for ticket | ใบ |
| **bài (7)** | *afternoon* | บ่าย |
| **bee-a sǐng (4)** | *Singha Beer* | เบียร์สิงห์ |
| **ber (7)** | *number* | เบอร์ |
| **bOO-rèe (10)** | *cigarette* | บุหรี่ |
| **bor-ris-sùt (1)** | *company* | บริษัท |
| **bòrk (wâh) (9)** | *to say, tell (that)* | บอก (ว่า) |
| **bung-ga-loh (15)** | *bungalow* | บังกาโล |
| **bpai (3)** | *go* | ไป |
| **... bpai nòy (2)** | *a little too ...* | ... ไปหน่อย |
| **... bpai tahng nǎi? (5)** | *which way is it to ...?* | ... ไปทางไหน |
| **bpàirt-sìp (2)** | *eighty* | แปดสิบ |
| **bpen (1) (8)** | *to be; to be able to* | เป็น |
| **bpen yung-ngai? (9)** | *how is it?* | เป็นอย่าง |
| **bpép-sêe (4)** | *Pepsi* | เป๊ปซี่ |
| **bper sen (14)** | *per cent* | เปอร์เซ็นท์ |
| **bpèt (4)** | *duck* | เป็ด |
| **bplah (12)** | *fish* | ปลา |
| **bplair (12)** | *to translate* | แปล |
| **... bplair wâh a-rai? (12)** | *what does ... mean?* | แปลว่าอะไร |
| **bplào (8)** | *no* | เปล่า |
| **bplèe-un (14)** | *to change* | เปลี่ยน |
| **bplòrt-pai (14)** | *safe* (adj) | ปลอดภัย |

| | | |
|---|---|---|
| **bpóht-gáht (6)** | *postcard* | โปสการ์ด |
| **bporn (6)** | *pound* | ปอนด์ |
| **bpra-mahn (5)** | *about* | ประมาณ |
| **bpra-tâyt lao (15)** | *Laos* | ประเทศลาว |
| **bprai-sa-nee (5)** | *post office* | ไปรษณีย์ |
| **bprùp ah-gàht (14)** | *air-conditioned* | ปรับอากาศ |
| **bpun-hǎa (15)** | *problem* | ปัญหา |
| **cháh (12)** | *slow* | ช้า |
| **chahm (4)** | *bowl* | ชาม |
| **châht (1)** | *nation* | ชาติ |
| **chái (13)** | *to use* | ใช้ |
| **chái way-lah (13)** | *to take time* | ใช้เวลา |
| **chái dâi (9)** | *reasonable, acceptable* | ใช้ได้ |
| **châi mái? (1)** | *isn't that so?* | ใช่ไหม |
| **chai ta-lay (15)** | *seaside* | ชายทะเล |
| **cháo (13)** | *morning* | เช้า |
| **chèet (14)** | *to spray, inject* | ฉีด |
| **chék bin (10)** | *can I have the bill?* | เช็คบิล |
| **chék dern-tahng (6)** | *traveller's cheque* | เช็คเดินทาง |
| **chern (8)** | *please; to invite* | เชิญ |
| **chêu (1)** | *first name, to have the first name ...* | ชื่อ |
| **chêu-a (12)** | *to believe* | เชื่อ |
| **chôhk dee (3)** | *good luck* | โชคดี |

| | | |
|---|---|---|
| **chôo-a-mohng (9)** | *hour* | ชั่วโมง |
| **chôo-ay ... (6)** | *please ...; to help* | ช่วย ... |
| **chôrp (9)** | *to like* | ชอบ |
| **chún (5)** | *floor, level; class* | ชั้น |
| **chút (8)** | *clear* | ชัด |
| **dâi (2)** | *can* | ได้ |
| **... dâi mái? (2)** | *can you ... ?* | ได้ไหม |
| **dee (7)** | *good* | ดี |
| **děe-o ... (6)** | *wait a moment; in a minute* | เดี๋ยว ... |
| **dern (5)** | *to walk* | เดิน |
| **dern tahng (13)** | *to travel* | เดินทาง |
| **deu-un (8)** | *month* | เดือน |
| **dèuk (9)** | *late at night, dark* | ดึก |
| **doo (4)** | *to look at* | ดู |
| **dôo-ay (4)** | *too, also* | ด้วย |
| **doo-ung (6)** | classifier for stamps | ดวง |
| **dung (7)** | *loud* | ดัง |
| **dtàhng jung-wùt (9)** | *up-country* | ต่างจังหวัด |
| **dtàir (9)** | *but* | แต่ |
| **(dtàir) cháo (9)** | *(from) early morning* | (แต่)เช้า |
| **dtàirng ngahn (8)** | *to be married* | แต่งงาน |
| **dtee hâh (13)** | *5.00 a.m.* | ตีห้า |
| **dtee nèung (13)** | *1.00 a.m.* | ตีหนึ่ง |
| **dtem (laír-o) (13)** | *full* | เต็ม(แล้ว) |

| | | |
|---|---|---|
| **dtèuk (9)** | *concrete building* | ตึก |
| **dtèun (9)** | *to wake up* | ตื่น |
| **dtìt (9)** | *to stick, be stuck* | ติด |
| **dtìt air (14)** | *to be air-conditioned* | ติดแอร์ |
| **dtìt dtoo-a (13)** | *on you, with you* | ติดตัว |
| **dtòk long (2)** | *agree(d)* | ตกลง |
| **dtôm yum gÔOng (10)** | *shrimp 'tom yam'* | ต้มยำกุ้ง |
| **dtôn-mái (9)** | *tree* | ต้นไม้ |
| **dtôo sáyf (14)** | *safe* (noun) | ตู้เสฟ |
| **dtǒo-a (13)** | *ticket* | ตั๋ว |
| **dtoo-a (13)** | *body* | ตัว |
| **... dtòr nèung bporn (6)** | *... to the pound* | ... ต่อหนึ่งปอนด์ |
| **dtorn (7)** | *period of time* | ตอน |
| **dtorn bài (7)** | *afternoon* | ตอนบ่าย |
| **dtorn née (9)** | *now* | ตอนนี้ |
| **dtôrng (9)** | *have to, must* | ต้อง |
| **dtrong (13)** | *straight, exact* | ตรง |
| **dtrong-née (3)** | *right here* | ตรงนี้ |
| **dtùm (11)** | *low* | ต่ำ |
| **dtung (4)** | *money, satang* | สตางค์ |
| **èek (3)** | *again; further* | อีก |
| **èek tee (12)** | *again* | อีกที |
| **eng (13)** | *self* | เอง |
| **èun (14)** | *other* | อื่น |

| | | |
|---|---|---|
| **fa-rùng (7)** | *westerner* | ฝรั่ง |
| **fàhk (14)** | *to deposit* | ฝาก |
| **fai sǔn-yahn (5)** | *traffic lights* | ไฟสัญญาณ |
| **fairn (8)** | *boy/girlfriend; spouse* | แฟน |
| **gài (4)** | *chicken* | ไก่ |
| **gâir (14)** | *to fix, repair, mend* | แก้ |
| **gâir-o (4)** | *glass* | แก้ว |
| **gairng (10)** | *curry* | แกง |
| **gairng gài (10)** | *chicken curry* | แกงไก่ |
| **gèe (8)** | *how many?* | กี่ |
| **gèe mohng? (13)** | *what time?* | กี่โมง |
| **gée-o náhm (4)** | *won ton soup* | เกี๊ยวน้ำ |
| **gèng (8)** | *to be good at something* | เก่ง |
| **gèp (4)** | *to collect, keep* | เก็บ |
| **gèp wái (14)** | *to keep* | เก็บไว้ |
| **... gern bpai (10)** | *too ...* | ... เกินไป |
| **gèrt (9)** | *to be born* | เกิด |
| **glâi glâi (3)** | *near* | ใกล้ๆ |
| **glai (5)** | *far* | ไกล |
| **gloo-a (11)** | *to be afraid* | กลัว |
| **glôo-ay (2)** | *banana* | กล้วย |
| **glôrng tài rôop (14)** | *camera* | กล้องถ่ายรูป |
| **glôrng tài wee-dee-oh (14)** | *video camera* | กล้องถ่ายวีดีโอ |
| **glùp (7)** | *return* | กลับ |

| gOO n-jair (14) | key | กุญแจ |
| gÔO ng (4) | shrimp | กุ้ง |
| gôr ... (9) | well ... | ก็ ... |
| ... gôr láir-o gun (2) | I'll settle for ... | ... ก็แล้วกัน |
| gòrn (7) | before, first | ก่อน |
| grOO ng-tâyp (5) | Bangkok | กรุงเทพฯ |
| gum-lung ... (11) | to be in the process of ... | กำลัง |
| gùp (1) | with | กับ |
| ... gwàh (9) | more than ... | กว่า |
| hâh-sìp-jèt (3) | fifty-seven | ห้าสิบเจ็ด |
| hâhm (15) | to forbid | ห้าม |
| hâi (10) | to get someone to do something | ให้ |
| hâi (14) | for | ให้ |
| hòk-sìp (2) | sixty | หกสิบ |
| hǒo-a hǐn (15) | Hua Hin | หัวหิน |
| hôrng (5) | room | ห้อง |
| hôrng náhm (14) | toilet, bathroom | ห้องน้ำ |
| hun-loh (7) | hello (on telephone) | ฮันโล |
| ìm (10) | to be full | อิ่ม |
| ja (7) | future time marker | จะ |
| jàhk (1) | from | จาก |
| jahn (4) | plate | จาน |
| jâo-nâh-têe (15) | official | เจ้าหน้าที่ |
| jèt-sìp (2) | seventy | เจ็ดสิบ |

| | | |
|---|---|---|
| **jing (9)** | *true, truly* | จริง |
| **jon těung (14)** | *until* | จนถึง |
| **jorng (13)** | *to book* | จอง |
| **jòrt (3)** | *park* (verb) | จอด |
| **jòt-mǎi ah-gàht (6)** | *aerogramme* | จดหมายอากาศ |
| **jung ler-ee (9)** | intensifier | จังเลย |
| **jung-wùt (15)** | *province* | จังหวัด |
| **kâ, ká, krúp (1)** | polite particles | ค่ะ, คะ, ครับ |
| **kâ (3)** | *yes* | ค่ะ |
| **ka-nǒm (10)** | *cake, dessert* | ขนม |
| **kâh (13)** | *cost* | ค่า |
| **kâhng bon (5)** | *upstairs* | ข้างบน |
| **kâhng nai (8)** | *inside* | ข้างใน |
| **kâhng nôrk (7)** | *outside* | ข้างนอก |
| **kâo (3)** | *to enter* | เข้า |
| **kâo jai (12)** | *to understand* | เข้าใจ |
| **káo (1)** | *he, she, they* | เขา |
| **kâo (4)** | *rice* | ข้าว |
| **kâo dtom (13)** | *rice porridge* | ข้าวต้ม |
| **kâo nâh bpèt (4)** | *duck rice* | ข้าวหน้าเป็ด |
| **kěe-un (11)** | *to write* | เขียน |
| **kem (12)** | *salty* | เค็ม |
| **ker-ee (11)** | *used to; to have ever done something* | เคย |

| | | |
|---|---|---|
| **ker-ee ... mah gòrn (11)** | *to have ever done something* | เคย ... มาก่อน |
| **kêun (13)** | *to get on* | ขึ้น |
| **kêun (14)** | *to go up* | ขึ้น |
| **keun (13)** | *night* | คืน |
| **kít (2) (7)** | *to think, charge* | คิด |
| **kít doo (15)** | *to think about, consider* | คิดดู |
| **klorng (9)** | *canal* | คลอง |
| **koh-lâh (4)** | *Coca-Cola* | โคล่า |
| **kong (11)** | *bound to be, sure to be* | คง |
| **koo-un (ja) (15)** | *should, ought to* | ควร(จะ) |
| **kòo-up (8)** | *year(s) old* | ขวบ |
| **kòo-ut (4)** | *bottle* | ขวด |
| **kon (1)** | *person* | คน |
| **koon (1)** | *you* | คุณ |
| **kŏr ... nòy (4)** | *I'd like ...* | ขอ ... หน่อย |
| **kŏr-tôht (1)** | *excuse me* | ขอโทษ |
| **kŏrng (5)** | *of* | ของ |
| **kŏrng (14)** | *things* | ของ |
| **kŏrng wǎhn (10)** | *sweet, dessert* | ของหวาน |
| **kòrp-kOOn (3)** | *thank you* | ขอบคุณ |
| **koy (7)** | *to wait* | คอย |
| **krai (7)** | *who?* | ใคร |
| **krêu-ung bprùp ah-gàht (14)** | *air-conditioner* | เครื่องปรับอากาศ |

| | | |
|---|---|---|
| **krêung (13)** | *half* | ครึ่ง |
| **krêung chôo-a mohng (13)** | *half an hour* | ครึ่งชั่วโมง |
| **kroo (11)** | *teacher* | ครู |
| **krôo (7)** | *a moment* | ครู่ |
| **krúng (9)** | *time(s)* | ครั้ง |
| **kum (12)** | *word* | คำ |
| **kwǎh (3)** | *right* | ขวา |
| **kwahm jing (11)** | *(in) truth; truly; actually* | ความจริง |
| **láir (6)** | *and* | และ |
| **lâirk bplèe-un (6)** | *to exchange* | แลกเปลี่ยน |
| **láir-o (3)** | *and then; already* | แล้ว |
| **láir-o ... lâ? (8)** | *and how about ... ?* | แล้ว ... ล่ะ |
| **láir-o gôr (4)** | *and* | แล้วก็ |
| **láir-o rěu yung? (8)** | *... yet (or not)?* | แล้วหรือยัง |
| **lée-o (3)** | *turn* | เลี้ยว |
| **lék (4)** | *small* | เล็ก |
| **lěr (2)** | question word | หรือ |
| **ler-ee bpai (3)** | *carry on, go on* | เลยไป |
| **lêrk (10)** | *to cease, give up* | เลิก |
| **leum (13)** | *to forget* | ลืม |
| **loh (2)** | *kilo* | โล |
| **loh la tâo-rài? (2)** | *how much a kilo?* | โลละเท่าไร |
| **long (13)** | *to get off (a bus)* | ลง |
| **long ta-bee-un (6)** | *register* | ลงทะเบียน |

| lôok (8) | child/children | ลูก |
| lôok chai (8) | son | ลูกชาย |
| lôok sǎo (8) | daughter | ลูกสาว |
| lorng chim (2) | to taste, try out | ลองชิม |
| lót (2) | to reduce | ลด |
| ma-hǎh-wít-ta-yah-lai (11) | university | มหาวิทยาลัย |
| mah (1) | to come | มา |
| mah těung (13) | to reach | มาถึง |
| mâhk (2) | very, much | มาก |
| ... mái? (2) | question word | ไหม |
| mài (7) | again; new | ใหม่ |
| mâi (2) | not | ไม่ |
| mâi bpen rai (5) | never mind | ไม่เป็นไร |
| mâi châi (1) | no (to châi mái? questions) | ไม่ใช่ |
| mâi dâi (2) | can't; no (in dâi mái questions) | ไม่ได้ |
| mâi dee (7) | bad | ไม่ดี |
| mâi dtôrng (11) | there's no need (to) | ไม่ต้อง |
| mâi kôy (9) | hardly, scarcely | ไม่ค่อย ... |
| mâi kôy ... tâo-rài (11) | not very ... | ไม่ค่อย ... เท่าไร |
| mâi ... ler-ee (9) | not at all | ไม่ ... เลย |
| mâi .. ròrk (3) | not at all | ไม่ ... หรอก |

| | | |
|---|---|---|
| **... mǎi-kwǎhm wâh a-rai? (12)** | *what does ... mean?* | ... หมายความว่าอะไร |
| **mâir (9)** | *mother* | แม่ |
| **may-noo (4)** | *menu* | เมนู |
| **mee (2)** | *have* | มี |
| **mee chêu sěe-ung (15)** | *to be famous* | มีชื่อเสียง |
| **mee-a (11)** | *wife* (informal) | เมีย |
| **mêu-rai? (7)** | *when?* | เมื่อไร |
| **mêu-a (9)** | *when* | เมื่อ |
| **mêu-a chún yung dèk (9)** | *when I was still a child* | เมื่อฉันยังเด็ก |
| **mêu-a gòrn (9)** | *formerly* | เมื่อก่อน |
| **měu-un (9)** | *like, similar, as* | เหมือน |
| **měu-un gun (8)** | *likewise* | เหมือนกัน |
| **... meu-un gun (9)** | *fairly ...* | เหมือนกัน |
| **meu-ung tai (8)** | *Thailand* | เมืองไทย |
| **mǒong lôo-ut (14)** | *mosquito screen* | มุ้งลวด |
| **mun (9)** | *it* | มัน |
| **ná (2)** | particle | นะ |
| **na-korn râht-cha-sěe-mah (13)** | *Nakhorn Ratchasima* | นครราชสีมา |
| **na-korn pa-nom (13)** | *Nakhorn Phanom* | นครพนม |
| **nâh bèu-a (9)** | *boring* | น่าเบื่อ |
| **nâh yòo (9)** | *habitable* | น่าอยู่ |

| | | |
|---|---|---|
| **nah-tee (5)** | *minute* | นาที |
| **nahm sa-gOOn (1)** | *surname; to have the surname* | ... นามสกุล |
| **náhm (4)** | *water* | น้ำ |
| **nahn (8)** | *a long time* | นาน |
| **nâir (14)** | *to be certain* | แน่ |
| **nâirn (9)** | *to be crowded* | แน่น |
| **nêe (2)** | *this* | นี่ |
| **nêe eng (15)** | *this very ...* | นี่เอง |
| **nee kâ/krúp (4)** | *here you are* | นี่ค่ะ/ครับ |
| **néu-a (10)** | *beef* | เนื้อ |
| **néu-a pùt núm mun hǒy (10)** | *beef fried in oyster sauce* | เนื้อผัดน้ำมันหอย |
| **nèung (4)** | *one, a* | หนึ่ง |
| **nin-tah (12)** | *to gossip* | นินทา |
| **nít nèung (3)** | *a little bit* | นิดหนึ่ง |
| **nít-nòy (8)** | *a little bit* | นิดหน่อย |
| **nǒo (4)** | way of addressing young waitresses | หนู |
| **nórng, nórng (10)** | *waiter!* | น้องๆ |
| **nórng chai (8)** | *younger brother* | น้อยชาย |
| **nórng sǎo (8)** | *younger sister* | น้องสาว |
| **nǒrng-kai (15)** | *Nongkhai* | หนองคาย |
| **nòy (2)** | *a bit* | หน่อย |

| | | |
|---|---|---|
| **nóy-nàh (2)** | *custard apple* | น้อยหน่า |
| **núk tÓO-rá-gìt (1)** | *businessman* | นักธุรกิจ |
| **núm kǎirng bplào (4)** | *iced water* | น้ำแข็งเปล่า |
| **núm ma-náo (4)** | *lemonade* | น้ำมะนาว |
| **núm mun hǒy (10)** | *oyster sauce* | น้ำมันหอย |
| **núm sôm (10)** | *orange juice* | น้ำส้ม |
| **núm sôm kún (10)** | *fresh orange juice* | น้ำส้มคั้น |
| **núng-sěu dern-tahng (6)** | *passport* | หนังสือเดินทาง |
| **ngahn (9)** | *work* | งาน |
| **ngâi (11)** | *easy* | ง่าย |
| **ngâi gwàh (11)** | *easier* | ง่ายกว่า |
| **ngêe-up (15)** | *quiet, calm* | เงียบ |
| **ngern deu-un (9)** | *salary* | เงินเดือน |
| **ngong (12)** | *to be dazed, confused* | งง |
| **oh kay (2)** | *O.K.* | โอ เค |
| **òrk (7)** | *to go out* | ออก |
| **pah-sǎh (8)** | *language* | ภาษา |
| **pâhk dtâi (9)** | *the South* | ภาคใต้ |
| **pàirn (6)** | classifier for aerogrammes | แผ่น |
| **pairng (2)** | *expensive* | แพง |
| **pêe-chai (8)** | *older brother* | พี่ชาย |
| **pêe-nórng (8)** | *brothers and sisters* | พี่น้อง |
| **pêe-sǎo (8)** | *older sister* | พี่สาว |
| **pèt (10)** | *spicy* | เผ็ด |

| | | |
|---|---|---|
| **pêu-un (7)** | *friend* | เพื่อน |
| **pìt (11)** | *wrong* | ผิด |
| **pǒn-la-mái (10)** | *fruit* | ผลไม้ |
| **pôo-doy-ee sǎhn (13)** | *passenger* | ผู้โดยสาร |
| **poo-gèt (9)** | *Phuket* | ภูเก็ต |
| **pôot (7)** | *speak* | พูด |
| **pôot lên (12)** | *to joke* | พูดเล่น |
| **pôr (9)** | *father* | พ่อ |
| **prór wâh (11)** | *because* | เพราะว่า |
| **prôong née (13)** | *tomorrow* | พรุ่งนี้ |
| **púk (13)** | *to rest; to stay* | พัก |
| **pùt (4)** | *to stir-fry, fried* | ผัด |
| **pút-ta-yah (15)** | *Pattaya* | พัทยา |
| **ráhn-ah-hǎhn (5)** | *restaurant* | ร้านอาหาร |
| **ráhn-ah-hǎhn kwǔn jai (5)** | *Khwan Jai Restaurant* | ร้านอาหารขวัญใจ |
| **ray-o (12)** | *quick* | เร็ว |
| **rêe-uk wâh ... (2)** | *(it's) called ...* | เรียกว่า ... |
| **ree-un (11)** | *to study, learn* | เรียน |
| **rêe-up róy (13)** | *safely* | เรียบร้อย |
| **rěu (4)** | *or* | หรือ |
| **... rěu bplào? (14)** | *... or not?* | ... หรือเปล่า |
| **rohng rairm (3)** | *hotel* | โรงแรม |
| **rohng rairm ree-noh (3)** | *Reno Hotel* | โรงแรมรีโน |
| **róo rêu-ung (12)** | *to understand* | รู้เรื่อง |

| | | |
|---|---|---|
| **róo-jùk (3)** | *to know* | รู้จัก |
| **róo-sèuk (9)** | *to feel* | รู้สึก |
| **ror (7)** | *wait* | รอ |
| **rorng táo (15)** | *shoes* | ร้องเท้า |
| **rót (9)** | *car* | รถ |
| **rót dtìt (3)** | *traffic jam* | รถติด |
| **rót may (13)** | *bus* | รถเมล์ |
| **rúp (10)** | *to receive, take* | รับ |
| **sa-àht (9)** | *clean* | สะอาด |
| **sa-bai (8)** | *to be well, comfortable* | สบาย |
| **sa-bai dee lěr? (8)** | *how are you?* | สบายดีหรือ |
| **sa-dairng (13)** | *to show* | แสดง |
| **sa-dtairm (6)** | *stamp* | สแตมป์ |
| **sa-gòt (12)** | *to spell* | สะกด |
| **sa-měr (11)** | *always* | เสมอ |
| **sa-nǎhm gee-lah hàirng châht (3)** | *National Stadium* | สนามกีฬาแห่งชาติ |
| **sa-tǎhn tôot (7)** | *embassy* | สถานทูต |
| **sa-wùt dee (1)** | *hello* | สวัสดี |
| **sǎhm-sìp-sǎhm (3)** | *thirty-three* | สามสิบสาม |
| **sâhp (7)** | *to know* | ทราบ |
| **sái (3)** | *left* | ซ้าย |
| **sǎi (7)** | *(telephone) line* | สาย |
| **say-wen up (4)** | *Seven-Up* | เซเวนอัพ |

| | | |
|---|---|---|
| **sěe dairng (2)** | *red* | สีแดง |
| **sèe tÔOm (13)** | *10.00 p.m.* | สี่ทุ่ม |
| **sèe tÔOm krêung (13)** | *10.30 p.m.* | สี่ทุ่มครึ่ง |
| **sèe-yâirk (3)** | *crossroads* | สี่แยก |
| **sěe-a (9)** | *to spend, waste* | เสีย |
| **sěe-a (14)** | *to be broken* | เสีย |
| **sěe-ung (11)** | *sound; tone* | เสียง |
| **sen chêu (6)** | *to sign* | เซ็นชื่อ |
| **sí (11)** | *particle* | ซิ |
| **sǒo-ay (2)** | *beautiful, pretty* | สวย |
| **sǒon (7)** | *zero* | ศูญ |
| **sǒong (9)** | *high* | สูง |
| **sòop bOO-rèe (10)** | *to smoke* | สูบบุหรี่ |
| **sÒOt soy (3)** | *end of the soi* | สุดซอย |
| **sòng (6)** | *send* | ส่ง |
| **sôrm (14)** | *to repair, mend* | ซ่อม |
| **sǒrn (11)** | *to teach* | สอน |
| **sǒrng (4)** | *two* | สอง |
| **sǒrng sǎhm (5)** | *two or three; a few* | สองสาม |
| **soy (3)** | *soi, lane* | ซอย |
| **soy ga-sǎym-sǔn (3)** | *Soi Kasemsan* | ซอยเกษมสรรค์ |
| **sùk (5)** | *(see Grammar, Unit 5)* | สัก |
| **sùng (10)** | *to order* | สั่ง |
| **ta-lay (15)** | *sea* | ทะเล |

| | | |
|---|---|---|
| **ta-na-kahn (5)** | *bank* | ธนาคาร |
| **ta-nǒn (3)** | *road* | ถนน |
| **ta-nǒn sÒO-kǑOm-wít (3)** | *Sukhumwit Road* | ถนนสุขุมวิท |
| **tâh (10)** | *if* | ถ้า |
| **tâh yàhng nún (10)** | *in that case* | ถ้าอย่างนั้น |
| **tǎhm (15)** | *to ask* | ถาม |
| **tahn (10)** | *to eat* | ทาน |
| **tahng née (5)** | *this way* | ทางนี้ |
| **tahng ah-gàht (6)** | *by air* | ทางอากาศ |
| **tahng reu-a (6)** | *by sea* | ทางเรือ |
| **tâo-nún (5)** | *only* | เท่านั้น |
| **tài rôop (15)** | *to take a photograph* | ถ่ายรูป |
| **tǎir-o née (5)** | *this vicinity* | แถวนี้ |
| **tâo-rài? (2)** | *how much?* | เท่าไร |
| **tee (12)** | *time* | ที |
| **têe-kèe-a bOO-rèe (10)** | *ashtray* | ที่เขี่ยบุหรี่ |
| **têe-nǎi? (5)** | *where* | ที่ไหน |
| **têe-nêe (3)** | *here* | ที่นี่ |
| **têe-nôhn (3)** | *over there* | ที่โน่น |
| **têe-o (15)** | *to visit, go out* | เที่ยว |
| **têe-ung krêung (13)** | *12.30 a.m.* | เที่ยงครึ่ง |
| **těung (3)** | *to reach* | ถึง |
| **toh (7)** | *to telephone* | โทร |
| **too-a (15)** | *tour* | ทัวร์ |

| | | |
|---|---|---|
| tòrt (15) | *to take off* | ถอด |
| tÓOk (9) | *every* | ทุก |
| tum ngahn (1) | *to work* | ทำงาน |
| tum-mai (11) | *why?* | ทำไม |
| tum-mai lâ? (14) | *why?* | ทำไมล่ะ |
| tûn (13) | *you* (polite) | ท่าน |
| túng ... láir ... (11) | *both ... and ...* | ทั้ง ... และ ... |
| túng mòt (4) | *altogether* | ทั้งหมด |
| ung-grìt (1) | *English* | อังกฤษ |
| ùt-dtrah (6) | *rate* | อัตรา |
| wâh (7) | *that ...* | ว่า |
| wâh (9) | *to think, say* | ว่า |
| wǎhn (2) | *to be sweet* | หวาน |
| wâhng (7) | *free, vacant* | ว่าง |
| way-lah (9) | *time* | เวลา |
| wěe la ... (2) | *... per bunch* | หวีละ ... |
| wun (9) | *day* | วัน |
| wun ah-tít (14) | *Sunday* | วันอาทิตย์ |
| (wun) la (14) | *per (day)* | (วัน)ละ |
| wun née (6) | *today* | วันนี้ |
| wun sǎo (14) | *Saturday* | วันเสาร์ |
| wun sǎo wun ah-tít (15) | *weekend* | วันเสาร์วันอาทิตย์ |
| wút tâht pa-nom (15) | *Wat That Phanom* | วัดธาตุพนม |
| yàh (12) | *don't* | อย่า |

| | | |
|---|---|---|
| **yah gun yOOng (14)** | *insecticide* | ยากันยุง |
| **yâhk (11)** | *difficult* | ยาก |
| **yàhk (ja) (6)** | *to want to* | อยาก (จะ) |
| **yài (4)** | *large* | ใหญ่ |
| **yái (9)** | *to move* | ย้าย |
| **yâir (9)** | *to be a nuisance, a hassle* | แย่ |
| **yér-yáir (15)** | *lots* | เยอะแยะ |
| **yòo (3) (8)** | *to be situated at; to live (in, at)* | อยู่ |
| **yÒOt (13)** | *to stop* | หยุด |
| **yung (15)** | *still* | ยัง |
| **yung-ngai? (9)** | *how?* | อย่างไร |

# GRAMMAR INDEX

Numbers in brackets refer to the unit in which each grammar point was first covered.

negative **mâi** (2)

> **mâi ... ròrk (3)**
> **mâi ... ler-ee (9)**
> **mâi kôy ...** (9)

noun+pronoun+verb (9)

numbers

> 1-10 (1)
> 20, 30, 40 ... 100 (2)
> 21, 22, 23-100 (3)

particles

> **kâ, krúp** (1); (3 meaning 'yes')
> ná (2)
> sùk (5)
> sí (10)

per: **la** (2)

polite commands: **choo-ay** (8)

polite requests:

> kǒr ... nòy (4)
> chôo-ay (6)

possession (5)

pronouns (1)

questions:

> **châi mái?** (1)
> **lěr** (2)
> **mái?** (2)
> **láir-o rěu yung?** (8)
> **reu bplào?** (14)
> hǒw? (12)
> how many? (8)
> how much? (2)
> what?(1)
> where?(5)
> who?(7)
> when?(7)
> why?(10)

reduplication (3)

seasons (14)

**sùk** (5)

telling the time (12)

**wâh** (7)

**yàh** (don't) (12)

**yàhk ja** (6)

# JAPANESE

## HELEN BALLHATCHET AND STEFAN KAISER

This is a complete course in spoken Japanese. If you have never learnt Japanese before, or if your Japanese needs brushing up, *Teach Yourself Japanese* is for you.

Helen Ballhatchet and Stefan Kaiser have created course that is both fun and easy to work through. They explain everything clearly along the way and give you plenty of opportunities to practise what you have learnt. Their course structure means that you can work at your own pace, arranging your learning to suit your own needs.

This course contains:

- Graded units of dialogues, culture notes, grammar and exercises

- An extensive Japanese-English vocabulary list

- A unique cross-referencing system to help you look up unfamiliar language

When you have finished *Teach Yourself Japanese* you'll be able to hold your own anywhere, from a karaoke bar to a business lunch.

£6.99
ISBN 0340 49245 7

# INDONESIAN

## J.B.KWEE

This course provides a sound working knowledge of spoken and written Indonesian.

The carefully graded lessons take the reader through pronunciation and word order, parts of speech and grammar, to the point where he or she will be able to take part in everyday conversations and read simple texts. There are exercises with answers at the end of each chapter. This course uses the authorised reformed spelling of Indonesian.

£8.99
ISBN 0340 20380 3

# CHINESE

### ELIZABETH SCURFIELD

Written for complete beginners, this book explains the complexities of spoken and written Modern Standard Chinese (otherwise know as Mandarin). Its logical and enthusiastic approach makes this notoriously difficult language straightforward and easy to learn.

Elizabeth Scurfield explains everything clearly along the way and gives you plenty of opportunities to practise what you have learnt. The graded structure means that you can work at your own pace, arranging your learning to suit your needs.

*Teach Yourself Chinese* has many unique features:

* You can decide whether or not to learn the script. If you don's need it, just follow the *pinyin* transcriptions.

* The summary of key grammar allows you to look up difficult points in seconds

* The extensive two-way vocabulary lists mean that this is truly a complete course in one volume

By the end of the course you will be able to take a fully active part in the life and culture of China and Chinese-speaking people everywhere.

£8.99
ISBN 0 340 51959 2

# Also in Thai

A cassette has been especially recorded to accompany this book and is available through all major bookshops or by post from Bookpoint as explained below.

0 304 59043 2 Teach Youself Thai cassette £9.99 (inc. £1.49 VAT)

Further titles from Teach Yourself

0 340 20380 3
Teach Yourself Indonesian £8.99 J.B.Kwee

0 340 49245 7
Teach Yourself Japanese £6.99 H.Ballhatchet and S.Kaiser
Also the book/cassette pack: 0 340 58513 7 £17.99 (inc. VAT)

All Teach Yourself books are available from your local bookshop or can be ordered direct from the publisher. Just tick the titles you want and fill in the form below. Prices and availability subject to change without notice.

To: Hodder & Stoughton Ltd, Cash Sales Department, Bookpoint, 39 Milton Park, Abingdon, OXON, OX14 4TD, UK. If you have a credit card you may order by telephone - 01235 831700.

Please enclose a cheque or postal order made payable to Bookpoint Ltd to the value of the cover price and allow the following for postage and packing:

UK & BFPO: £1.00 for the first book, 50p for the second book and 30p for each additional book ordered up to a maximum charge of £3.00.
OVERSEAS & EIRE: £2.00 for the first book, £1.00 for the second book and 50p for each additional book.

Name

Address

If you would prefer to pay by credit card, please complete:
Please debit my Visa/Access/Diner's Card/American Express (delete as appropriate) card no:

□□□□□□□□□□□□□□□□

Signature...........................................Expiry Date